EXODUS

PART II: FREEDOM

EXODUS 12:33-18:27

MINDI JO FURBY

KingsWynd exists to fight biblical illiteracy in our families, Church, communities, and world. Our goal is to help others love God and become more like Jesus through His Word. We accomplish this through publishing books, a podcast (Biblically Lit), articles, curriculum, and Bible studies used by individuals and churches throughout the world.

Mindi Jo Furby
For more information about Mindi Jo Furby, visit www.mindijofurby.com

Printed Worldwide
First Printing 2024
First Edition 2024
Published by: KingsWynd Books

ISBN: 978-1-943413-14-0

10 9 8 7 6 5 4 3 2 1

For more information about KingsWynd Books, visit www.kingswynd.org.

EXODUS
PART II: FREEDOM

TABLE OF CONTENTS

MAKE BIBLE STUDIES

The goal of every Christian is to glorify God and become more like Jesus. The process of realizing this goal is discipleship. Christ chose twelve disciples during His years of ministry on Earth and commissioned them to continue the process of making disciples—helping people become more like Him.

As a disciple of Christ, my prayer is to do the same.

Some attempt to condense the process of discipleship into a concise list with checkboxes in front of tasks like "read your Bible" and "attend church regularly," etc. While I encourage such spiritual disciplines, by themselves, they do not make disciples. We may gain knowledge, but in the end, we will resemble the Pharisees rather than becoming more like Jesus.

If we intend to become more like Jesus and help others do the same, we must follow His example. Jesus' method for discipleship was quite simple. He used relationships fueled by God's Word to produce disciples.

Jesus did not instruct His disciples to check off behavioral boxes as they went about their lives. He did not assign homework involving endless questions and intense reading. He lived with them, poured into their lives, and used their relationships (with Him and each other) as the conduit for spiritual growth and maturity.

If that's how He produced disciples, that's how we should too.

MAKE Bible Studies exist to make disciples by igniting relationships fueled by God's Word. These studies are intensely practical and applicable to life. They are intentionally designed with relationships in mind—first, your relationship with God, then your relationships with others in a group setting.

MAKE studies work because they're simple and to the point. They are designed to be the launching point for discussion, action, and transformation—

merging God's truth with life in practical, engaging ways. Be as involved as you want. You have the option of engaging in the personal Bible study and commentary before your group meets to work through the group study, or simply showing up on group nights for discussion. Homework is not necessary, though it is helpful. Like most things in life, the more you invest in your studies, the more you will reap.

The following resources are available for your convenience: an introduction to Exodus, personal Bible study questions, passage commentaries, and group study guides for each week. A special note to group leaders: read through the commentary and study guides before your group meeting. Pray over the material, make notes, and think of ways to instigate further discussion. Also, before beginning each week, discuss how your group members incorporated the prior week's challenges into their lives and faith.

Enjoy the journey of becoming more like Jesus through this study of the second part of Exodus. Keep your eyes open and your heart hungry for His transforming power in your life and the lives of your group members!

INTRODUCTION

As explored in the first volume of this study, "set apart" is both a theme and a hope within the book of Exodus. Nearly every stroke of the narrative displays someone being set apart—God, Moses, Israel, etc.—often in spectacular ways. God reveals Himself as the true God and formally stakes His claim on Israel, who remains distinct from the world for the rest of time.

Within Exodus, God also offers hope in being set apart. The biblical understanding of hope is not wishful thinking; it is a current and future reality for those who believe. Thus, God being set apart (or holy) from His creation offers hope because we trust the One Who is in control and stands outside of time and circumstance.

When we put our faith in Him, He gives us a new identity, which is the second source of hope. His people (Israel then, the Church now) are set apart from the world/sin and for God and His glory. The narrative of Exodus helps us realize just how holy He is. Then it reveals His invitation for people to join in holiness.

In the first volume, we learned about how God set apart numerous aspects of the narrative for His glory and to accomplish His purposes. He set apart people like the midwives, Jochebed, the Egyptian princess, Moses, Zipporah, and Israel to contribute to and advance His story. He also set apart people, (namely, Pharaoh), for destruction – using him as an example of what happens when we refuse God and His plan for our lives. God also set Himself apart, individually with Moses at the burning bush and publicly with the plagues, as He revealed His sovereign power over nature. God is not an element in this world; He is the Author, Sustainer, and King of it. Exodus Part 1 revealed this and invited us to join His story above our own with practical applications like tackling our choices and opportunities, saying yes, making commitments, investigating where truth meets friction, our habits, and our posture of submission to Him.

This second volume continues exploring how God sets Himself and His people apart, primarily through freedom. First (and finally!), He freed His people from Egypt. This, of course, was accomplished through a series of miracles that leaves us in absolute awe of God—Pharaoh's intense pursuit of Israel, God's cloud pillar protecting His people, the famous parting of the sea, and then closing the sea to seal the fate of countless Egyptian warriors.

But Israel's awe of God and praise for Him did not last long, unfortunately. Israel would succumb to slavery again but in a different way. Instead of needing freedom from Egypt, God would show Israel that they needed to experience freedom from themselves. Though they were free, they acted like slaves of sin—distrusting and disobeying God, grumbling against Him, and refusing to learn from their mistakes. Even Moses made some unwise decisions in his leadership that resulted in an enslaved schedule he did not break free from until his father-in-law showed up.

Fortunately, God's grace is greater than our worst failures, and His love remains steadfast. Israel experienced His grace and mercy over and over, along with His constant provision. He was wooing them and leading them painstakingly through the process of learning how to trust Him above and beyond all else. God knew they were set apart, but Israel had yet to learn what that meant.

Ultimately, a study through Exodus is really a study of God and His holiness. The more we realize His greatness, the more we can be transformed into His image. My prayer is that He will open your eyes to His holiness, awaken your heart to the ramifications thereof, and ignite a passion in your life to pursue the same.

WEEK ONE

TASTE OF FREEDOM

Exodus 12:33-13:16

PERSONAL BIBLE STUDY QUESTIONS

1. How did the Egyptians view the Israelites? (12:33)
   a. What were they afraid of? (12:33)
2. What had the Israelites requested from the Egyptians prior to this point in obedience to Moses and the Lord? (12:35)
3. How did the Lord bless their obedience? (12:36)
4. Where did the Israelites travel to? (12:37)
5. About how many men were in the Israelite group? (12:38)
6. Who/what else went with them? (12:38)
7. How long had the Israelites been in Egypt? (12:40-41)
8. Who was allowed to observe the Passover from that point forward? (12:43-45)
9. Where was it to be eaten? (12:46)
10. What was not to be broken of the sacrificial lamb? (12:46)
    a. Read John 19:31-37. What is the significance of the instruction regarding the Passover lamb in whom it foreshadowed?
11. What was the requirement for a sojourner to celebrate the Passover? (12:48)
12. How did the Israelites respond to the Lord's instruction? (12:50)
13. Who did God want sanctified for Him? (13:1)
14. The Israelites were leaving slavery in Egypt and going where? (13:5)
15. How long were they to eat unleavened bread as a part of the special feast? (13:6-7)
16. What were the Israelites supposed to tell their sons? (13:8)

17. How often were they to celebrate this ordinance? (13:10)
18. What/who was supposed to be consecrated to the Lord? (13:11-13)
19. What was the significance of the firstborn? (13:15-16)
20. Why was it important for the Israelites to remember such a time in their history?

COMMENTARY

Exodus 12:33–13:16

She could feel the pressure in her bones. It seemed as if, at any moment, she would be crushed, and her fight was starting to take flight. Hope, like a dainty bird, gracefully began to ascend beyond her reach, and though it was weightless, she just didn't have the energy to hold onto it anymore. Freedom was but a dream... and oh, how she longed to dream again! But insurmountable fatigue and defeat coiled around her body like snakes. She wasn't going anywhere; she couldn't. She simply wanted to give up and, in fact, pleaded for God to take her life. How could she be of any use to Him in this condition, anyway?

Welcome to my mind in the midst of my battle with anorexia over a decade ago. I rarely talk about it, but when I realized this chapter would focus on freedom, I revisited that experience from the recesses of my mind where it had been buried. Anorexia, like other disorders and addictions, seemed impossible to conquer, and at one point, I honestly didn't think I could. Freedom felt like an ethereal, mystical thought – splendid in theory but beyond my grasp. As a Christian, I, of course, understood the theological errors of such a conclusion, but my body was giving up. Weighing less than ninety pounds, my body was slowly shutting down. Fading into the Light seemed much more appealing (and possible) than fighting with any success. Obviously, God had other plans for me (I'm here!). Over the course of several years, He granted me freedom from anorexia bit by bit, taste by taste, and drew me closer to Him than I had ever been.

Freedom seems impossible for millions of people today. From relatively "minor" chains like anxiety and fear to weightier chains like full-blown addictions and human trafficking, the ways we can be enslaved are countless.

But regardless of the size and weight of our chains, we all seek one thing—freedom. We cling to hope, even if it is as delicate as a fragile bird the enemy is trying to snatch from our grasp.

The first volume of this study concluded with Pharaoh telling Moses, "Take both your flock and your herds, as you have said, and go, and bless me also." After ten devastating plagues that brought Egypt to its knees, Pharaoh finally gave in and wanted the Israelites gone. Losing his firstborn proved to be too much for the leader of Egypt; he wanted Israel out, and out now.

It was time for Israel to taste freedom for the first time in four hundred years – for the first time in any of their lives. Freedom had seemed like a cruel mirage until then. Moses and Aaron had come with its promise, but the battle for it had dragged on as each plague consumed Egypt with another expression of God's wrath. But now, the time had come... now they would finally leave.

Exodus 12:33–41

The Egyptians urged the people, to send them out of the land in haste, for they said, "We will all be dead." (12:33)

Our narrative begins with a shift from Pharaoh to his people, the Egyptians, both of whom shared a common goal—to get the Israelites out of Egypt. As often happens, what began with the leader filtered down to the common people. Pharaoh clearly and finally desired Israel's departure; his people now shared this desire with fervor and determination. They strongly **urged** the Israelites to leave. The Hebrew word for **urged** (*hazaq*) conveys the idea of exerting pressure.[1] While they were too afraid to be impolite (fearing that another plague might befall them), the Egyptians were nonetheless resolute in their insistence that their Israelite workforce should leave. They were not content to sit by and wait patiently for the Israelites to depart; they actively pressured them to do so.

Another instance where the Hebrew word *hazaq* is used can be found in Judges 19. It is a graphic story, but communicates the nuances of what **urged** means. A Levite man had a concubine who cheated on him and ran away to her father's house. The Levite found her and wanted to take her back, but her father detained (*hazaq*) her master/husband. He urged her husband to stay as long as possible because he knew his daughter's life was at stake due to her infidelity. He undoubtedly wanted to protect his daughter as much as possible and knew that nothing would happen to her as long as she remained under his roof. So he stalled firmly until he could not anymore. As it turned out, his premonitions were correct. His daughter left with her husband, and that night, wicked men surrounded the house they were staying in. They demanded to have sex with the husband. To escape the situation, the man seized (*hazaq* again) his concubine, shoved her out the door, and into the hands of the evil men who then "raped her and abused her all night until morning" (Judges 19:25). Sadly, she died from her injuries. It is an awful story that communicates the deplorable state of Israel at the time. But twice, we encounter the word *hazaq*. The father urged the husband to stay to protect his daughter; the husband urged the concubine out the door to her tragic fate. To "urge" in this context meant to pressure someone physically or with words. It is an active and relentless action, much like the Egyptians' posture toward the Israelites: they wanted them out of Egypt.

Not only did Egypt want Israel out, they wanted them out *now*. Determination married swiftness in the Egyptians' actions. They had been pummeled hard over the last year or so, economically, spiritually, emotionally, physically, and now in mourning as each household was touched by the deaths of their firstborns. Israel needed to leave immediately, and the Egyptians were emphatic about it. They reasoned, **"we will all be dead"** if the Israelites do not go. More death was the only logical conclusion of what would happen if Israel did not leave. Again, the Egyptians had lost their crops, livestock, health in many ways, and the death of countless firstborns; the only thing worse would be more death, and Egypt was wholeheartedly tapping out. They recognized their defeat and were willing to do anything necessary to evict Israel before more harm befell them.

So the people took their dough before it was leavened, with their kneading bowls bound up in the clothes on their shoulders. Now the sons of Israel had done according to the word of Moses, for they had requested from the Egyptians articles of silver and articles of gold, and clothing; and the Lord had given the people favor in the sight of the Egyptians, so that they let them have their request. Thus, they plundered the Egyptians. (12:34-36)

Israel reciprocated the Egyptians' urgency and headed out. They did not need or want to linger – freedom was waiting for them; they only had to get up and take it. And take it they did. The **people took their dough before it was leavened,** along with their other belongings, and began to head out. As we thoroughly discussed in the last volume, unleavened bread was a significant aspect of God's deliverance of Israel from His final plague on the Egyptians. Along with killing a one-year-old spotless lamb, the Israelites were instructed to only consume unleavened bread and bitter herbs (think, salad) with it. God also announced a new feast that Israel would observe every year for generations to come: the Feast of Unleavened Bread. Not a single bit of leaven would be found anywhere within the houses of the Israelites for the seven-day duration of this feast; only unleavened bread was permitted to be consumed. This was done, of course, to remind Israel (and also to teach their children) of what God had done for them in bringing them out of Egypt.

Preparing bread without leaven signified the haste with which Israel left. They simply did not have time to wait for leavened dough to rise before it was baked. They had waited long enough; now it was time to make haste **with their kneading bowls bound up in the clothes on their shoulders** and leave. As a mother of four girls, I have begun to learn the art and science of packing for trips, which lately means dance conventions. Enormous strategy goes into packing suitcases, especially since the girls are not able to carry a whole lot on their own. Thus, if I don't want to break my back lugging everything to the hotel myself, I need to consolidate what we have into the smallest amount of space possible.

While I now have the benefit of experience in this regard, we must remember that the Israelites had never packed for anything. They had been slaves; traveling was not exactly a perk they were allowed to enjoy (not that tourism was a big industry back then, anyway). In addition to the idea of freedom, the specifics of actually getting there were all new to them too. Men were likely responsible for the animals, tools, and such; women were responsible for packing everything needed to establish a home in the new land. Even though they were rushed, this required strategy, especially since they would be carting or carrying everything themselves. Binding up **kneading bowls ...in their clothes on their shoulders** killed two birds with one stone, so to speak. They used their clothing as packing material to keep the unleavened bread from spoiling.[2]

With that, we have a slight shift from practical luggage to that of wealth. But first, a reminder **that the sons of Israel had done according to the word of Moses, for they had requested from the Egyptians articles of silver and articles of gold, and clothing; and the Lord had given the people favor in the sight of the Egyptians, so that they let them have their request. Thus, they plundered the Egyptians.** Despite their moments of doubt and backlash before, Israel did obey God's command of asking their Egyptian neighbors for items of material wealth. God told them to do so before the Passover in Exodus 11:2, and with their obedience came the fulfillment of a prophecy that God made to Moses way back at the burning bush:

> But every woman shall ask of her neighbor and the woman who lives in her house, articles of silver and articles of gold, and clothing; and you will put them on your sons and daughters. Thus you will plunder the Egyptians. (Exodus 3:22)

Both Moses and the Israelites had come a long way and changed significantly since the day God called Moses on Mount Horeb. Moses, the coward who had tried everything he could think of to evade the call God had placed on his life, was now a strong, confident leader whom God had used to defeat one of the world's strongest empires. The Israelites had transformed from timid slaves into pioneers, boldly asking their former masters for the wealth they had worked a lifetime to accrue. Transformation is inevitable when we obey God's call. I do not know how introspective Moses and the Israelites were regarding their transformation thus far, but we have been given the benefit of inspired insight on their behalf, and it sheds a blinding light on the true Protagonist of the narrative.

God was accomplishing exactly what He said He would, as He always does. He did so with the plagues, with Pharaoh's flip-flopping mind, with Moses, and now with the abundant wealth Israel plundered from Egypt. Again, all the Egyptians wanted at this point was to survive. They had lost so much and, at God's sovereign nudge, had freely given much of what they had left to the Israelites. Israel had entered Egypt as a wealthy family who had earned even more prestige and favor through Joseph. Although they had been stripped of that as slaves, God was re-establishing them with abundant resources as they prepared to leave. They were leaving as they had come in—wealthy and with heads held high. They were God's people, set apart for His purposes, and He deserves all the credit and glory for Israel's burgeoning portfolio as they walked into their freedom.

Now the sons of Israel journeyed from Rameses to Succoth, about six hundred thousand men on foot, aside from children. (12:37)

And just like that, the Israelites walked out of Egypt to begin their journey of autonomy as a new nation. Their voyage began with a stint **from Rameses to Succoth** (see map)[3], which scholars believe was about a day's journey.[4] The exact location is impossible to pinpoint because of the inaccuracy and the total absence of maps from that time, but Tel el-Maskhuta, the modern-day site some scholars believe was preserved from ancient Succoth, is about 25 miles from Rameses.[5]

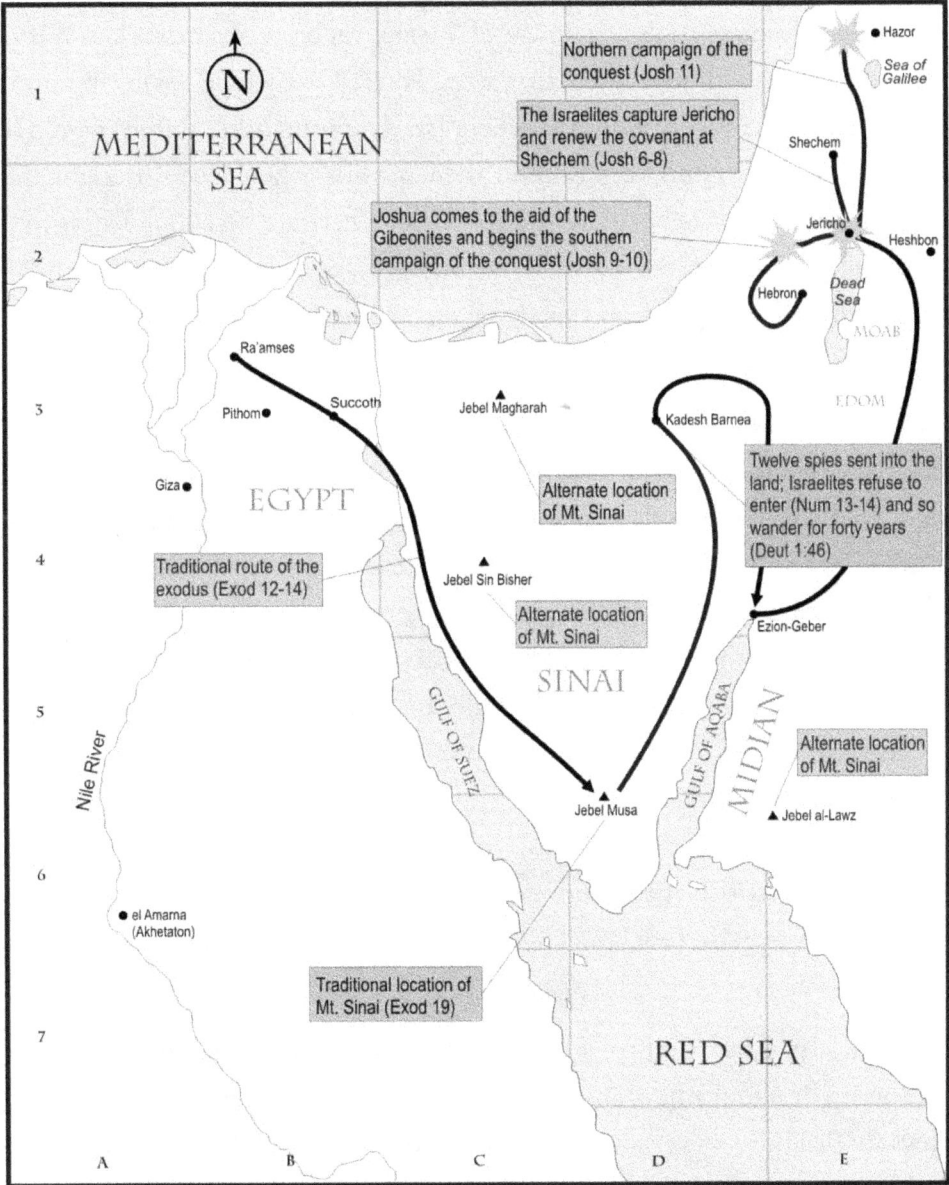

Northern campaign of the conquest (Josh 11)

The Israelites capture Jericho and renew the covenant at Shechem (Josh 6-8)

Joshua comes to the aid of the Gibeonites and begins the southern campaign of the conquest (Josh 9-10)

Twelve spies sent into the land; Israelites refuse to enter (Num 13-14) and so wander for forty years (Deut 1:46)

Traditional route of the exodus (Exod 12-14)

Alternate location of Mt. Sinai

Alternate location of Mt. Sinai

Alternate location of Mt. Sinai

Traditional location of Mt. Sinai (Exod 19)

MEDITERRANEAN SEA

Hazor
Sea of Galilee
Shechem
Jericho
Heshbon
Hebron
Dead Sea
MOAB
EDOM

Ra'amses
Pithom
Succoth
Jebel Magharah
Kadesh Barnea
Giza
EGYPT
Jebel Sin Bisher
SINAI
Ezion-Geber
Nile River
GULF OF SUEZ
GULF OF AQABA
MIDIAN
Jebel Musa
Jebel al-Lawz
el Amarna (Akhetaton)
RED SEA

N

1 2 3 4 5 6 7
A B C D E

Like everything else in our narrative, God wastes no detail. The word Succoth in Hebrew is *sukka* and refers to a booth or temporary shelter that both animals and soldiers took advantage of.[6] Israel then "took shelter" away from Egypt for the first time as their first stop. Later, God would establish another celebration, the "Feast of Booths," where Israel, among other things, would live in booths to mirror this very time in their history, when God "brought them out from the land of Egypt" (Leviticus 23:43). There are no coincidences in the providence of God. God led them to Succoth for a specific reason, and He would continue leading them exactly where and how He deemed best.

Having been informed of the location of Israel's first stop, God then revealed approximately how many people were in this traveling party: **about six hundred thousand men on foot, aside from children.** Scholars have had lots of fun with these few words, sometimes getting into heated debates about the accurate meaning and translation of nearly every term in Hebrew. The most traditional translation is the one presented here—**about six hundred thousand men on foot**, which would bring the total amount of people (including women and children) to approximately two million.[7] That is an enormous number of people, just under the current total population of Houston, Texas.[8] Some scholars doubt the feasibility of such a large group doing what Israel did—wandering around the desert for forty years as God-ordained nomads. We will briefly explore critics main arguments against the two most debated terms, **thousand** and **men on foot**, and conclude with the most probable interpretation and its relevance.

Some argue the validity of the term **thousand** for the Hebrew word *eleph,* and suggest it should be translated as "squad" or "unit" because the Hebrew allows for flexibility in certain instances.[9] If correct, the total number of Israelites would be brought down astronomically to about 25,000.[10] The main reasoning behind such arguments is that two million people are simply too many to handle.

In their minds, there is just no way that such a large group could have traveled together as Israel did, nor did the wilderness have enough resources to support them.

The phrase **men on foot** has also caused some disagreements over the years. Translations vary, with numerous interpretations ranging from just "men" to "soldiers on foot."[11] Some have even proposed that it could mean both men and women, making clarity on the issue that much more elusive.[12]

Asking questions, thinking critically, and studying God's Word deeply are all admirable endeavors and ones I pray more Christians start taking seriously. However, we should never get so caught up in textual criticism that we miss the point of what God is trying to communicate. The world of language is vast, peculiar, and will always have hidden pockets of subjective nuances. In our examples, it is true that the Hebrew term used for **thousand** (*eleph*), can be translated in numerous ways depending on the context.[13] But just because it is technically possible for it to be translated more than one way, it does not mean that it is probable or responsible to translate it any other way than the most obvious one. It makes the most sense to translate it as the overwhelming majority, if not all, translations have been done for hundreds of years– as **six hundred thousand.**

If we want to get technical for a moment, we can observe that the text states **about six hundred thousand.** Nowhere does it claim to be a precise, detailed number. It is, in fact, narrowed down to 603,550 later in Numbers 1:46. Furthermore, the authors of Scripture in ancient times used numbers differently than we do today. As one scholar explains:

> In the Bible, the numbers are correct, but they are correct in asserting what they actually meant, and this is not necessarily the same as what we think they meant.

If we do not know how the authors computed their numbers or what, to them, was the significance of the numbers. In that case, our interpretations will be wrong, even when we read a text that to us seems obvious and unambiguous in its meaning. And in fact, we probably do not understand the reasoning behind some of the biblical numbers. [14]

The basic rule of thumb for proper hermeneutics is to take Scripture literally unless the context demands otherwise. Sometimes, the text we are reading seems to contradict another text elsewhere, and since we know Scripture is inerrant and infallible, we are left to figure out what it means through deeper study. But here is the non-negotiable principle: our job is to discover what Scripture says in order to apply it to (and subsequently transform) our lives. We are never at liberty to make judgments about it simply because it does not satisfy our immediate understanding, or worse, our preferences. If a particular text does not initially make sense, we dig deeper; we do not disregard it or change the text to make it more convenient to understand.

Our text says **about six hundred thousand,** and that is accurate, making the total number of the traveling party around two million. Such a number makes sense and is supported by several additional factors. First, while Israel only numbered seventy when they entered Egypt, that was four hundred years prior—more than enough time to multiply at great numbers. This is especially true when considering that God had directly and purposefully increased their numbers when they became slaves as an affront to Pharaoh (Exodus 1:7, 12, 20). If you recall, Pharaoh said:

> "Behold, the people of the sons of Israel are more and mightier than we. Come, let us deal wisely with them, or else they will multiply and in the event of war; they will also join themselves to those who hate us, and fight against us and depart from the land." (Exodus 1:9-10)

Pharaoh would not have been afraid of 25,000 people. But he would have been terrified of almost 2 million and the threat they could pose to Egypt.

Secondly, "the demographic data given for the forty years of the wilderness wanderings are more or less internally consistent and accord with this [2 million] figure."[15] Scripture is consistent about the number of men being around 600,000 (Numbers 1:46; 2:32); the logical conclusion is that with women and children, that number would be at least tripled.

Lastly, the main reason behind critics' doubts about such a large number of people is quite disappointing. Ultimately, the argument boils down to the Israelites not being able to move or acquire proper sustenance in such great numbers. Frankly, that is a challenge to God's sovereignty. God provided everything they needed thus far, accomplishing one of the most significant rescue missions the world had ever seen. Also, God has been providing for everyone and every creature since the beginning of time:

> For this reason I say to you, do not be worried about your life, as to what you will eat or what you will drink; nor for your body, as to what you will put on…Look at the birds of the air, that they do not sow, nor reap nor gather into barns, and yet your heavenly Father feeds them. Are you not worth much more than they? (Matthew 6:25a, 26)

He has, is, and will continue to provide everything Israel (and we) need. As we will see in the coming chapters, He does exactly that repeatedly for Israel in the wilderness. To cast doubt on portions of Scripture simply because we do not think it is feasible means that we are putting ourselves in authority over God. It indicates that we think we know better, are smarter, and somehow have deeper knowledge than the omniscient God. This was Satan's tactic in the Garden of Eden and is one he uses again and again because of its success rate. Fight against it. Think critically, not foolishly.

We now turn our attention to the second term of discord, **men on foot**. Historically, this term has military undertones, and some suggest a more restrictive translation like "six hundred thousand young foot soldiers" to more accurately reflect the Hebrew verbiage and context.[16] The reason this is somewhat important is because 600,000 able-bodied men (basically, every man able to walk between the ages of 20-100) provides a much different total number than 600,000 young foot soldiers (likely between the ages of 20-40). The former keeps the total number at around two million; the latter would make the number much higher.

In accordance with the majority of translations, it seems most likely that the standing translation is accurate. Most obviously, because it is doubtful that Israel would have had any kind of established military yet or were even thinking about it. They were literally just leaving slavery for the first time in generations. That kind of military organization requires time and attention, and at the moment, they were preoccupied just trying to get out. Therefore, it seems like the 600,000 approximation refers to men "of age" who were able to be **on foot**, not necessarily young men who were trained as soldiers.

Complicating the matter even more is the next verse:

> **A mixed multitude also went up with them, along with flocks and herds, a very large number of lives. (12:38)**

The Israelites were not the only ones to leave Egypt, which is often a neglected detail in Exodus studies. Unsurprisingly, many theories exist regarding who these people were and why they joined Israel. Among some of the most plausible are: (1) slaves of other ethnicities who took advantage of the post-plague chaos and decided to join with Israel for freedom,[17] (2) people of mixed ethnicities who were living in Egypt and witnessed God's power firsthand, choosing to align themselves with Israel as His followers,[18] or (3) people who simply took advantage of an exciting opportunity when they saw it. Egypt was, after all, a destitute mess, and people would have had little motivation to stick around and help rebuild.[19]

Regardless of the motivation, we know two things about this group of people with certainty: first, that they were of **mixed** nationalities and ethnicities; and second, that there were a lot of them, increasing the number of travelers even more. We have already seen a glimpse into foreigners being among the Israelites in God's instructions about the Passover and Feast of Unleavened Bread. In Exodus 12:22, God states that anyone who eats leavened bread during the seven-day feast will be cut off from Israel "whether they are an alien or a native of the land." Instructions regarding foreign residents are addressed in the books of the law, leaving us to believe that foreigners were always among the Israelites to some extent. Perhaps they were sprinkled among the Israelites as slaves when Egypt conquered their native people, and they eventually struck up friendships with the Israelites. Or maybe they were just respectable neighbors who lived civilly near the Israelites in Egypt, saw God's obvious hand moving on their behalf, and wanted to associate themselves with them more than Egypt. Regardless, these people would have had different cultural and religious practices, which God would address numerous times in the coming years. These foreigners would have different rules than the Israelites when it came to obedience to God's law, but they were to be treated with respect among the Israelites (Leviticus 19:33).

While usually portrayed in a neutral light, one danger that foreigners posed to Israel was their foreign gods. The foreigners, at this point, had seen God's hand at work and were obviously in favor of it enough to follow Israel out of Egypt. But was their favor enough to totally convert their faith? Did they give up every one of their idols and previous beliefs? Not likely. Rather, they probably added God to their belief system, which, if anything like the rest of the world at the time, was highly polytheistic. In other words, they might have adapted their religious beliefs to include God, but God did not completely rebuild and become the center of their belief system.

The presence of idols would be a point of consternation throughout the future generations of Israel because they wanted to be like the people around them. They would be tempted to set aside their belief in God in order to pursue (or additionally include) false ones. Warnings against such a danger will be issued later in this volume, but it is wise to note it here because this **mixed multitude** inevitably included their idols.

Along with **a multitude** of people also came a large number of **flocks and herds**. If you recall, the fifth plague was a fatal pestilence that attacked the Egyptians' "livestock which were in the field, on the horses, on the donkeys, on the camels, on the herds, and on the flocks" (9:3). All of their livestock died, which was an enormous blow to their economy on several fronts. But God spared Israel's livestock, and "not one died" (9:6b). Israel entered Egypt as shepherds, an occupation that was "loathsome to the Egyptians" (Genesis 46:34). God had certainly blessed Jacob with the gift of shepherding (Genesis 30:25-43), and it is safe to assume that the gift continued to produce large numbers of flocks and herds as the Israelite population grew. This made their traveling caravan enormous indeed, containing a **very large number** of lives, both man and beast alike.

> **They baked the dough which they had brought out of Egypt into cakes of unleavened bread. For it had not become leavened, since they were driven out of Egypt and could not delay, nor had they prepared any provisions for themselves. (12:39)**

The haste with which the Israelites left is reflected here in the lack of leaven for their bread. **Cakes of unleavened bread** were much faster to bake than leavened ones, for they had no need to rise. Further, they were new to traveling and had not **prepared any provisions for themselves.** God had provided what they needed with the plunder from the Egyptians, along with their flocks and herds. However, they were receiving a crash course on how to prepare food "on the road," so to speak.

Although I am a decent cook, I don't enjoy it much. Part of the reason is that it is very time-consuming, and we have it so easy in our modern world of grocery stores and appliances. Still, it requires planning, shopping, preparing, storing, and then washing dishes. Add that to an already full plate (pun accidental, but it works) of being a homeschooling mom of four, it's just something I do not find enjoyment in. Just thinking about learning how to plan and prepare meals without modern-day conveniences, all while walking with an enormous caravan, gives me slight heart palpitations. This journey was going to be a struggle for "Type A" people who thrived on routine and order. They were going to need to learn a new rhythm of spontaneity, thinking quickly on their feet, and providing for their families in new ways. **Unleavened bread** was step one in letting go of their former routines and embracing new ones, an invitation to exchange comfortable familiarity with courageous obedience as they followed God to freedom.

> **Now the time that the sons of Israel lived in Egypt was four hundred and thirty years. And at the end of four hundred and thirty years, to the very day, all the house of the Lord went out from the land of Egypt. (12:40-41)**

"And the grand total is…" Those words carry a sense of anticipation in any context. In the form of a bill, it is anticipatory dread; in the form of an accomplishment, it is an anticipated measure of pride. For Israel, it was an anticipated sigh of relief and realized hope. The grand total? **Four hundred and thirty years**. Israel had been in Egypt for nearly half a millennium, with numerous generations living and being enslaved in a foreign land.

At first glance, the number **four hundred and thirty** poses a problem of inconsistency for the astute reader because in Genesis 15:13, God told Abraham that his descendants "will be strangers in a land that is not theirs, where they will be enslaved and oppressed for four hundred years." There seems to be a thirty-year discrepancy. But when we look deeper, as many scholars have, we find a simple solution to the apparent problem. The Israelites lived in Egypt as favored citizens before they became enslaved; thus, it is likely that they lived in Egypt for four hundred and thirty years but were enslaved in Egypt for four hundred years of those years. God had fulfilled His promise to Abraham as well as to his descendants – after hundreds of years in a foreign land, **all the house of the Lord** went out to embrace the freedom He was offering.

Exodus 12:42-51

Weddings are perhaps the most anticipated events in one's lifetime. Little girls dream and plan for their weddings from a very early age – imagining details from the dress to the flowers. Once engaged, the dream becomes an impending reality as the bride and groom navigate through those details and make final decisions. Anticipation is high as both families and friends excitedly prepare for the big day, marking the beginning of two lives becoming one. When the day finally comes, it is a blissful blur as we try to savor each moment but are also caught almost floating from one part to the next.

The actual moment of the Exodus must have been similarly surreal. Like a wedding, I imagine the Israelites were in a state of reverie. Each step they took fulfilled the dream that both they and their ancestors had longed for throughout generations. So many thoughts must have been competing for their attention, from last-minute checklists to absorbing the historic moment as best they could.

They did not want to forget, and God did not want the significance of this moment to be forgotten either. He had already prescribed new ordinances regarding the Passover and Feast of Unleavened Bread that the Israelites would celebrate every year indefinitely. He now provides a literary interlude in the narrative before reminding Moses and Aaron of more details regarding the Passover.

> **It is a night to be observed for the Lord for having brought them out from the land of Egypt; this night is for the Lord, to be observed by all the sons of Israel throughout their generations. (12:42)**

A wise bride and groom will realize early on that their special day, while about them, is really for their families and friends. It provides a formal chance to celebrate, and it is enjoyed just as much (or even more) by the families and friends as it is by the bride and groom. Though the Passover night was meant to be remembered, celebrated, and rejoiced over by the Israelites (and certainly for their benefit), the true focus of celebration was to be the Lord. This night was **to be observed for the Lord**; it is, as reiterated just words later, **for the Lord.**

Unfortunately, English translations differ on this verse, which sometimes lead us to miss the full point of what is being communicated. Another translation reads, "That was for the Lord a night of vigil to bring them out of the land of Egypt; that same night is the Lord's, one of vigil for all the children of Israel throughout all the ages."[20] The NIV translation communicates it in another way that is easier to understand: "Because the Lord kept vigil that night to bring them out of Egypt, on this night, all the Israelites are to keep vigil to honor the Lord for generations to come." God watched over them, now it was their turn to keep watch for Him and honor Him for generations to come.

Both Israel's rescue and the command for them to remember it were for the purpose of glorifying God. The theme weaving itself throughout the whole book of Exodus is the idea of being set apart, and God begins by setting Himself apart. He is wholly distinct and unmatched from His creation. Everything we do, from every word that passes through our lips to every action taken with our hands, should shine a light on His holiness. God was making Israel an enormous, wandering beacon shining light on His presence in the world—proving that He was holy and like no other. As Jesus tells us in Matthew 5:14-16:

> You are the light of the world. A city set on a hill cannot be hidden; nor does anyone light a lamp and put it under a basket, but on the lampstand, and it gives light to all who are in the house. Let your light shine before men in such a way that they may see your good works, and glorify your Father who is in heaven.

Who we are, what we say, how we act, and what we do is all **for the Lord.** He wanted the Israelites to remember the Exodus as a prominent anniversary, so they would keep Him at the forefront of their minds and hearts **throughout their generations.**

> **The Lord said to Moses and Aaron, "This is the ordinance of the Passover, no foreigner is to eat of it; but every man's slave purchased with money, after you have circumcised him, then he may eat of it. A sojourner or a hired servant shall not eat of it." (12:43-45)**

These verses refer to the **mixed multitude** we chatted about earlier in 12:38 who went with Israel out of Egypt. While they were welcome to join Israel, they were not welcome to participate in the Passover. **No foreigner is to eat of it,** nor **a sojourner or a hired servant.** The only non-Israelite who was permitted to participate in the Passover was a **man's slave purchased with money,** and only then after he was **circumcised.** God did not hit Egypt with detrimental plagues over the course of the year for the sake of foreigners. He was not setting apart sojourners and hired servants. He rescued and set apart *His* people. His people (and those properly grafted in) were the only ones permitted to celebrate a feast of remembrance for it.

Circumcision, while not a particularly pleasant topic to think about (especially for our male readers), was the way that God chose to set apart His people, beginning with Abraham in Genesis:

> This is My covenant, which you shall keep, between Me and you and your descendants after you: every male among you shall be circumcised. And you shall be circumcised in the flesh of your foreskin, and it shall be the sign of the covenant between Me and you. And every male among you who is eight days old shall be circumcised throughout your generations…a servant who is born in the house or who is bought with money shall surely be circumcised; thus shall my covenant be in your flesh for an everlasting covenant." (Genesis 17:10-12a, 13)

God uses the same language in Genesis as He does here in Exodus to describe the slaves permitted to join the family of Israel, so to speak, and therefore become a part of their covenant community. God's people were to reflect God in His holiness. Joining Israel's covenant community required the physical removal of the foreskin to, in part, represent the individual's removal from the world and dedication to God.

The same is true when someone comes to faith in Christ today. As we discussed, we cannot simply add God to our already-established philosophies and worldviews. He is not an accessory that adorns our lives and adds a nice little addendum to our resumes. He becomes our life and authors our resume from that point forward. The foreskin was (and still is) the most tender, vulnerable part of a man, the part he would naturally choose to protect and hold onto at all costs. Cutting it off was a powerful act, symbolizing that he was willing to give it all in order to follow the Lord and be a part of His covenant community. People who wanted to join Israel and celebrate God with them in these contexts had to give it all. They had to make themselves vulnerable and remove a part of the most well-protected member of their bodies to symbolize their willingness to shed their old worldview and allow God to shape their new one.

> **It is to be eaten in a single house; you are not to bring forth any of the flesh outside of the house, nor are you to break any bone of it. (12:46)**

Continuing with His instructions for the Passover, God clarifies three important points regarding the Passover lamb. First, **it is to be eaten in a single house**, which aligns with His previous instruction to keep it within individual families. The only exception mentioned in 12:4 is when a household is too small for a lamb. In such cases, "he and his nearest neighbor" were instructed to share a lamb. We discussed the importance of the family in the first volume of this study, and its echo here confirms that this celebration was meant to be personal and confined to individual families rather than a congregational gathering.

Secondly, the Israelites were **prohibited from taking any of the flesh outside of the house**. Most obviously, the meat was to remain inside because the

Israelites needed to stay indoors during the tenth plague. The lamb's blood, spread on the doorposts and lintel of their houses, provided protection from God's wrath that swept through Egypt and claimed the lives of their firstborns. Remaining indoors was not negotiable; it was how they stayed under the protection of the blood. Another reason for keeping the meat inside was to safeguard it from unwelcome, unqualified individuals, animals, or accidents.[21] The meat became sacred due to its association with the Passover celebration and had to be treated as such. It was set apart, just as the people set God apart in their worship and remembrance of what He had done for them. It was always to remain in the house, protected and treated with respect for what it represented—a sacrifice that spared them from death.

The reason for such care is culminated in Who the last piece of instruction represents. The Israelites were not **to break any bone** of the lamb, just like the ultimate Lamb, Jesus Christ, would not have any bones broken in His sacrifice on the cross (John 19:36). The Passover was celebrated not only for what God did in the tenth plague (which certainly would have been enough); but also, and more importantly, for what the tenth plague represented as a future reality of the gospel for those who would believe. The lambs sacrificed in the Passover were without blemish, but were unwilling participants in the salvation of those their blood redeemed. Jesus, however, was both a perfect and willing sacrifice—laying down His life so others may come to life in Him. The Passover was the gospel in symbolic and anticipatory form, which is why God was adamant about its careful and consecrated observation.

Freedom from Egypt was made possible through the Passover. Without God's provision of sacrifice on Israel's behalf, they would not have been able to even dream of freedom, much less experience it. The point here and for us is that salvation is costly because sin is costly. In Exodus, it cost the destruction of one of the most powerful kingdoms in the world and the personal sacrifice of families' choicest lamb. In God's kingdom, it cost the death of His Son—the only One who did not deserve it—the Lamb of God who takes away the sin of the world (John 1:29).

The symbolism in the Passover is an endless spring of water beckoning us to drink deeply. With each sip, we become simultaneously satisfied and addicted, wanting more. Israel did not fully realize the depths of the Passover waters, but their obedience would reveal more as they participated and taught their children to do the same for generations to come.

> **All the congregation of Israel are to celebrate this. But if a stranger sojourns with you, and celebrates the Passover to the Lord, let all his males be circumcised, and then let him come near to celebrate it; and he shall be like a native of the land. But no uncircumcised person may eat of it. The same law shall apply to the native as to the stranger who sojourns among you. (12:47-49).**

Though the Passover was meant to be celebrated intimately among individual families, it was also a congregational celebration in the sense that everyone participated at the same time. Think of it loosely in terms of Christmas morning – celebrating Christ coming to Earth with our immediate families, yet uniting with the Church worldwide by observing it simultaneously. Passover was both intimately familial and a corporate act of worship.

Additionally, it was not optional: **all the congregation of Israel was required to celebrate it**. Today, we have a lot of freedom in how we worship. However, during the time of Exodus, formal worship was more regulated (as we will see later in our study). The Passover, along with other celebrations to be detailed later, was a prescribed and mandatory way that Israel was supposed to worship.

God then reiterates the importance of circumcision, stating that only those who are circumcised would be allowed to **come near and celebrate it**. Everyone was welcome, but joining the covenantal community through circumcision was a non-negotiable requirement. Once again, the Passover was an intimate act of worship where the Israelites looked back on what God did for them in Egypt and then looked forward to a Savior who would offer total and final freedom for them. It required reverence and strict compliance with the laws God prescribed.

Then all the sons of Israel did so; they did just as the Lord had commanded Moses and Aaron. And on that same day the Lord brought the sons of Israel out of the land of Egypt by their hosts. (12:50-51)

These verses immediately remind me of the old hymn, "Trust and Obey:" [22]

> When we walk with the Lord
> In the light of His Word,
> What a glory He sheds on our way!
> While we do His good will,
> He abides with us still,
> And with all who will trust and obey.
> Trust and obey
> For there's no other way
> To be happy in Jesus
> But to trust and obey.

While not perfect every step of the way, Moses, Aaron, and the Israelites ultimately trusted and obeyed God—**they did just as the Lord had commanded**. Is there a sweeter, more satisfying triumph? Any eulogy with those words would reflect the life of a soul most accomplished, someone who achieved transcendent success.

Observe the relationship between Israel's obedience and their reward: **on that same day, the Lord brought the sons of Israel out of the land of Egypt by their hosts**. Let's be clear: God accomplished so much for them before they ever did anything for Him. He raised up Moses, inflicted the plagues upon Egypt, dealt with Pharaoh's stubborn heart, etc. That represents what He does for us in the gospel. He always makes the first move because we are dead in our sins, rendering us unable to ever make the first move. While God saves and frees us from our sins for eternity, He expects us to live free of our sins here and now.

While we are still on Earth, we are expected to live out practically who He declares us to be in Christ, and that always involves obedience.

God saved Israel from Egypt and clearly instructed them to comply with His Passover instructions as a way to worship and remember His holiness, provision, and salvation in their lives. God had given them everything; all they had to do was respond and accept it. This meant obeying. Generally speaking, obedience precipitates rewards, and disobedience bears consequences. If they wanted to embrace and live in the freedom He made possible, they had to trust and obey Him. If they did, they could experience freedom and a brand new life better than what they ever could have imagined possible. Though it would not always be the case, in this instance, Israel opted for obedience and received freedom for it. Would they have been freed if they had not obeyed? We are in no position to speculate, but then, we do not need to. They obeyed. After four hundred and thirty years of being homeless—without a land of their own—they officially began the journey of establishing their own nation, following God every step of the way.

Exodus 13:1-16

Then the Lord spoke to Moses, saying, "Sanctify to Me every firstborn, the first offspring of every womb among the sons of Israel, both of man and beast; it belongs to Me." (13:1-2)

Perspective is the riverbank of our thoughts, keeping them focused and flowing in the right direction. We cannot control many of the circumstances in our lives, but we can control how we react and respond to them. Much anxiety, stress, and angst in life can be avoided simply by maintaining a biblical perspective. Aligning our thoughts with God's Word will keep our lives on track, as the Israelites did when they decided to trust and obey God.

God's command here might jolt us a bit upon the initial reading. He tells Moses that every firstborn, **both man and beast**, must be sanctified (set apart) to Him because it/he belongs to Him. Such a command flies in the face of our natural, sinful perspective because we like to believe that what we have belongs to us—that we somehow actually own and are in control of what we have. We cling onto our relationships, things, and portfolios, hardly willing to relinquish them for any reason unless, as a material good, we get a significant return for them.

But what does **sanctify** in this context actually mean? With children, it most certainly did not mean sacrificing them as an offering like some cultures did in ancient times. It also did not mean, with very rare exceptions (1 Samuel 1:11), that God wanted the families to give up their firstborns to serve in special service to Him, removed from their homes for their entire lives. Rather, it meant a shift in perspective, dedicating their firstborn children to God in recognition that 1) they were a gift from God to begin with, 2) that everything in this world and our possession rightfully belongs to Him anyway, and 3) that they were in submission to God—a posture that is "so important for salvation, personal discipline, and blessing."[23]

Firstborns bore special responsibilities and represented their whole families in ancient times.[24] Part of sanctifying them, or setting them apart, meant redeeming and consecrating them. While not specified here, this act of redemption would eventually require payment,[25] as seen in the case of Jesus in Luke 2:22-24:

> And when the days of their purification according to the law of Moses were completed, they brought Him up to Jerusalem to present Him to the Lord (as it is written in the Law of the Lord, "Every firstborn male that opens the womb shall be called holy to the Lord"). And to offer a sacrifice according to what was said in the Law of the Lord, "A pair of turtledoves or two young pigeons."

Jesus, of course, is the perfect example of the sanctification of the firstborn for more than one reason. He was the embodiment and culmination of what this practice represented. The Passover required the deaths of the firstborns in

Egypt and the deaths of unblemished lambs—sacrifices necessary to save God's people. Just the same, but even more so, Jesus became the ultimate firstborn and unblemished Lamb sacrificed on our behalf:

> If God is for us, who is against us? *He who did not spare His own Son, but delivered Him over for us all*, how will He not also with Him freely give us all things? (Romans 8:31b-32, emphasis added)

Sanctifying their firstborn children served many purposes for the Israelites. First, it gave them a reason to pause, remember, and meditate on what God did for them in bringing them out of slavery in Egypt. Next, it challenged them to reorient their perspective and align it with God's. "The earth is the Lord's, and all it contains," beginning with our children, whom we cherish most (1 Corinthians 10:25). We own nothing in the true sense of the word. We are merely stewards of what He has given us, and God expected Israel to formally recognize this by dedicating their firstborn to Him. Lastly, this act of sanctification pointed to Jesus, whom God gave up for us. Jesus' sacrifice paved the way for our own sanctification—we can now be set apart in Him, and join with Him in advancing the gospel here on earth.

Along with their firstborn children, Israel was also to sanctify **the first offspring of every womb** among beasts as well. Most commonly, these animals were destined to be sacrificed as an offering (Deuteronomy 15:19-20), unless they were redeemed (purchased) with something else (Numbers 18:15-16).

Sacrificing the firstborn of an animal served as a powerful means of commemorating Israel's own redemption from Egypt and renewing their perspective to align with God's will. He is the Author, Ruler, Sustainer, and Owner of the world; everything we have originates from and belongs to Him.

Moses said to the people, "Remember this day in which you went out from Egypt, from the house of slavery; for by a powerful hand the Lord brought you out from this place.

And nothing leavened shall be eaten. On this day in the month of Abib, you are about to go forth. It shall be when the Lord brings you to the land of the Canaanite, the Hittite, the Amorite, the Hivite, and the Jebusite, which He swore to your fathers to give you, a land flowing with milk and honey, that you shall observe this rite in this month. For seven days you shall eat unleavened bread, and on the seventh day there shall be a feast to the Lord. Unleavened bread shall be eaten throughout the seven days; and nothing leavened shall be seen among you, nor shall any leaven be seen among you in all your borders. (13:3-7)

One element of creation not often referenced is that of memory. The all-knowing God made a way for His created beings to learn and remember what they learn by uniquely designing our brains to function collectively and progressively. From a baby learning how to articulate her mother's name to an astronomer studying details of the universe unknown throughout most of history, the human mind, and particularly our ability to remember, is no small feat. It illuminates the mastery of God's imagination and power in creating us in His image.

But memory is neither simple nor predictable. Sometimes, we remember what we do not want to, or cannot for the life of us recall things that we want to (and should!) remember. A German psychologist, Hermann Ebbinghaus (1850-1909),[26] studied and proposed several widely referenced theories on memory, including a fascinating "Forgetting Curve," which aims to show the declining relationship between the information we retain and the period of time we retain it.[27]

Ebbinghaus Forgetting Curve

Retention (%)

100% — 100%
80%
60%
40% — 58%
20% — 44% 36% 33% 28% 25% 21%
0%

immediately · 20 minutes · 1 hour · 9 hours · 1 day · 2 days · 6 days · 31 days

Elapsed Time Since Learning

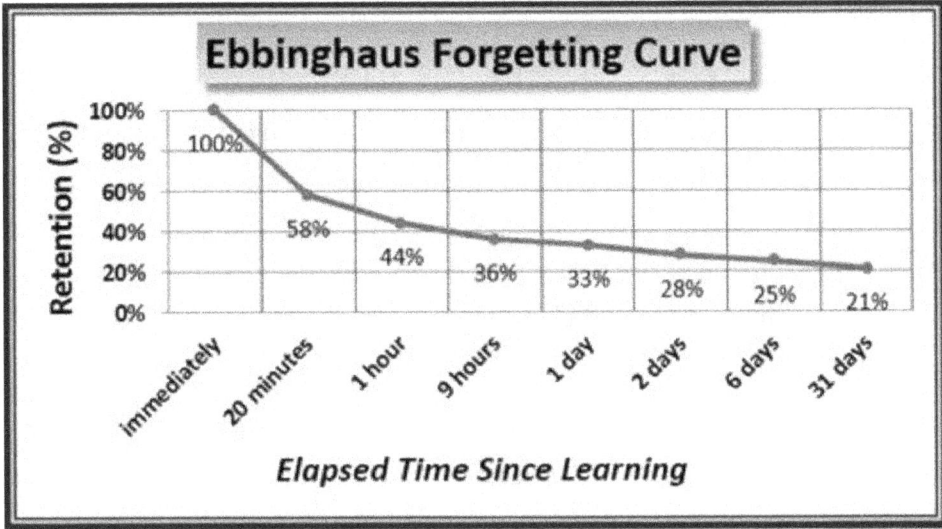

This graph reveals what we all know to be true: we actively retain very little of the information we receive, especially as more time passes. We are easily distracted, forgetful people. Though our memories are powerful, and we will inevitably remember specific, momentous life events, no subject is totally immune to our forgetfulness. Unless we repeat something every day, it often fades from our ability to remember what it is or how to do it.

Consider your wedding day. Most people, especially brides, can recall many details; they did, in fact, plan for months leading up to the day. But can we remember every single detail? I can't. My memory is like a highlight reel, shining a spotlight on many details throughout the day, but I cannot remember the entirety of our pastor's message; I even struggle to remember the songs played during the ceremony and reception.

Though we probably all remember our wedding day with more clarity than we do most others, we also likely do not sit around and dwell on it too often. Anniversaries are obviously the most natural occasion to do so, but as years go by, the details seem to fade in importance as you now actively engage in what your life has become together. As time goes on, we begin to forget even the most significant moments in our lives unless we actively pursue their memory. If we do not actively engage in remembering, we will passively forget.

The Exodus was not an event the Israelites were going to truly forget. It was a once-in-a-million-lifetime kind of event that they were blessed enough to experience. The experience was likely seared into their souls. But as the years went by, the vibrancy of the details would begin to fade. The transparent, clean stream of their memory would cloud with debris the further downstream they went.

To keep their memories unpolluted, God established several "washing stations"—ways for Israel to deliberately and intentionally meditate on the exodus and what it signified, salvation for their souls. God wanted them to **remember this day**, how they **went out from the house of slavery…by a powerful hand.** The first way they would remember it (as we have studied before), was that **nothing leavened shall be eaten.**

As with any anniversary, this act of purposeful remembrance would occur at the same time every year, specifically **on this** [the 15th] **day of the month of Abib.** As discussed in the first volume of our study, God was establishing a new calendar with the Israelites, their new beginning would coordinate with how they would measure time. This foreshadows another major calendar beginning that would correspond with a God-event, the birth of Jesus Christ. Jesus' birth changed the calendar of the world and how we measure history from B.C. to A.D. It is fitting that He would prelude such a historical moment with a similar event, just like the sacrifice of Christ was foreshadowed by the Passover.

God frames His instructions in the context of an already articulated promise—**when the Lord brings you to the land of the Canaanite, the Hittite, the Amorite, the Hivite and the Jebusite, which He swore to your fathers to give you, a land flowing with milk and honey, that you shall observe this rite in this month.** We discussed these people groups in the first volume of this study when we came to Exodus 3:8, so I will not repeat all the details. The point here is that Israel's promised land was currently occupied, but God would take care of it. If Egypt was not a formidable foe to God, these smaller people groups certainly would not be. God had reserved that land for His people, and it was a good land, **a land flowing with milk and honey.** It would be a land where Israel would prosper and enjoy living. Unlike Egypt, where all their efforts benefited the Egyptians, they would reap all the benefits of their efforts in the land of promise.

The Israelites were not just being saved from something (slavery); they were being saved *for* something—to be God's representatives on Earth. Like He promised Abraham (Genesis 15:18-21), He would establish His people in their own land, a land they would enjoy as long as they remained faithful to His covenant with them. In this land, the fulfillment of God's promise is where Israel was to celebrate the Feast of Unleavened Bread.

Instructions concerning the feast are then re-articulated. Israelites were to eat unleavened bread **for seven days, and on the seventh day, there shall be a feast unto the Lord.** As an extra precaution, every ounce of leaven was to be removed from their homes and placed outside their borders. Leaven was an ingredient the Israelites used and worked with daily. It is not difficult to imagine someone waking up and beginning daily food preparations, accidentally forgetting the temporary ban, and making their bread with leaven out of habit. This feast was to be observed with utmost diligence; temporarily removing all the leaven from within the borders of Israel would help them remain faithful in their obedience.

Banning leaven served the purpose of remembering what God had done, but it also served another purpose—one of instruction to the younger generations of Israelites who had not experienced the exodus themselves.

You shall tell your son on that day, saying, "It is because of what the Lord did for me when I came out of Egypt." And it shall serve as a sign to you on your hand, and as a reminder on your forehead, that the law of the Lord may be in your mouth; for with a powerful hand the Lord brought you out of Egypt.

Therefore, you shall keep this ordinance at its appointed time from year to year. (13:8-10)

Herein lies the crux of parenthood and discipleship in general—teaching children (either literally or in faith) the truths of God's Word. Discipleship is Scripture being lived out in the context of relationships. It is when we are both learning the truth of God's Word and simultaneously applying it to our lives as we walk alongside others. Parenthood is a form of discipleship. Contrary to what some elements of society would like us to believe, parents are responsible for their children. This includes, but is not limited to their health, well-being, diets, shelter, clothing, social life, education, development of worldview, and theological instruction.

Far too often, parents send their children to school and wash their hands of the education they receive. "After all," they reason, "it's the school's and teachers' responsibility to educate my children. That's what we pay them for!" Or, a family will arrive at church only to be immediately segregated, each going to their "age-appropriate" class. The assumption is that the volunteers and/or staff members will teach their children biblical principles and subsequently, lay the theological framework that is supposed to be the foundation of their faith. The same thing happens with sports, music lessons, art classes, and any other extracurricular activities. Parents delegate their responsibility to someone else so they can work or pursue other endeavors.

While some of these are necessary (we cannot, after all, be teaching experts at every venture our children desire to explore), the danger is that parents are no longer bearing the active, primary responsibility of raising and disciplining their children. The fact is that children are parented by whoever is around them the most. When children spend more time with their teachers, recreational program staff members, adult volunteers, and coaches, they are being parented by those adults, not their parents. Eventually, their concept of home will more closely resemble a rental unit. Their family members will be more like roommates who only come together to eat, sleep, and occasionally play.

God's original design for the family was much different and significantly better than what our culture has stripped the family down to. A family begins with one biological man and one biological woman who are committed to each other within the lifelong covenant of marriage (every aspect of this, unfortunately, is being viciously attacked in our culture today). Both spouses are to be fully committed to God first and to each other second as they harmoniously live together with complementary roles, embrace and share the gospel through active discipleship within the church, and work hard to fulfill the calling God has placed on their lives professionally. Two lives become one in Christ and mirror the beautiful relationship that Christ has with His church.

If God blesses the couple with children, one major role is added to their purpose—training and equipping their children to know and love Christ through the process of discipleship. Time restricts me from sharing my full philosophy of parenting, but one major tenet of it is seen in our current passage—**You shall tell your son on that day, saying, "It is because of what the Lord did for me when I came out of Egypt."** At its core, the Feast of Unleavened Bread and the Passover were to be opportunities for parents to teach their children about God and His salvation. They were designed to give parents a straightforward and obvious reason to disciple their children.

The term **son** here is not gender specific (not only for sons); it also includes daughters, so the word "child" would be a more appropriate English translation.[28] Every child in a family was to be taught about God and reminded of His power, faithfulness, and holiness every time they celebrated this feast.

It is also worth noting the use of the singular pronoun in this verse: **me**. It does not say what the Lord did for *us* when *we* came out of Egypt (though it will in verse 14), but rather, **what the Lord did for me when I came out of Egypt.** This was personal. We discussed about the personal and intimate familial aspect of the Passover in the first volume and saw a glimpse of that here again. Faith in God and our worship of Him is first personal. We are saved individually and then made members of His family. God does not save us in bulk. We do not get into heaven one day because of our proximity to another believer.

God desired the intimacy of His salvation to be passed down in an intimate setting. Fathers taking time to speak with their children about what God had done for them individually would have had a much more profound impact on the children than hearing it in a corporate setting. Don't get me wrong—corporate worship is absolutely crucial for the development and nurturing of our faith. However, we tend to grow the most in more intimate settings with people we know personally, love, and admire. The Israelites experienced freedom personally as well as corporately, and God wanted the personal aspect of it to be handed down to future generations in an intimate way.

We have similar opportunities to celebrate God in personal ways through dedicated celebrations today. Holidays like Easter and Christmas are theologically obvious, but discipleship can be advanced through other holidays too, such as Thanksgiving, Labor Day, Valentine's Day, and more. Each of these holidays can serve as a catalyst to launch fruitful discussions with our children, exploring the truth behind each and how we can bring God glory in and through our celebration of them. The problem, however, is that we (as parents) rarely take the time to be purposeful about them.

Even mandated and regulated celebrations run the risk of not being taken seriously by Israel, just as they are for us. We can go through the motions easily enough—we can read Luke's account of Christ's birth every Christmas, just like the Israelites could have put away their leaven and told the story of the Exodus to their children by rote memory. But both miss the mark. God wants full, intentional, and enthusiastic discipleship of children by their parents who are fully, intentionally, and enthusiastically in a thriving relationship with Him.

Parents who are active disciples in Jesus will inspire active discipleship in their children. Children observe both the actions and words of their parents; they know when we are faking it or when something is forced. We need to live out the faith we want our children to have. Our lives should be the runway from which they learn to take flight and then soar.

Such discipleship should come as naturally as dressing ourselves every day: **it shall serve as a sign to you on your hand, and as a reminder on your forehead, that the law of the Lord may be in your mouth.** Dressing ourselves every morning is hardly something we would forget to do. Some of us may put more effort into it than others (I once knew a young woman who would strategically plan out her wardrobe and paint her nails daily to match!). Regardless of the amount of effort, we all are intentional enough about it to ensure we do not walk out the door naked.

The **sign** on **your hand** likely refers to accessories like rings, and the **reminder on your forehead** (more accurately, "between the eyes") represents headwear and also the symbolic placement of God's truth as our primary focus. Both of these serve the purpose that **the law of the Lord may be in your mouth** that we speak of it often, both in personal meditation, corporate worship, and instruction to our children.

Later, Jews would take these instructions more literally and begin writing this and other similar passages on pieces of parchment paper to be worn in boxes (called phylacteries) on their foreheads and left arm.[29] While a bit much, Jesus never condemned the practice itself, but rather their motivation behind it— "they do all their deeds to be noticed by men; for they broaden their phylacteries" (Matthew 23:5). It is one thing to wear something as a physical reminder to worship, and we do this often with cross necklaces, purity rings, etc. As Calvin writes:

> The sum is that in the Passover, a monument of God's grace should exist so that it might never sink into oblivion, just as ornaments which appear on the forehead and on the fingers awaken the attention by their being constantly beheld.[30]

When we adorn ourselves with these items for the purpose of appearing holy, the effect is rendered mute. Such accessories should be worn to remind us to worship. If their effectiveness diminishes, if we become accustomed to them, or worse, if we start using them to promote the illusion of piety, we should set them aside and refocus on redirecting our affections to Christ.

Certain accessories may serve as legitimate reminders to our ever-wandering minds and hearts. The key, however, is to remain grounded and dedicated in our worship of the Lord. Our relationships with God, meditation upon His Word, and subsequent discipleship of our children should be as intentionally routine as clothing ourselves, lest we begin the day spiritually naked—exposed and unable to protect ourselves from the elements of this world.

The Israelites were able to adorn their hands because of the **powerful hand** with which God brought them **out of Egypt**. Thus, they **shall keep this ordinance at its appointed time from year to year**. While God's law should be on His people's lips daily, these specially appointed times throughout the year inspire us to reflect more profoundly on specific aspects of His character and story. For Israel, the Passover served as a reminder of how God powerfully secured their freedom from the chains Egypt held them in for centuries.

> **Now when the Lord brings you to the land of the Canaanite, as He swore to you and to your fathers, and gives it to you, you shall devote to the Lord the first offspring of every womb, and the first offspring of every beast that you own; the males belong to the Lord. But every first offspring of a donkey you shall redeem with a lamb, but if you do not redeem it, then you shall break its neck; and every firstborn of man among your sons you shall redeem. (13:11-13)**

In this chapter of Exodus, we observe a bit of back and forth—instructions about the firstborn, references to the Promised Land, further details about the Feast of Unleavened Bread, additional instructions concerning children, and yet another reference to the promised land and the firstborn of both man and beast. These practices were to be officially established in the Promised Land (though presumably before that as well), Israel **shall devote to the Lord the first offspring of every womb**, specifically **the males**.

The firstborn of every clean, domestic animal was supposed to be dedicated to the Lord through sacrifice. However, one domestic animal, the donkey, was considered unclean and unworthy of being offered as a sacrifice.[31] The first male offspring of a donkey was to be redeemed **with a lamb**, which means a lamb must be sacrificed in its place. If no such act of redemption took place, the Israelites were commanded to **break its neck.** It belonged to God.

Human beings, quite obviously, were never intended to be sacrificed to God (despite other cultures practicing such rituals with their false gods in biblical times). To **devote** the firstborn child to God at that time required redeeming him with a clean animal. A price had to be paid for the firstborn of both children and animals, serving as a demonstration of the parents' or owners' dedication and an act of worship to the Lord. As Mackay observes:

> God was the giver of life, and the first life was specially consecrated to him as a token of gratitude. This pointed repeatedly in the life of Israel to the significance of God as the Creator. But the LORD's claim went beyond what was his right as Creator. It was also grounded in what he had done for the people in the Exodus.[32]

Both the Feast of Unleavened Bread and the consecration of the firstborn (child and animal) were constant and perpetual reminders of what God had done for Israel in the Exodus. The Feast was to be observed at a specific time each year, never wavering. Firstborn children and animals were born throughout the year on their own schedule. Yet with each, the Israelites were to reflect on the Passover and reorient their perspectives to God's. From Him comes all things:

> For by Him all things were created, both in the heavens and on earth, visible and invisible, whether thrones or dominions or rulers or authorities—all things have been created through Him and for Him. (Colossians 1:16)

Naked I came from my mother's womb, And naked I shall return there. The Lord gave and the Lord has taken away. Blessed be the name of the Lord. (Job 1:21)

Dedicating portions of our gifts back to Him is a privilege, not a burden. It belongs to Him anyway.

Finally, these acts of redemption are steeped within the tenth plague of the Exodus. God's "firstborn," Israel, was redeemed from the plague of death that God poured over Egypt. Israel's firstborns were redeemed through a sacrificial lamb on the night of the plague. The act of redemption was being set as a foundational tenet of the Christian faith, one that would point to Christ's ultimate act of redemption on the cross and with His resurrection.

And it shall be when your son asks you in time to come, saying, "What is this?" then you shall say to him, "With a powerful hand the Lord brought us out of Egypt, from the house of slavery. It came about, when Pharaoh was stubborn about letting us go, that the Lord killed every firstborn in the land of Egypt, both the firstborn of man and the firstborn of beast. Therefore, I sacrifice to the Lord the males, the first offspring of every womb, but every firstborn of my sons I redeem. So it shall serve as a sign on your hand and as phylacteries on your forehead, for with a powerful hand the Lord brought us out of Egypt." (13:14-16)

Teaching occurs in various forms, from structured planning to impromptu discussions. God has already addressed the former. By establishing strict recurring feasts and sacrifices, Israel was to educate their children about God and what He had done through the Exodus. In the midst of these celebrations, astute children would become curious, ask questions, and initiate deeper discussions: **"What is this?"** "Why do we do this?" "How did it happen?" Parents were to take full advantage of such curiosity and use it to deepen the entire family's understanding and appreciation of God's powerful hand.

The mention of Pharaoh also helps the Israelites (and us) remember that in every story, there is a villain. Pharaoh was the physical villain representing the ultimate spiritual one—the devil. If you recall, one of Pharaoh's first acts in the Exodus narrative was to order the deaths of Israel's newborns. He had hoped to halt Israel's rapid growth, but little did he know that he was foreshadowing his own demise—God would (and did) take the life of his son as well.

Pharaoh also serves as a reminder that salvation necessitates freedom from something. Freedom is costly, and many times we cannot afford to pay its price ourselves. Israel certainly could not. They were so burdened by their chains of slavery that they did not have the physical, economic, or motivational capital to free themselves.

Slavery is both a literal and a metaphorical reference to sin. The Israelites were literal slaves to Egyptians for hundreds of years. Their labor was far from easy; they were not merely bondservants working off a debt. They were forced to do what Egypt wanted them to do and did not profit from their toil. To be freed from slavery was a real and potent liberation. It was a physical, mental, emotional, psychological, and economic escape from the bondage to which they had been captive for centuries.

But their slavery extended deeper than the physical realm. They, like every other human, were also slaves to sin. They, like Egypt, stood guilty and in need of redemption. If they had not sacrificed the lamb, they would not have been spared. Isn't it interesting that God 1) informed them of their need for redemption, 2) provided them with the necessary sacrificial lambs (He protected and preserved their livestock during the plague of pestilence), and 3) instructed them on how to properly offer the lambs to Him? He does the same for us through Christ. He informs us of our need for Him, provides the only Lamb worthy and able to redeem us, and tells us how to accept His sacrifice—through belief in and submission to Jesus Christ as our Lord and Savior.

> All of us like sheep have gone astray, Each of us has turned to his own way; But the Lord has caused the iniquity of us all To fall on Him. (Isaiah 53:6)

If you confess with your mouth Jesus as Lord, and believe in your heart that God raised Him from the dead, you will be saved. (Romans 10:9)

The **powerful hand** that brought the Israelites **out of Egypt** is the same powerful hand that saves us today. He saved Israel from physical and spiritual slavery, just as He saves us from our spiritual slavery to sin. He had something so much better in mind for His people (the Promised Land) and has something so much better for us (eternal life with Him). We, like Israel, need to remind ourselves of the gospel on a regular basis, and diligently teach these truths to our children as well.

Summary

The first taste of freedom after a lifetime of slavery must have been exhilarating and surreal for the Israelites. They must have asked themselves, "Is this real? Can this actually be happening?" Many probably never even allowed themselves to consider freedom as a realistic possibility in their lifetimes. It took hundreds of years and scathing plagues unleashed against the Egyptians, but Israel was now tasting the freedom their hearts had longed for.

And they were not the only ones who wanted them to leave.

Filled with a sense of dread regarding what would happen if the Israelites stayed, the Egyptians **urged the people, to send them out of the land in haste**. After everything they had endured and lost (most grievously, the loss of their firstborns), Egypt wanted the Israelites gone and gone quickly. They were afraid that if the Israelites stayed, they would **all be dead** in due time. That was the only logical conclusion after everything they had been through. They no longer cared whether or not they had slaves. At this point, it was the Egyptians who wanted to be free—free from the continued wrath of God.

Unsurprisingly, the Israelites had no problem acquiescing to their request. They **took their dough before it was leavened**, packed up what they could reasonably transport and carry, and left. Prior to the Passover, they had obeyed

God by asking their Egyptian neighbors for **articles of silver and articles of gold, and clothing.** They were not leaving empty-handed. Quite the opposite, actually. When Jacob's family originally came to Egypt, they came with wealth that was eventually stripped away as they became slaves. But in another glorious act of redemption, God provided them with great wealth once again. They were leaving as they came in—with heads held high and abundant coffers.

The first leg of their journey was from **Succoth to Rameses**, probably around a day's journey. Though it may have taken slightly longer due to the enormity of their traveling party—**about six hundred thousand men on foot, aside from children**. This would put the approximate total number of Israelites at about 2 million. Further, **a mixed multitude also went up with them, along with flocks and herds, a very large number of livestock.** We are not sure who the **mixed multitude** was comprised of, but it is reasonable to assume that they were slaves of other nationalities that had found themselves in Egypt. Or perhaps sojourners who lived in Egypt, seeing what God did to the Egyptians with the plagues, and were smart enough to want to follow Him from that point on. This was an enormous group of people and beasts. They probably were not the fastest excursion, but they were motivated and in a hurry.

Since they left with such haste, their bread remained unleavened. As they went, **they baked the dough which they had brought out of Egypt into cakes of unleavened bread.** They dined on unleavened bread to celebrate the Passover, and doing so now would further remind them of what they were experiencing—God was actually freeing them. They were living through one of the most iconic historical moments the world had ever known.

And it had been a long time coming. **The time that the sons of Israel lived in Egypt was four hundred and thirty years**, and they had left Egypt **on the very day** of that four hundred and thirty years. Initially, there seemed to be a bit of discrepancy with that number because, in Genesis 15:13, God told Abraham that his descendants would be "strangers in a land that is not theirs, where they will be enslaved and oppressed for four hundred years." The easiest way to resolve that apparent tension is to suggest that Israel lived in Egypt for four hundred and thirty years but were only slaves for four hundred of those years. They did live in Egypt for a bit before a new Pharaoh arose who "did not know Joseph," and therefore, turned against the Israelites by enslaving them (Exodus 1:8).

At this point in the narrative, God provides us with an instructional interlude about the Passover and the consecration of firstborns to Him. The night the Israelites left Egypt was one **to be observed by all the sons of Israel throughout their generations**. Foreigners, slaves, sojourners, or hired servants were not permitted to participate in the celebration of the Passover unless they were first circumcised. Circumcision was a powerful act symbolizing someone's willingness to give it all to follow the Lord and be a part of His covenant community. People who wanted to join Israel and celebrate God in these contexts had to be fully committed. They had to make themselves vulnerable and remove part of the most well-protected members of their bodies to symbolize their willingness to discard their old worldview and allow God to shape their new one.

Holiness, or being set apart, is a major theme throughout the book of Exodus. God sets Himself apart, sets Pharaoh and Egypt apart for His wrath, and sets Israel apart for His glory. Another way He establishes rhythms of holiness in their lives is the consecration of the firstborns to Him. **The first offspring of every womb among the sons of Israel, both man and beast**, belonged to the Lord. Obviously, no humans were to be offered as sacrifices to the Lord, so each firstborn was to be redeemed with an animal sacrifice.

Furthermore, the Israelites would celebrate the Feast of Unleavened Bread, **where unleavened bread shall be eaten** throughout the seven days after the Passover. God was so serious about them using unleavened bread that He forbade leaven from being anywhere in their homes or even borders. Perhaps He did not want it to be a temptation or the command to be accidentally broken out of habit.

Regardless, the Feast of Unleavened Bread, the Passover, and the consecration of the firstborns to Him were all for the sake of remembering what God had done for them in Egypt. The Israelites were commanded to tell their children, **"It is because of what the Lord did for me when I came out of Egypt."** Memory was affected by the fall, like every aspect of life and this world. God knows that we are forgetful people. Even something as monumental as the Exodus would fade with time, especially for subsequent generations who did not experience it firsthand. Thus, God established these observances to help them remember and teach their children about Him and what He had done for Israel.

God gave Israel their first taste of freedom, but it came at a cost. It cost the lives of untold Egyptian firstborns and unblemished lambs of the Israelites. "The wages of sin is death," and blood must be shed in order for sin to be atoned for (Romans 6:23). This, of course, foreshadowed Christ, who was the ultimate "Lamb of God who takes away the sin of the world" (John 1:29). Jesus did eternally what the Passover lambs could only do temporarily. He took the sin of the world, bore our punishment, and set us free:

> Surely our griefs He Himself bore, and our sorrows He carried; Yet we ourselves esteemed Him stricken, smitten of God, and afflicted. But He was pierced through for our transgressions, He was crushed for our iniquities; the chastening for our well-being fell upon Him, and by His scourging we are healed. All of us like sheep have gone astray, each of us has turned his own way; But the Lord has caused the iniquity of us all to fall on Him. (Isaiah 53:4-6)

It was **with a powerful hand the Lord brought** the Israelites **out of Egypt**, and they needed to meditate on it intentionally and repetitively in order to worship Him appropriately. Freedom is something only truly available in God, and Israel was getting their first taste of what that meant as they began their journey to their promised land.

GROUP STUDY

Introduction

Freedom is constructed on the foundation of victory.

We never experience freedom without first experiencing a fight. Indeed, the concept of freedom is predicated on the assumption that we desire to be freed *from* something. We've all experienced freedom to some degree or another. Sometimes, achieving it is easy, and other times, it can be exceedingly difficult.

- Share a time in your life when you've experienced freedom.
  - Was it easy or difficult to achieve? Why?

The Word

God granted Israel the freedom they had been praying about for over four hundred years, but it didn't come without a fight. Egypt first learned this lesson through the plagues that God pummeled them with. By the end of those, God had completely shifted the dynamic between Egypt and Israel. Exodus began with Pharaoh killing the Israelite babies; now God had taken the lives of the Egyptian firstborns. Egypt had once been dominant, strong, and in control; now, they were weak and trembling.

> **The Egyptians urged the people, to send them out of the land in haste, for they said, "We will all be dead." (Exodus 12:33)**

- Why did the Egyptians want Israel gone immediately?
  - What does this shift reveal about the power of God?

Israel responded well to this shift. While it posed a logistical challenge, they loaded up and headed out. They were finally free, yet their freedom wouldn't be enough. God expected them to remember His victory in their lives forever.

> **It is a night to be observed for the Lord for having brought them out of the land of Egypt; this night is for the Lord, to be observed by all the sons of throughout their generations. (Exodus 12:42)**

But if a stranger sojourns with you, and celebrates the Passover to the Lord, let all his males be circumcised, and then let him come near to celebrate it; and he shall be like a native of the land. But no uncircumcised person may eat of it. (12:48)

- Who was the Passover supposed to be observed for first?
  - Why is that significant in light of what He had done for the Israelites?

- What did God require of anyone who celebrated the Passover?
  - What does this reveal about the holiness (set-apartness) of God and His people?

- How long was Israel supposed to celebrate the Passover (12:42)?
  - Why would that be a challenge without dedicated annual celebrations?

While Israel did nothing to earn or fight for their freedom (God accomplished it all on their behalf), they would have to fight to remember it. The Passover, Feast of Unleavened Bread, and consecration of the firstborns (both man and animal) each had different requirements, but all served the purpose of reminding Israel of what God had done for them in the exodus. It was important not only for their personal faith, but also for the development of their children's faith.

You shall tell your son on that day, saying, "It is because of what the Lord did for me when I came out of Egypt." (Exodus 13:8)

And it shall be when your son asks you in time to come, saying, "What is this?" then you shall say to him, "with a powerful hand the Lord brought us out of Egypt, from the house of slavery." (Exodus 13:14)

- Why was it important to pass down their knowledge of God and what He'd done to future generations?
- Notice the pronoun change in these verses, from singular to plural. Why is that significant?

Apply

> So if the Son makes you free,
> you will be free indeed.
> Jesus, John 8:36

> I shall remember the deeds of the Lord;
> Surely I will remember Your wonders of old.
> Asaph, Psalm 77:11

God sovereignly orchestrated every detail of Israel's freedom, from sparing Moses' life as a baby to leading them out of Egypt with great wealth after 430 years of slavery. But freedom was not the end of their story, just as a wedding isn't the end of a love story. Israel needed to remember this moment; God wanted it to fundamentally shape their faith and inspire new depths of faith in their children.

Our first "moment" was when we came to faith in Christ. It's when we experience true freedom for the first time because we were freed from spiritual death. Yet we often neglect to remember it. We tend to keep our salvation in our pockets as a "get out of hell free card" and then move on with our lives.

- Read Romans 8:1-4. What has Christ done for us?
  o Why is it important for us to remember and dwell on this often?

Our freedom in Christ needs to be remembered, but it also needs to be shared.

- Read 1 Peter 3:15 and Psalm 78:2-7. How are you (or should you be) telling others of what Christ has done for you?
  o What hinders you from doing so?
- How can you combat those things?

WEEK TWO

REDIRECTING FEAR

Exodus 13:17-14:31

PERSONAL BIBLE STUDY QUESTIONS

1. Why did God not lead the Israelites through the most convenient/shortest way? (13:17)
2. What did Moses bring with him and why? (13:19)
3. How did God lead them? (13:21-22)
4. What did God tell Moses to tell the sons of Israel? (14:1)
5. What reason did He give Moses for doing so? (14:1-3)
6. Why was Pharaoh mad about letting Israel go (what were they missing out on because Israel left)? (14:5)
7. What did Pharaoh take with him? (14:6-7)
8. Where did the Egyptians catch up with the Israelites? (14:9)
9. What was Israel's reaction upon seeing Pharaoh and his men? (14:11-12)
   a. Was it an appropriate reaction? Why or why not?
10. How did Moses respond to the Israelites? (14:13-14)
11. What did God tell Moses to do? (14:16)
    a. What do you think was going through Moses' mind at that instruction?
    b. What would have been going through yours?
12. What was God going to do in the meantime? (14:17)
13. Who was going to get the honor from this episode? (14:18)
14. How did God keep the Egyptians away from Israel at first? (4:19-20)
15. How long did it take for the sea-land to dry? (14:21)
16. When did God look down on the Egyptians? (14:24)

17. How did God thwart the Egyptians' pursuit once again? (4:24-25)

18. How did God take care of the pursuing Egyptians once and for all? (4:27-28)

19. What was Israel's response to their salvation? (4:31)

COMMENTARY

Exodus 13:17-14:22

Shannon was a single mother who suffered from severe anxiety. Her anxiety began over big things that were totally outside of her control—what if the coming hurricane destroys her house? What if another economic crisis hits her country? What if her car broke down, and she could not afford to repair it or get a new one? She began to live in the world of "what ifs," and it slowly started consuming her daily life.

Worry over big things transformed into worry over everything until she could barely leave the house. She didn't want to drive, terrified that something might happen to her, her daughter, or their car. She couldn't eat and couldn't sleep. She was afraid of going anywhere, meeting new people, or even growing in the relationships she already had. Her world became smaller and smaller until it crippled her.

Fear can do that. It is a poison that seeps into the deepest crevices of our minds and starts paralyzing us. We may not have experienced anxiety like Shannon, but we have all had what I call "2 a.m. moments." These moments (typically in the middle of the night when everything seems more dramatic than it actually is) leave us scared and worrying about something. Sometimes, it's finances—should we have made that big purchase? Are we going to have enough for retirement? Are we saving enough for our kids' college? Other times, it's our relationships—did he take that the wrong way? I can't believe I said that! What did she mean by that? What if he doesn't like me anymore? Or perhaps it's our children—he has been making such bad decisions lately...what have we done wrong in raising him? What can we do to help him make wise choices? What if it's too late?

Questions like these can rage like wildfires in our minds in the wee hours of the morning, crippling us with fear and robbing us of rest. In these moments, it is tough to distinguish reality from the world of "what ifs." The dangers of such thinking are vast, but a huge one is that fear robs us of worship. When we get so consumed with worry, it means we are not so consumed with God—trusting Him and embracing the peace He offers us through Christ.

Israel had finally experienced freedom. God had fought Egypt on their behalf and had been overwhelmingly victorious. They walked away with heads held high and full of expectation—both of what was to come and how God expected them to remember what He had done for them. They were finally free; they no longer had to fear. But just because they were no longer slaves did not mean they would not face trials. The enemy never seems to let us enjoy our freedom for very long, does he? Would Israel trust God or cave to fear? When their 2 a.m. moment came (which was admittedly intense), would they succumb to their fear or put their fear in subjection to God? Let's find out.

Exodus 13:17-22

> **Now when Pharaoh had let the people go, God did not lead them by the way of the land of the Philistines, even though it was near; for God said, "The people might change their minds when they see war, and return to Egypt." Hence God led the people around by the way of the wilderness to the Red Sea; and the sons of Israel went up in martial array from the land of Egypt. (13:17-18)**

God's sovereignty reaches into the depths of eternity's ocean, yet it is also seen dancing amidst the waves of the shore. We just read about the Passover and the depths of the theological and Christological truths offered within it for Israel to dive into with their families for generations to come. Now, we pull back and see Him working among practical issues Israel would face as they leave.

First, we read another brief reference to **Pharaoh** letting **the people go.** In the first volume, we studied this intensely, recognizing that Pharaoh's stubborn mind was engaging in a bit of tango with God's sovereignty with each plague. With some plagues, Pharaoh hardened his heart and refused to let Israel go. With others, God hardened his heart because He was not finished with him yet. But God allowed Pharaoh's hardened heart to break with the last plague, with the death of the firstborns. **Pharaoh had let the people go**, but we know that it was really God who caused him to do so.

Pharaoh letting them go was perhaps expected at that point, but what happened next was not: **God did not lead them by the way of the land of the Philistines, even though it was near.** Lest we be tempted to forget, we are reminded that **God** is the one leading the Israelites. He had been from the beginning and will continue to do so (in rather intriguing ways, as we will see) for the rest of time.

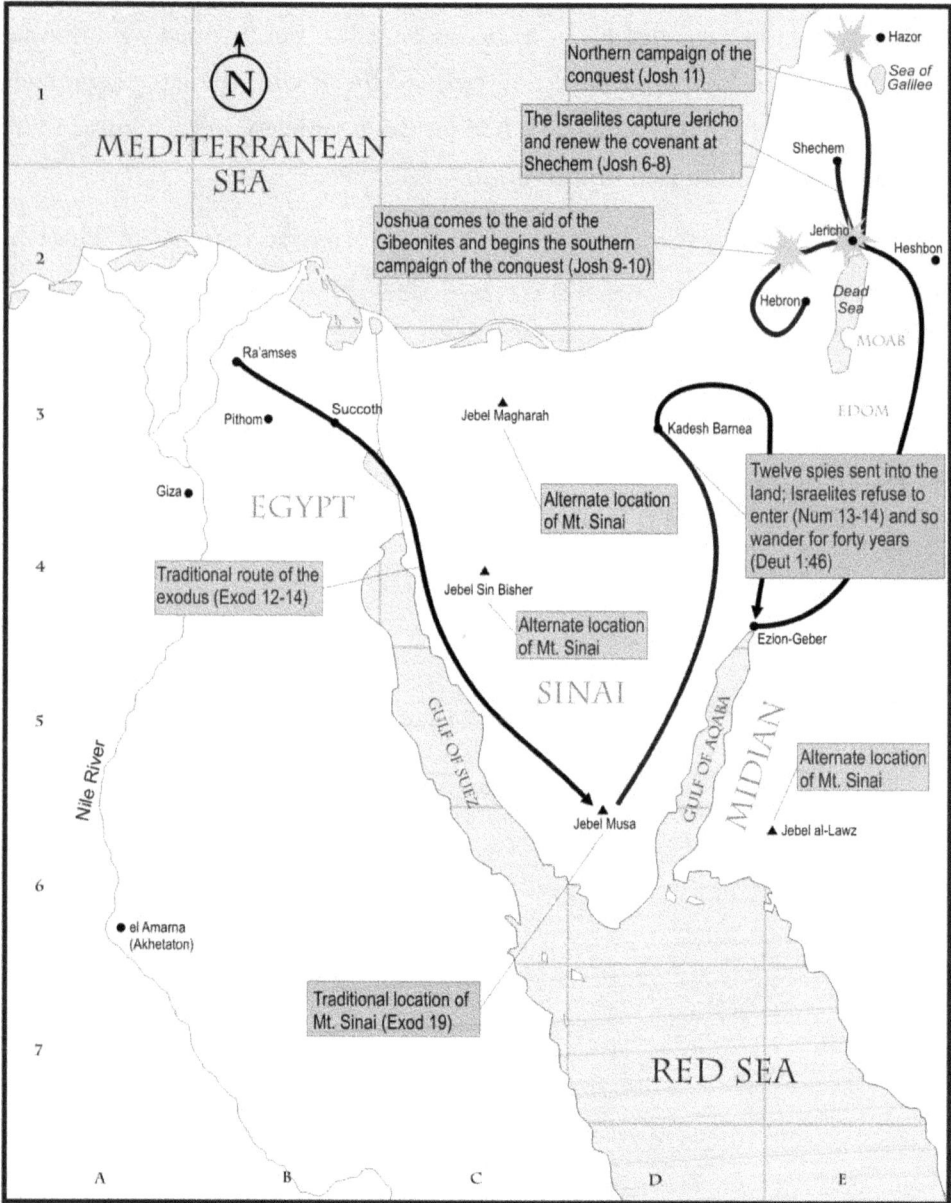

In His infinite wisdom, God chose not **to lead them by the way of the land of the Philistines, even though it was near.** The most logical route would have been through the land of the Philistines. While scholars debate the exact route, many agree that it would have been directly across the top of the Sinai Peninsula, keeping close to the shore of the Mediterranean Sea[33] (see map for visual reference).[34] This route was crucial for trade in ancient times, "several Egyptian forts, way stations, and watering places were located along this vital route from Egypt to Canaan," where the Israelites would eventually end up.[35]

Speculation also arises regarding the mention of the Philistines. Some believe it references the traditionally held Philistine people, "Sea Peoples who arrived on the Mediterranean coast of Palestine about 1200 BC".[36] Others, however, believe that the Philistine reference is of little importance, asserting that the Egyptians still posed the biggest threat to Israel if they had taken the conventional and shorter route. Instead, these scholars argue that "the most likely source of military opposition to the Israelites would have been Egyptian troops stationed in forts established to guard Egypt's north-eastern border."[37] This theory is supported by the fact that there were numerous points of known Egyptian military presence along that route. Regardless of who posed the biggest threat, the point here is that there was a threat, and God knew what He was doing by taking them the long way.

God provides us with a reason, albeit not very specific, for His decision to take a longer route: **"The people might change their minds when they see war, and return to Egypt."** If the Egyptians were still the main threat, then **war** would primarily refer to further conflict with the Egyptians, which would make Israel want to turn back. At first glance, it is difficult to imagine that Israel would even think about turning back so soon after their enormous victory over Egypt. The plagues, Passover, and the fact that the Egyptians were begging them to get out—and fast—would lead us to believe that fear of the Egyptians would be eradicated from the Israelites' minds. Unfortunately, that would be an erroneously optimistic perspective to maintain:

Would Israel really be so inconsistent as to give up their conquest and return to Egypt—of all places? And would they do so after all they had seen and experienced in the ten plagues? The answer is yes—decidedly yes. Not only did this very plan to return to Egypt actually occur less than two years later (Numbers 14:3, 14), but one must not forget that the Israelites were accustomed only to Egypt; they had lived nowhere else for 430 years. A properly chastised Egypt, which had perhaps "learned its lesson" about mistreating the Israelites by force of the plagues, might have seemed to them the very place they would now be most safe and happy. [38]

Israel's grumbling and complaining against Moses and God would, regrettably, begin soon enough; God knew that their hearts were not nearly as steadfast as His word on the matter.

The reference to war may also pertain to witnessing the ever-constant conflicts of the Philistines and other neighboring people groups in the ancient Near East. Wars were a pervasive part of life, and the Israelites were relatively inexperienced in this regard since they had never witnessed or been involved in a war themselves. However, some of them would be perceptive enough to realize that they would eventually have to engage in warfare, as they needed to take control of the land God had promised to them. Thus, if they were exposed to war too early, God knew **the people might change their minds …and return to Egypt.**

Though it is fairly certain that the Israelites did not travel along the Mediterranean Sea, scholars are not in total agreement on the exact route they took. God simply states that He **led the people around by way of the wilderness to the Red Sea**. The exact identity of this body of water has been the subject of much debate among scholars. Some emphatically believe that it should be translated and understood as the Red Sea as it is known today. Others argue that it should be more appropriately translated as the Sea of Reeds, contending that it does not refer to the main body of the Red Sea due to linguistic, historical, and other practical reasons. [39]

We must also consider the probability that the landscape has changed over time. Perhaps the sea was much larger in some places back then than it is now, or vice versa. I believe the ambiguity of the location is actually a good thing for this very reason. What if we knew the exact geographical coordinates, but today, it is a total dried-out desert with little evidence of erosion? That would fuel skeptics and inject confusion into the study. Ultimately, therefore, I do not think the exact identity of this body of water matters all that much. Whether it was the Red Sea as we know it today or another large body of water within the same region is not relevant. What does matter is that it was a body of water physically impossible for a group that size to cross on their own, as we will soon see.

Much debate has also surfaced over how the Israelites went up from Egypt **in martial array.** Bible translations vary widely in their interpretations of this term in Hebrew, *hamusim.* Some translations include: "went up harnessed out of the land" (KJV), "went up in orderly ranks" (NKJV), "went up out of Egypt ready for battle" (NIV), "went up...equipped for battle" (ESV), "went up armed" (ASV), and "like an army ready for battle" (NLT). To be fair, it is an unclear term in Hebrew, used only three other times in Scripture. The term shares the same root as the number five in Hebrew,[40] leaving some to believe they went out in groups of fifties. However, most agree that it "does not literally refer to groups of fifty men but is part of the 'thousand-hundreds-fifties-tens' language employed to delineate military units."[41]

Since God just made it clear that the Israelites were not even ready to witness war, much less take part in it, it would be naive to consider this term as indicative of Israel's readiness for battle (despite what some translations lead readers to believe). Again, these people were slaves for the past several hundred years and shepherds before that. While they may have been gifted some weaponry from the Egyptians on their way out, they were hardly an elite military force ready to conquer a new land for themselves. This point is further illustrated in later narratives, where Israel would have been easily conquered without God's direct and divine intervention. [42]

The term *hamusim*, then, should be understood in terms of organization rather than military prowess. Instead of an enormous mob of people traveling in chaos, Moses ensured they were organized and proceeded "in an orderly fashion" **from the land of Egypt.** [43]

Weaponry, riches and material belongings were not all the Israelites took with them from Egypt. Moses was also careful to fulfill a promise made by his predecessors to take something else of great importance with them as well:

> **Moses took the bones of Joseph with him, for he had made the sons of Israel solemnly swear, saying, "God will surely take care of you, and you shall carry my bones from here with you."** **(13:19)**

Joseph's words were recorded originally in Genesis 50:24-25:

> Joseph said to his brothers, "I am about to die, but God will surely take care of you and bring you up from this land to the land which He promised on oath to Abraham, to Isaac, and to Jacob." Then Joseph made the sons of Israel swear, saying, "God will surely take care of you, and you shall carry my bones up from here."

If you are not familiar with Joseph's story, I highly recommend that it be your next study. His life was marked by excruciating, confusing trials and unmatched, deeply profound blessings. He lived a life supernaturally orchestrated by God. He did not always understand what was happening, but even at the peak of his success in Egypt, he knew that his people did not belong there. Despite Egypt being the place he lived for most of his life, he did not want it to be where he remained after he was gone. So he made his brothers promise to take his bones with them when their descendants left one day.

Joseph exuded more faith than most in our Exodus narrative thus far. Perhaps the midwives of chapter one come the closest, choosing to stand firm in their faith regardless of the consequences. Moses certainly was not a beacon of faith to emulate at the beginning (and at more than one point along the way), nor were the Israelite elders or people in general, for that matter. But Joseph believed what God said. He knew God would lead his people out one day and so desperately wanted to be a part of it that he made it his last request.

To Moses' credit, he kept the promise of his heritage and **took the bones of Joseph with him.** I love what Victor P. Hamilton observes in this act:

> Canaan represents one's future, where one is headed. Joseph's bones represent one's past, where one has come from. Here the future and past are wedded without either consuming the other.[44]

Taking Joseph's bones was another way of purposefully remembering the past and what God had done for them. Just like the Passover and Feast of Unleavened Bread, Joseph's bones (in whatever container they were held) would be a tangible reminder of where Israel came from, God's established covenant with them, the miracles He had done on their behalf, and His commitment to securing their future with Him. Those dry old bones hopefully sparked life in the Israelites, serving as a powerful reminder that the God who wrote Joseph's story was also writing their own.

> **Then they set out from Succoth and camped in Etham on the edge of the wilderness. The Lord was going before them in a pillar of cloud by day to lead them on the way, and in a pillar of fire by night to give them light, that they might travel by day and by night. He did not take away the pillar of cloud by day, nor the pillar of fire by night from before the people. (13:20-22)**

Their story continues as **they set out from Succoth and camped in Etham.** The exact (or even probable) location of Etham is unknown.[45] All we know is that it was **on the edge of the wilderness,** which meant the Israelites were officially leaving Egypt and its outskirts behind.[46]

When I was much younger, I went through a phase where I found myself preoccupied with knowing God's will, specifically the day-to-day, moment-to-moment decisions we all make. Did He want me to wear this shirt or that one? Should I go sit with this friend or that one? Which Scripture should I read today? I often wished God would communicate with me through post-it notes—a note on my pillow every morning with the verses He wanted me to read, a note near my closet for wardrobe choice, and notes sporadically throughout the day preempting every decision He deemed important. I quite obviously had an immature understanding of God, His sovereignty, and the Holy Spirit. Nonetheless, I was terrified of making imperfect, God-unordained decisions.

What I would have given to experience God like the Israelites did in this time of their history! My legalistic, anxious heart would have been soothed and strengthened. All I would have had to do was look straight ahead to witness God's reassuring presence, and what a powerful way He did so: **the Lord was going before them in a pillar of cloud by day ...and in a pillar of fire by night to give them light**. Those pillars were way better than any post-it note. God used them **to lead them on the way**, the exact way He wanted them to go.

These pillars have been the subject of much study over the years, and we benefit immensely from the results. To begin our brief study, let's focus on the pillars themselves. While some critics claim they were merely strange weather patterns, we know that to be false. Weather patterns may occur randomly, but these pillars were distinct and continuous. For forty years, they led the Israelites through a barren desert; no random act of nature could achieve such a feat for that length of time.[47]

Further, the pillars were organized and structured enough to be labeled as a **pillar**, which has a form. They were not just bursts of sporadic clouds just happening to ebb and flow in the same general direction.[48] On a more technical note, while I have been referring to them as plural (cloud by day and fire by night), it was most likely just one pillar that transformed with daylight.[49] During the day, it appeared as a distinct cloud formation that the Israelites could clearly see and follow. At dusk, it would transform into a pillar of fire, or perhaps the fire would illuminate the cloud structure. The Israelites traveled both day and night, and the pillar of fire would have been bright enough to light a clear path for them to follow. Given the number of people, it is easy to imagine that the pillar was quite large. It had to be visible to at least the front line of travelers, assuming the rest carried torches as they walked during the darkness.

We are not told much about the physical structure of the pillar, but some speculate that it was not visible to everyone in its full grandeur. Because the Egyptians were not recorded as fearing it, nor were the Israelites completely emboldened by its presence, some scholars believe that it "was far more subtle and less threatening than we might imagine. It was able to block the Egyptian advance, but apparently did not appear as awesome or even supernatural."[50] That conclusion, however, is short-sighted. It is far more probable that the pillar's grandeur rose in proportion to the viewer's lens of faith.

This observation turns our attention from the physical to the supernatural and spiritual elements of the pillar. The term theophany refers to a "God sighting" in the Old Testament—a physical manifestation of God in some form, tangibly interacting with someone in the narrative. The first theophany of our Exodus study was the burning bush with Moses back in Exodus 3:

> The angel of the Lord appeared to him in a blazing fire from the midst of a bush, and he looked, and behold, the bush was burning with fire, yet the bush was not consumed…God called to him from the midst of the bush and said, "Moses, Moses!" And he said, "Here I am." (Exodus 3:2, 4b)

Moses was amazed by this sight, and it was from this miracle that God chose to first reveal Himself and speak to Moses. The pillar of cloud and fire was another miraculous theophany—a physical manifestation revealing God in a form that interacted with His people. It actively and consistently led the people, protected the people (as we will observe soon), and guided them for over four decades in the wilderness.

God will continue to use storm theophanies throughout the book of Exodus—a thick cloud descending on Mount Sinai (19:9, 24:16, 34:5, 40:34-38), thunder and lightning flashes within a thick cloud (19:16), and smoke (19:18). Each of these was a powerful display of God's power and identity, and they seem to build upon each other as the narrative unfolds.

> The burning bush is a theophany, that is, a manifestation of God's presence with his people. The pillars of cloud and fire take us to the next level of intensity of God's presence with his people, an intensity that will reach its climax at Mount Sinai, where that presence will be too much for the people to bear (20:18-19). For now, the presence of God in the cloud and fire is meant to be unbearable not for the Israelites, but for the Egyptians, as the subsequent narrative makes clear. [51]

Before we delve into that, we must note that ancient peoples associated their gods with elements of nature. As we observed in our first volume of study, each of the plagues attacked one or more of the Egyptian gods. For example, the plague of darkness was an affront to Ra, the Egyptian god of the sun, who was supposed to be the most powerful god of all. In each plague, God demonstrated His sovereign and unmatched power over every other "god," revealing and confirming His supremacy.

Similarly, "in the figurative language of ancient Near Eastern religions, a theophany...is frequently expressed in terms of storm phenomena." [52] Understandably, gods and idols were associated with objects and phenomena beyond human control and were, therefore, objects of worship. The sun, moon, stars, wind, storms, water, and even fertility were subjects of worship as people attempted to control them through sacrifices and other sacrilegious offerings. We know, of course, that they were worshiping the creation instead of the Creator (Romans 1:25) and, in all their efforts, achieved nothing of positive, eternal worth.

While God reveals Himself in figurative ways that may seem in alignment with such pagan thinking, He is actually asserting His ownership of such natural phenomena. He uses storms and fire (each considered their own "god" according to ancient pagan beliefs) to reveal mere aspects of His power. Far more potent than the most formidable of storms, God reveals Himself in a controlled storm to display His unmatched might. God can control what no human can. The continued use of such imagery, both literally and figuratively throughout Scripture, reveals even more:

> Of course, in biblical poetic texts, this highly figurative language has been cut loose from any pagan moorings, emptied of mythic content, and monotheized. This is one of the remarkable characteristics of biblical literature: it can employ literary fragments, images, and phrases that are meaningfully literal in pagan compositions, and it can transform them and reuse them as mere colorful poetic imagery.[53]

God created and sustains the world and everything in it. He is so far beyond our comprehension that He graciously uses objects within our intellectual capacity to reveal His nature and allow us to be in a relationship with Him. In the case of the pillar, He used two of the most powerful forces of nature, clouds and fire, to reveal His power and sovereignty over His creation.

The pillar revealed God in some ways but also served another purpose: to remind His people of His continued presence in their lives. This brings us back to the earlier reference to the lens of faith. It is entirely possible that the visibility of the pillar was directly proportional to the amount of faith the viewer had. We will see this confirmed in the next chapter. When the Egyptians started pursuing Israel, Israel panicked, but Moses did not. Furthermore, when the pillar moved behind Israel to block the Egyptians, there was no record of the Egyptians doing anything but stalling. If that pillar was as big and threatening as it seems to have been, one would think Israel would be courageous, and the Egyptians would have fled outright (it would have reminded both of God's power recently unleashed through the plagues). But that is not what happened. This leads me to believe that those with greater faith were able to see the pillar for what it was (and how vast it was), while those with little to no faith saw it only in a vague part.

This theory bears substance in other narratives in Scripture as well. Consider the account of Elisha and his servant when the king of Aram tried to capture them:

> He [the king] sent horses and chariots and a great army there, and they came by night and surrounded the city. Now when the attendant of the man of God had risen early and gone out, behold, an army with horses and chariots circling the city. And his servant said to him, "Alas, my master! What shall we do?" So he answered, "Do not fear, for those who are with us are more than those who are with them." Then Elisha prayed and said, "O Lord, I pray, open his eyes that he may see." And the Lord opened the servant's eyes and he saw; and behold, the mountain was full of horses and chariots of fire all around Elisha." (2 Kings 6:14-17)

Elisha had more faith than his servant and was therefore permitted to see what his servant could not—an army of the Lord surrounding and protecting them from the comparatively puny army of Aram.

Of course, the ability to see "behind the curtain" of eternity is only possible if God first ordains it. It is not as if we can peel back the curtain on demand and see whatever we want as soon as our mustard seed of faith sprouts to a certain size. The principle, however, is both noteworthy, intriguing, and fitting within our narrative. It will remain speculative, yet entirely possible, that the pillar's visibility directly corresponded to the amount of faith the people had in God.

One final note about the pillar: while it far surpasses any post-it note system my immature mind could devise, it was also surpassed exponentially by the Holy Spirit after Christ's ascension.

In the new covenant, after Christ's earthly ministry and ascension, we now have something better, namely, the Holy Spirit indwelling individuals…God was *with His people* (as exemplified with the cloud) but not *in His people* (with the exceptional case of the mediators). That all changed in the new covenant.[54]

To be with God and reminded of His presence by way of a pillar of cloud and fire would be remarkable and undoubtedly was for those who experienced it fully. But we, as Christians, get to experience God on a whole new level—to be indwelled permanently by His very Spirit. Instead of God's presence resting upon a physical tabernacle or temple that we can gather around to witness and worship, He allows His presence to dwell within us:

> Do you not know that your body is a temple of the Holy Spirit who is in you, whom you have from God, and that you are not your own? (1 Corinthians 6:19)

The pillar guided the Israelites physically, but the Holy Spirit "will guide you into all the truth" (John 16:13). What I missed as a child in faith was that the power of the Spirit living within me is far greater than any fiery pillar seen by the Israelites. He leads, empowers, and transforms us into the image of God. We have direct and unobstructed access to God through the power and indwelling of the Holy Spirit—an unmatched and priceless gift to every believer. And like our theory about the pillar, the more we understand and get to know the Spirit through prayer, studying the Word, and fellowship with other believers, the stronger our faith will grow and the more we will be able to see His presence in our lives.

God **did not take away the pillar of cloud by day, nor the pillar of fire by night from before the people** for several decades to come. Even more remarkably, He never takes His Spirit away from those who believe. We "were sealed in Him with the Holy Spirit of promise, who is given as a pledge of our inheritance, with a view to the redemption of God's own possession, to the praise of His glory" (Ephesians 1:13-14).

Exodus 14:1-12

> Now the Lord spoke to Moses, saying, "Tell the sons of Israel
> to turn back and camp before Pi-hahiroth, between Migdol
> and the sea; you shall camp in front of Baal-zephon, opposite
> it, by the sea. For Pharaoh will say of the sons of Israel, 'They
> are wandering aimlessly in the land; the wilderness has shut
> them in.' Thus I will harden Pharaoh's heart, and he will chase
> after them; and I will be honored through Pharaoh and all his
> army, and the Egyptians will know that I am the Lord." And
> they did so. (14:1-4)

In an unexpected turn of events, the Lord told Moses to tell Israel **to turn back and camp before Pi-hahiroth, between Migdol and the sea; you shall camp in front of Baal-zephon, opposite it, by the sea.** Unsurprisingly, scholars have various opinions about the locations of each of these places. Ultimately, however, we can neither be certain about the location nor is it all that relevant. The most important points to note here are 1) that God is still intentionally leading Israel, and 2) He wants them **to turn back and camp...by the sea.**

Turning **back** means turning back toward Egypt, back the way they just came, regardless of the specific locations named. The first route out of Egypt did not make much sense from a worldly perspective because it was not the shortest distance from the starting point to the final destination. But at least they were moving forward. Now, God confuses them even more by having them retrace the ground they have already covered, only to end up at a "dead end" **by the sea.** This was intentional, first because God was leading them, and second because He instructed them to **camp** there.

Can you imagine being one of the Israelites hearing Moses' instructions? Turn back? Make camp at a decidedly vulnerable spot where there was nowhere to flee should trouble arise? I would certainly have questions, as I am sure many of them also did.

But God had a plan, and He cued Moses into it. Just as He knew Israel would change their minds if they saw war, He knew Pharaoh was going to change his mind about letting Israel go. Pharaoh thought Israel was **wandering aimlessly in the land,** and he would partially be right with this latest move. To Pharaoh and the rest of the world, it sure looked like Israel had no idea what they were doing or where they were going.

This still happens quite frequently in the lives of believers today, by the way. God says, "the foolishness of God is wiser than men...God has chosen the foolish things of the world to shame the wise" (1 Corinthians 1:25, 27). Sometimes God calls us to do something that makes zero sense to the world (or even to us, if we are honest).

I had a thriving photography business for the past several years. It was a wonderful second source of income for our family and a creative outlet for me. It was not difficult, but it took up quite a bit of my time, which is ever fleeting around here. For the last couple of years, I have felt a "nudge" to step away from it in order to focus all my extracurricular (meaning in addition to being a wife and mother) efforts on my writing. I started to do so slowly, cutting my sessions in half for the year. Then, I cut them in half again. But the nudge only grew stronger.

So, I recently decided to give it up altogether. It was painful, mostly for selfish reasons (having that extra income was very nice!). And to the world, it did not make sense. Why would someone give up a successful part-time job and a second source of income? Why trade the easy for the difficult? A profitable business for a non-profit ministry? The decision made zero sense from a worldly perspective, but it makes all the sense in the world to someone trying her best to follow God's lead.

Israel's route made zero sense to anyone watching from the outside, and likely to many on the inside as well. But that did not matter. They were following the only Navigator worth listening to—the One in control of the universe. He will always honor our trust and obedience.

Pharaoh scorned the Israelites, and God turned his mocking speculations into stubborn resolve once more—God would **harden Pharaoh's heart** one final time, and Pharaoh **would chase after Israel**. God had hardened Pharaoh's heart several times throughout the plagues, and while it seemed like the last plague of death would be the undoing of any sane person, as it turns out, that was not quite the case. Pharaoh was not finished with Israel, and God was not finished with Pharaoh.

I just finished an excellent biography of President Abraham Lincoln.[55] He was a fascinating man, growing up extremely poor and rising to the highest position in our great nation. His time as president, of course, was fraught with angst, as his main goal was keeping the United States together as they battled fiercely in the Civil War. One fact I had never realized before reading that biography is that the Union had more than one chance to win the war long before 1865. While speculative to some extent, one example many historians (and President Lincoln himself) agree upon is that General McClellan could have ended the war in 1862 after his victorious battle at Antietam if he had pursued the Rebels as they retreated. The North had achieved a decisive victory over the South in that battle, and McClellan just let the South walk away. McClellan was an expert in defense but had not a single offensive bone in his body, and thus, he let the Confederates and the victory of the whole war slip through his grasp.

God and Pharaoh battled it out numerous times over the course of several months during the plagues, with God winning every battle without question. But God knew that the war was not over. He was not just out to conquer a few battles, no matter how spectacular and victorious. He would do what McClellan would not—He would finish off the enemy and leave them with no recourse to strike again.

Pharaoh's heart would be hardened, and he would pursue Israel again so God would **be honored through Pharaoh and all his army, and the Egyptians would know that** He was **the Lord.** Moving Israel back and rendering them as "sitting ducks" by the sea, as well as hardening Pharaoh's heart, were all careful orchestrations of God to end the war once and for all. He would make it painfully and finally obvious that He, and He alone, is the Lord.

> **When the king of Egypt was told that the people had fled, Pharaoh and his servants had a change of heart toward the people, and they said, "What is this we have done, that we have let Israel go from serving us?" So he made his chariot ready and took his people with him; and he took six hundred select chariots, and all the other chariots of Egypt with officers over all of them. The Lord hardened the heart of Pharaoh, king of Egypt, and he chased after the sons of Israel as the sons of Israel were going out boldly. Then the Egyptians chased after them with all the horses and chariots of Pharaoh, his horsemen and his army, and they overtook them camping by the sea, beside Pihahiroth, in front of Baal-zephon. (14:5-9)**

A bit of debate surrounds Pharaoh's thought process within the context of these verses. Two main arguments present themselves. The first argues that Pharaoh had all along only expected the Israelites to be gone for three days to celebrate a feast in the wilderness, as indicated in Moses' initial request (Exodus 5:1,3). This argument explains why Pharaoh had to be **told that the people had fled**, meaning "that after three days have elapsed…they have kept right on going."[56] After all, why would Pharaoh have to be told they left? He was the one who originally sent them away!

While this argument has merit, it is hard to believe that Pharaoh really did not believe, or at least highly suspect, that Israel would be gone for good when he sent them away. Enduring several months of intense, costly, debilitating plagues for only a three-day release stretches the bounds of even the most stubborn mind. The fact that he would risk and subsequently forfeit his son's life on top of everything else over only three days is hard to fathom. Furthermore, Pharaoh and the Egyptians sent the Israelites away with everything they (and nearly all the Egyptians!) owned. It is doubtful that even a mind wrought with debilitating mental illness would go to such lengths as to not recognize the finality of their flight.

Far more likely is that Pharaoh knew Israel would be gone for good. Being **told that the people had fled** was a confirmation that they were really gone, and the proclamation flipped his switch from grief to vengeance and anger. Subsequently, **Pharaoh and his servants had a change of heart toward the people, and they said, "What is this we have done, that we have let Israel go from serving us?"** This seems to be far more of a wake-up call to the consequences of their own previous decisions than a new understanding that Israel somehow deceived them and had no intention of coming back.

Regardless of the context of their mindset leading up to this switch, Pharaoh and his servants played right into the hand God had sovereignly dealt. Pharaoh **made his chariot ready and took his people with him, taking six hundred select chariots, and all the other chariots of Egypt with officers over all of them.** Pharaoh's immense reaction reveals and confirms several details. First, and unsurprisingly, Pharaoh's intention was to capture Israel by force, take them back to Egypt, and reinstate them as slaves. Part of his grief-to-anger switch probably included the realization that Egypt needed to be rebuilt from the ground up in many respects. While seemingly obvious, the force of that realization came from understanding they would have to do it themselves.

The reason for their indignation is that they had let **Israel go from serving** them. For the last several centuries, Egypt did not have to do the majority of their own menial labor—they did not have to build storehouses or fill them; they did not have to tend to flocks on their own—they had hundreds of thousands of slaves to do it for them. Rebuilding would cost them nearly as much as its destruction, for they would have to do it themselves.

Another detail confirmed with Pharaoh's intense action is the number of Israelites they were going after.[57] If, as some scholars suggest, the number of Israelites was as small as a few thousand, Pharaoh would hardly need to take such severe measures to pursue them. Israel was not an army; they could put up no serious or even probable defense if their numbers were insignificant. Further, the Egyptians **overtook them camping by the sea** relatively quickly. What had taken the Israelites days at best due to their number likely took this Egyptian military force only hours at most.

Finally, thought should be given to the haste of Pharaoh's reaction.[58] Neither Pharaoh nor his advisors took time to think through the ramifications of their decision. Once they realized the gravity of what it meant to be without slaves, they went full throttle into battle mode in an attempt to undo what they had previously done. Unfortunately for them, no "five-second rule" applies. While they will attempt it, the Egyptians cannot snap their fingers and reinstate life as they knew it before. The irony is that the haste in which they sent Israel out, urging them to leave (12:33), has now come full circle in the haste in which they **chased after them.**

As promised, **the Lord hardened the heart of Pharaoh**, and allowed the hearts of the Egyptians to follow suit. One commentator notes the distinct lack of mention of the whole Egyptian army, at least in these initial verses. His **people** should not be translated as army, as some English translations do.[59] Rather, the term refers most certainly to his officers and "functions as a reminder that the Egyptian *people* in general were of a mind to pursue and recapture the Israelites. Pharaoh's policy was, in other words, a popular one."[60] God hardened the heart of Pharaoh, and his callousness spread like a scabbing disease over the hearts of the rest of the Egyptian people. Where leaders go, the people follow.

One final note to mention is the description of Israel **going out boldly** when Pharaoh began chasing after them. Several different translations have been applied to this phrase, including "Israel went out with a high hand" (KJV), "going out defiantly" (ESV), "marching out boldly" (NIV), "going out with an exalted hand" (LSB), and "left with fists raised in defiance" (NLT). The Hebrew is literally, "with upraised hand" and is likely a metaphor "drawn from the depiction of ancient Near Eastern gods menacingly brandishing a weapon in the upraised right hand."[61]

While the timing may seem confusing at first glance, we need to understand that this was Israel's posture *before* they had any knowledge of Pharaoh changing his mind and coming after them. Israel did leave Egypt with confidence—their God had defeated Egypt with a mighty hand and set them free. However, as one commentator wisely notes, the inclusion of this **going out boldly** remark may suggest "that they considered themselves, rather than YHWH, to have won the victory."[62] This misplaced arrogance becomes evident in the coming verses when terror seizes their hearts upon the realization that Pharaoh is coming back. Israel left with boldness, but the source of their confidence was misplaced. Instead of their boldness being grounded in God, they grew arrogant, acting as if they played any role in their own deliverance. They were about to experience quite the reality check.

> **As Pharaoh drew near, the sons of Israel looked, and behold, the Egyptians were marching after them, and they became very frightened; so the sons of Israel cried out to the Lord. Then they said to Moses, "Is it because there were no graves in Egypt that you have taken us away to die in the wilderness? Why have you dealt with us in this way, bringing us out of Egypt? Is this not the word that we spoke to you in Egypt, saying, 'Leave us alone that we may serve the Egyptians'? For it would have been better for us to serve the Egyptians than to die in the wilderness." (14:10-12)**

Since there were no cell phones, tablets, or other ways to receive instant communication, Israel had no idea that Pharaoh had changed his mind until they could see him—until it was too late for them to do anything to avoid him. Of course, God knew and had orchestrated this, just like He had the entire narrative thus far. But God is not where Israel looks when they see the Egyptians. Rather, **the sons of Israel looked, and behold, the Egyptians were marching after them, and they became very frightened**.

Their reaction is, in part, understandable. It is certainly natural to be afraid when an intimately known enemy is seen coming after you. Yet God is anything but natural, and He calls His followers to be the same. God had just spent months showing both Israel and Egypt that He was the epitome of the supernatural—He bent this natural world and the phenomena within it to His will. In ten epic displays of power, God was inviting Israel to see Him, to see that He was greater than even the most cruel taskmaster. He invited them to see and behold Him, to fear Him in admiration instead of fearing the Egyptians in distress.

Israel did turn their attention to God, but unfortunately, it was only long enough for them to be freed from slavery. As soon as they tasted the briefest morsel of freedom, they turned the gaze of their hearts away from God and back to this world. How often do we do the same? We turn to God for the salvation He offers, yet are quick to revert back to our old vision—our old ways of doing life—until we encounter conflict and need His salvation again.

That is where we find Israel, only worse. Instead of calling on Him in a declaration of faith and reliance, **they cried out to the Lord** in fear and distrust. Instead of uttering petitions for another brilliant deliverance, they blaspheme His sovereign provision in the series of questions they launch at Moses.

God has blessed my husband and me with four daughters. Our house overflows with glitter, tulle, ballet shoes, and…emotions. They are still young at the moment, which makes it that much more difficult for them to control their feelings. I was in another room the other day when our three-year-old got so upset that I was sure one of her limbs must be being torn from its socket. Hurrying to her, expecting to see some kind of carnage and seeing none, I quickly investigated the source of her anguish only to realize it was because our five-year-old was "looking at me!" (her words). Yep. Hollyn was looking at Maelee, apparently in a way Maelee deemed unacceptable. I never figured out exactly what look constituted such a visceral reaction, but it did not really matter for the ensuing "talk" that followed.

It is a battle we strategically fight every day, teaching our girls to destroy "speculations and every lofty thing raised up against the knowledge of God, and we are taking every thought captive to the obedience of Christ" (2 Corinthians 10:5). We talk through the gospel in the context of whatever emotional situation we find ourselves in—what has Jesus done for us? What does He continue doing for us today and every day? What are ten things you're grateful for that He has given you? What would Jesus do in this situation? In light of all of that, how should our hearts and minds act, even in difficult circumstances? We are trying to teach our girls that we are to think before we act (and react), and that every response should be first filtered through the lens of the gospel.

The Israelites' response to seeing Pharaoh reminded me of Maelee's little outburst. Granted, it must have been scary seeing the Egyptians coming at them full speed. Nevertheless, the Israelites were not three-year-old little girls, and their response should have been much different than immediate and utter despair. As we discussed in the previous volume, we should all strive to purposefully *respond* to situations in light of the gospel, not just *react* to them on an emotional whim. Israel reacted impulsively, and it revealed where their hearts are with God:

> **"Is it because there were no graves in Egypt that you have taken us away to die in the wilderness? Why have you dealt with us in this way, bringing us out of Egypt? Is this not the word that we spoke to you in Egypt, saying, 'Leave us alone that we may serve the Egyptians'? For it would have been better for us to serve the Egyptians than to die in the wilderness." (14:11-12)**

Not only were they completely beside themselves in fear, the Israelites were also being sarcastic in their spew of hateful questions to Moses and were exaggerating well beyond what the situation warranted. They made a number of immediate (and false) assumptions that led to their childish tantrum. First, they assumed that the Egyptians were coming to kill them instead of what they were actually trying to do—recapture them and force them back into slavery. Again, it would have been intimidating, seeing the Egyptian chariot force coming full throttle at them. However, automatically assuming the Egyptians were going to kill them is a puny display of the next erroneous assumption they made: that a massacre was a foregone conclusion. They assumed that death was inevitable, that they would **die in the wilderness**, and Moses became the object of their scorn.

Israel's third error was not an assumption as much as a flagrant error. They flashed back to when they told Moses to "**leave us alone so that we may serve the Egyptians**." While there is no record of those exact words being spoken, the thought is conveyed on two occasions earlier in Exodus. When Pharaoh first refused to let Israel go and then made their labor harder, the Israelite foremen angrily confronted Moses with, "May the Lord look upon you and judge you, for you have made us odious in Pharaoh's sight and in the sight of his servants, to put a sword in their hand to kill us" (5:21). That over-exaggeration is one they are repeating currently in the wilderness—that the Egyptians are going to kill them. While Pharaoh had killed their babies for population control, he had never made so daring a move as to begin slaughtering adults. After all, they did all his work! Pharaoh's fear from the beginning was that "they would multiply, and in the event of war, they will also join themselves to those who hate us, and fight against us and depart from the land" (1:10). While Israel did not know his intentions, Pharaoh always feared Israel leaving; there was no profit in their absence.

The second earlier occasion records Israel's refusal to listen to Moses: "they did not listen to Moses on account of their despondency and cruel bondage" (6:9). Israel was in a dark place, no question. It is somewhat understandable why they would not listen to Moses at the beginning—at that point, he had been all words. He said great things about God fulfilling His promise of freedom, but all that had happened until that point was an increase of labor and hardship.

But (and that is a very important conjunction), Israel was not in the same position now as they were in when they first uttered their lack of faith. God had obliterated the Egyptians with the plagues and crushed their souls with grief over losing their firstborns. Israel witnessed every plague and its gruesome effects for months as God fought for them. They saw the effort the Egyptians had to exert to find clean water from blood. They saw the Egyptians, their belongings, crops, food, houses, beds, and clothing covered in frogs, lice, flies, and locusts. They cringed, seeing the pus-dripping boils that consumed the Egyptians' flesh. They watched as the Egyptians' livestock were supernaturally poisoned by a disease that left them dead, and likely smelled the stench of their bodies either decaying or being burned to be disposed of. They heard the deafening sound of hail as it pummeled the earth and residences of the Egyptians, and the screams of those who had not listened and taken cover. They saw God literally blot out the sun from Egypt and smother them with darkness so potent they could feel it. They also heard the cries of agony as Egyptians woke to find their firstborns without a pulse or breath—the final nail in the coffin of Egypt's enslavement of Israel.

These miracles were a testament to God's unmatched power and dedication to Israel, and they witnessed each one firsthand. Further, they felt the dusty earth under their feet as they walked out of Egypt, free and wealthy beyond their imagination. By this point, Israel knew enough both intellectually, experientially, and spiritually to trust God. Herein lies their third and most egregious assumption: that God was either incapable or unwilling to rescue them (again). They had made this mistake once at the beginning of Exodus, and were apparently so dense that not even witnessing the wrath of heaven itself descending on the Egyptians was enough to solidify their faith in God.

Now, God wanted to bury the coffin of the Egyptians' enslavement of Israel so deep that no one would ever find it. But Israel is not getting it. They immediately snuff out any light of faith that had been lit and fueled by the plagues. Instead of letting the Light of Life guide their way, they turn into their understanding darkened by depravity. Instead of rising above the confines of their earthly vision, they belly flop into it, so immersed in fear that they quench even the possibility of God having a bigger plan. They lose their minds in sheer panic when they should have grounded themselves in the hope and promise they had recently found in Him.

We do the same thing far too often. Like our daughter Maelee, we react impulsively rather than respond purposefully when situations do not go our way. And like the Israelites, we rely on our own (grossly limited) understanding of circumstances rather than placing our trust in the One who controls them. Like both, we do not stop to assess the situation through the lens of Scripture—taking our thoughts captive to the obedience of Christ. We should do what Israel did not: throw ourselves into His Word and upon His promises. We need to start telling our problems how big God is instead of the other way around.

Exodus 14:13-22

But Moses said to the people, "Do not fear! Stand by and see the salvation of the Lord which He will accomplish for you today; for the Egyptians whom you have seen today, you will never see them again forever. The Lord will fight for you while you keep silent." (14:13-14)

I teared up reading these verses because Moses has come such a long way since God first called him. He was scared as a chicken and stubborn as a mule when God told him to go back to Egypt. Then he tried to weasel his way out of the call, utilizing every ounce of creative energy he had. His trepidation continued into Egypt and the initial confrontations he had with Pharaoh and the Israelite leaders. But slowly (ever so very slowly), he began trusting God and embracing His call on his life.

Moses did what Israel should have done here—he evaluated the situation in light of God's word and clung to His promises more than his fear. I wholeheartedly agree with one commentator: "this speech of Moses represents perhaps his finest hour yet in the leadership of Israel." [63] Contrary to his actions when God first called him, Moses now tells the Israelites not to **fear**. How could they fear when they had God as their leader and defender? Fear only belongs to those who stand against God.

Israel was then given two instructions that are quite similar. First, Moses told them, **"Stand by and see the salvation of the Lord, which He will**

accomplish for you today." In other words, Israel did not have to do anything! They literally just had to **stand by** and watch God's salvation unfold for them once again. Moses finally understood that it is not by man's power, shrewdness, or talent that God's will gets done. It is **the Lord** who **will accomplish** salvation.

Our hearts cannot help but flutter when thinking about the salvation we also receive in Christ. Our salvation, too, is not of ourselves, it is "not as a result of works, so that no one may boast" (Ephesians 2:9). Rather, it is by grace that we have been saved. It is an act of God alone through Christ alone, empowered by the Spirit alone in our lives. We contribute nothing to salvation except the sin that made it necessary in the first place. Our task, like Israel's, is to **stand by and see the salvation of the Lord.**

Israel was not an active participant in attaining their rescue, but they had the privilege of watching it happen. Sight is one of the best gifts God gives us. For those of us fortunate enough to have physical sight, we can behold the wonders of His creation—tangible items, people, and places where He has left His fingerprints. However, physical sight alone is limited. Helen Keller once said, "If the blind put their hands in God's, they find their way more surely than those who see but have no faith or purpose." Our physical sight was designed to awaken our spiritual sight. Just as we are supposed to take every thought captive in obedience to Christ, we are wise to take every sight captive and see through it to its transcendent reality in Jesus.

A little while back, we were driving to a dance convention (such is my current mom life), and we happened to be driving down a road that offered the most glorious view of the sunset. I watched the sky turn into a fire raging among the clouds as the sun descended in its last burst of glory for the day. Reds and oranges slowly morphed into purples and blues, welcoming sparkling stars that seemed to dance among the calm night sky. As a photographer, I started thinking about how even the best lens could not capture such magnificence the way our eyes can. This guided my thoughts to the design of the eye and how utterly beyond my comprehension God is. People have studied the eye—its design, function, etc.—for hundreds of years. But even the most educated, practiced experts cannot make a blind man see. They can help improve sight, but they cannot create it. The eye is just one of the trillions of aspects of creation that God designed in mere moments. We could spend lifetimes studying each element of creation and barely scratch the surface of them, yet He breathed them into existence with a word.

I beheld that sunset with my physical sight, but before long, I was ushered into His presence with thanksgiving and praise through the spiritual sight bestowed upon me. That is what our eyes should do; that is what God wanted Israel's eyes to do. He wanted them to **see the salvation of the Lord**—to witness something tangible through a spiritual lens. He wanted them to interpret what they saw through His Word, recognizing that He was fulfilling His promises.

In a similar directive, Moses makes a promise: **the Egyptians whom you have seen today, you will never see them again forever.** Israel was seeing the Egyptians solely with their physical eyes, resulting in their fear, distrust, and disrespect toward God. They allowed their sight to be dictated only by worldly circumstances, detached from the reality and power of God. Moses' promise that the Israelites will never see them again is physical, but had a spiritual invitation attached to it. No, the Israelites would never see those Egyptians again first, because they were going to receive total and final freedom, and second, because the Egyptians' doom was impending. This circumstantial threat was going to be obliterated by God.

Yet, and perhaps unrealized to them at the time, Israel was going to face new enemies. The threat of the Egyptians would be replaced by other challenging circumstances, as well as by several other people groups and nations as they traveled through the wilderness and eventually began to conquer the promised land. Moses' promise subtly invites them to start implementing their spiritual sight now, so that they can do so with confidence later. Our lives are never void of threats, conflict, or temptation because we live in a sinful world. But seeing each of these dangers through the lens of our spiritual reality in Christ gives us the ammunition to fight them and to witness His salvation unfold again and again in our lives.

Moses concludes his brief speech with a final reassurance: **the Lord will fight for you while you keep silent.** There was to be no confusion about who was going to do the fighting (and who should consequently receive the glory for the victory). God is the sole warrior and conqueror in this narrative; Israel was "to be witnesses, rather than participants in the battle."[64] I do love (and chuckle at) the not-so-subtle instruction for Israel to **keep silent.** They just threw quite a dramatic tantrum, shouting a whole lot of noise at Moses as they saw only through their physical eyes of fear. Moses now tells them they need to be quiet if they want to watch God fight on their behalf. Also, and in a more practical sense, their "silence before the Lord was necessary before they could hear the word to 'move on.'"[65] They could not hear God's instruction if they were too busy running their mouths at Him. They needed to **stand by** and **keep silent**, ready to **see the salvation of the Lord.**

> **Then the Lord said to Moses, "Why are you crying out to Me? Tell the sons of Israel to go forward. As for you, lift up your staff and stretch out your hand over the sea and divide it, and the sons of Israel shall go through the midst of the sea on dry land." (14:15-16)**

At first glance, God's question to Moses here seems kind of harsh. This is especially true since Moses just displayed a great measure of faith by criticizing the Israelites' lack thereof. The "you" here is singular, confirming that God is, in fact, addressing Moses individually. Is God annoyed with Moses, then? Not exactly; we just need to look at the greater context to figure that out. Many scholars agree that by this point, Moses is so established as Israel's representative that sometimes he and Israel are interchangeable as objects of God's attention:

Moses was consistently identified with the character and fate of the people as a whole; as their leader, he had to accept criticism leveled at them even if he himself was not responsible. Moses knew that whatever God said to *him* was normally meant also for *them*. The first half of v. 15 is thus meant as a rebuke to the Israelites, not…to some lack of faith on Moses' part. [66]

Also supporting this is the fact that **crying out** is the same verb that the Israelites used in verse 10 – "the sons of Israel *cried out* to the Lord" when they saw the Egyptians. Thus, it seems most probable that while God is speaking directly to Moses (as He normally did), His reproof is directed primarily toward the Israelites.

One more possibility exists, though admittedly less likely. Some speculate that "maybe there is some unrecorded prayer that Moses has lifted heavenward on behalf of his beleaguered people." [67] If so, God's question is really directed at Moses, urging him to stop praying and start taking action. While Moses may have been praying and awaiting instruction from God, it is unlikely that he has reached a level of desperation eradicating the confidence he just showed the Israelites. Thus, in all probability, God is here referencing the Israelites' lack of faith and is now turning His attention to them openly.

God wanted Moses to **tell the sons of Israel to go forward.** Time does not permit any more whining; they need to move and move now. In their minds, however, the blaring question is, "to where are we moving?" The Egyptians were fast approaching from one side, and on the other was the sea. They did not have time to go around it; they did not have boats or other means to go through it. How were they supposed **to go forward**?

The question is answered before anyone can speak it out loud. God tells Moses to **"lift up your staff and stretch out your hand over the sea and divide it, and the sons of Israel shall go through the midst of the sea on dry land."** God wanted Israel to **go forward** to the sea and watch Him do the impossible. This is not the first time Moses has lifted up his staff or stretched out his hand to unleash God's power into a situation. If you recall, his staff was the same one he used as a shepherd. When God called him at the burning bush, God ordained that staff to be a tangible instrument of His power. He transformed it into a serpent and then back to a staff again at Moses' touch (4:2-4). From that point on, Moses took his staff with him everywhere, and it remained a symbol of God's power, being used in some capacity to initiate several of the plagues.

Stretching out one's hand also bore significance. A man's hand was an extension of his arm—a representation of his strength and power. Back in Exodus 3:20, God told Moses, "I will stretch out My hand and strike Egypt with all My miracles which I shall do in the midst of it; and after that he will let you go." With His mere hand, God would accomplish what all of Egypt and the very forces of nature could not. Moses' hand did not have any special or innate powers; it merely represented the hand of God, who holds all power in it. As one commentator notes, stretching out his hand was "a visible motion to reassure him and those watching that the power of an invisible God was at work."[68]

Moses was to stretch out his hand **over the sea and divide it** so the Israelites could **go through the midst of the sea on dry land.** I chuckle pondering what I would have thought if I were in Moses' sandals. "What did God just say?!" Moses just watched God accomplish a lot through the plagues, but his eyes had to widen just a bit of what God was telling him to do—"go on, split the sea in two and dry out the land so hundreds of thousands of people can walk across it. Get on it!" Obviously, God was the One accomplishing everything; He was merely telling Moses what He was going to do through Moses' rather unremarkable actions of lifting his staff and hands. But still, I wonder if some part of Moses, either upon hearing it or recalling it afterward, made his jaw drop or his eyes bulge slightly at such a command.

Like He did with the plagues, God informed Moses of what was going to happen before it happened. However, the rate at which the news spread among the Israelites is unknown. It is highly improbable that everyone knew what was going to happen until they saw it begin to transpire. Remember, there were a lot of people, and a distinct lack of cell phones. In their minds, they were still stuck and had no idea what God was saying or if He had said anything at all. I also do not know if all the Israelites were able to physically see the waters start to divide when they did. Not being certain of the terrain, it may be that many of the Israelites did not even know what was happening until it was their turn to walk through the sea. While details like that do not matter much to the narrative, it is interesting to ponder as we consider applications for our own lives.

On this side of heaven, we need to accept the fact that we are often not going to be privy to God's thought process or sovereignty in any given situation. Consider Job, who went through earthly hell and never found out why. The apostle Paul likely never understood why he endured quite as much persecution as he did (though God did inform him he should expect some). John the Baptist never understood why he ended up in prison and was eventually beheaded for speaking the truth. Countless biblical and modern-day examples communicate the fact that we are simply not at liberty to know all the inner workings of God. But they also all confirm this fact: we do not need to.

We do not need to know all the details because we know and trust the One who does. We do not need to have a hand in the minutia because we love the One who controls every detail effortlessly. We do not need to exhaust ourselves figuring out why because He knows and is working all things "together for good to those who love God, to those who are called according to His purpose" (Romans 8:28). If you find yourself, as I often do, wondering what He is doing, especially when you cannot see evidence of His hand; keep trusting. He is at work, He is moving, and He is accomplishing His purposes. Just because we cannot see it (yet!) does not mean it is not there. That is faith. "It does not require faith to begin a journey when I can see all the way through; but to begin when I can merely see the first step, this is faith."[69] Trust His heart when you cannot see His hand.

God gave Moses instructions that He prefaced with, **"As for you..."** He outlined specific steps for Moses to follow in obedience. All Moses had to do was lift his staff and reach out his hand over the water. God would do the rest and more:

> **"As for Me, behold, I will harden the hearts of the Egyptians so that they will go in after them; and I will be honored through Pharaoh and all his army, through his chariots and his horsemen. Then the Egyptians will know that I am the Lord, when I am honored through Pharaoh, through his chariots and his horsemen." (14:17-18)**

Moses received instructions for dealing with one of the Israelites' problems: the sea. Now God reveals more of His agenda regarding the more intense threat: the Egyptians. Once again, God **will harden the hearts of the Egyptians.** He had already hardened Pharaoh's heart back in 14:8, and now He was hardening the hearts of the remaining Egyptians who went with him. What would their hard hearts embolden them to do? They would bravely chase after the Israelites into the sea.[70] Ordinary, "unhardened heart" people would pause when they came upon the sight of the sea being divided and the Israelites walking through it safely. Common sense would dictate that they at least consider the possibility that the walls of water could crash down at any moment and that they should perhaps use caution in continuing their pursuit. But no. God hardened their hearts to such an extent that they were driven by blinding selfishness, not self-preservation.

The reason for this, and any other God-ordained action, is for God **to be honored**. The word for **honored** here, *kabed*, communicates "the concept of a 'weighty' person in society, someone who is honorable, impressive, worthy of respect. This latter usage is prevalent in more than half the occurrences in the Old Testament."[71] If ever someone was deemed worthy of honor, it is God. His glory outweighs every other aspect of His creation, including one of the most powerful nations on earth at the time. While we typically think of honor in constructive terms (honoring those we esteem and think highly of), God receives honor in destructive ways as well. **Pharaoh and all his army…his chariots and his horsemen** were all people and symbols of power who foolishly had no respect for God, nor did they have any intention of showing Him honor. But God would take it anyway. Through the destruction of the Egypt's power, God would be honored.

At long last, **the Egyptians will know that** God is **the Lord.** They should have known this by now after suffering the long and debilitating effects of the plagues. But God was leaving no room for them to rally again. Like General McClellan should have done in ending the Civil War with a final pursuit of the Rebels, God was going to end every ounce of Egypt's interest (and delusion) in Israel's slavery once and for all. And He would receive every ounce of honor they should have given Him voluntarily.

> **The angel of God, who had been going before the camp of Israel, moved and went behind them; and the pillar of cloud moved from before them and stood behind them. So it came between the camp of Egypt and the camp of Israel; and there was the cloud along with the darkness, yet it gave light at night. Thus the one did not come near the other all night. (14:19-20)**

As promised, God takes action, and begins with the pillar. Interestingly, **the angel of God** is used synonymously with **the pillar of cloud** here. The first and only reference thus far to the angel of the Lord in Exodus was back in 3:2 when He appeared to Moses from the midst of the burning bush. While it is uncertain how exactly the angel of the Lord is distinguished from God in Scripture, it is relatively accepted that the angel is an extension and representation of God Himself. As we noted in the burning bush narrative (in the first volume of this Exodus study), God's presence was first mentioned as the angel of the Lord. But soon thereafter, the text says that "*God* called to him [Moses] from the midst of the bush" (3:4, emphasis added), indicating no real or meaningful distinction between the two. In that narrative, I proposed that the angel of the Lord acted as an agent preparing the way for the Lord—going before Him in a sense to get Moses' attention and prepare him to listen. The same could be said here. The angel of God moved within the pillar like with the burning bush, and prepared the way for God Himself (14:24).

While the mention of **the angel of God** is interesting, it is not the primary point of these verses. The main focus here is that God moved the manifestation of His presence **from before them** to stand **behind them.** The Israelites had been following God; now they have instructions to move forward while God protects them from the Egyptians behind them.

As we observed before, we are not sure of the exact size or look of the cloud other than the reference to some kind of pillar. Also, since the Egyptians were not stricken with fear upon seeing it, it is possible that the ability to perceive the intensity of the cloud directly correlated with a person's "lens of faith." Perhaps for the Egyptians, it just appeared as fog they were unable to penetrate, and they decided to wait until it let up. I am not sure what they thought about the cloud giving **light at night**, but they knew enough to realize that it was not wise (or possible) to try to go through it.

Regardless of the details, the pillar of cloud successfully protected the Israelites from the Egyptians **all night**. This reveals not only the power of God, but His provision and answer to prayer as well. He provided the Israelites with exactly what they needed when they needed it. The pillar faithfully led them where God wanted them to go thus far, and when they needed protection, it moved to serve that function. It also was His answer to their faithless prayer. He answered their cry better than they could have imagined, and He was not stopping there. He does the same for us today. He provides us with what we need when we need it, whether or not we are aware of it. And He does not stop. Israel was protected from behind as God turned His attention once more to the next phase of His plan—clearing their path ahead.

Then Moses stretched out his hand over the sea; and the Lord swept the sea back by a strong east wind all night and turned the sea into dry land, so the waters were divided. The sons of Israel went through the midst of the sea on the dry land, and the waters were like a wall to them on their right hand and on their left. (14:21-22)

Moses obediently **stretched out his hand over the sea,** and God took action. He **swept the sea back by a strong east wind all night and turned the sea into dry land, so the waters were divided.** Moses' outstretched hand, paired with the **east wind,** brings us back to the plague of the locusts:

> So Moses *stretched out his staff over the land* of Egypt, and the Lord directed an *east wind* on the land all that day and all that night; and when it was morning, the *east wind* brought the locusts. (Exodus 10:13, emphasize added)

The **east wind** that ushered in consuming swarms of locusts was the same **wind** God used to divide the sea. This "dry, hot piercing wind" was either from the wilderness or the desert and blew "intermittently between April and June and during the latter part of September."[72] This term, *quadim*, is used in nearly twenty verses in the Old Testament, and almost every one of them holds a destructive tone. In the interpretation of Pharaoh's dream, the thin ears of grain were "scorched by the east wind" (Genesis 41:6, 23). It is with "the east wind" God is said to "break up the ships of Tarshish" (Psalm 48:7). God will scatter people "like an east wind" before their enemies (Jeremiah 18:17), and "the east wind" breaks others (Ezekiel 27:28). It was also referred to as "the wind of the Lord" when used as an instrument of His judgment.[73] The **east wind** was a powerful force often used by God to accomplish supernatural purposes, just as He does here to part the sea.

We must not underestimate the power of this **wind,** especially at the behest of its Conductor. Many people argue about the amount of water that was parted that night. Some think it was only a trickle (which is ridiculous); others believe it was a substantial part of the sea with significant depth and breadth. It was quite certainly the latter. If it were merely a stream, the Israelites would not have had any trouble crossing it, nor would the Lord have found it necessary to part it. But a vast amount of water would have required hurricane-like winds to both part and dry up.

Our house is built with a crawl space underneath because our lot is at a low elevation and collects a surprising amount of water during bouts of heavy rain. After some storms, about half our backyard turns into a pond several inches deep (which makes for wonderful puddle jumping for our daughters). Usually, after a storm, strong winds come to blow it away. They bring sunshine, which is lovely, and also begin the drying-out process for the drenching rain left behind. The winds are not at hurricane speeds, but they are pretty strong, and it takes two to three days for it to dry up that little pond. I cannot imagine how strong the **east wind** must have been to dry up a sea to the point of dry land on the bottom!

Also, did they feel it? Did the Israelites and Egyptians feel the wind, or did God keep it directed only at the water? Even if He kept it pointed directly at the water, it must have been deafening. I wonder if that was also why the Egyptians temporarily stopped their pursuit. They could not see where they were going because of the cloud, but perhaps the roar of the wind cemented their decision to wait it out. It also probably shut them up. That many Egyptians and chariots racing after the Israelites was probably pretty loud. The noise of the horses and racing footsteps alone would have been substantial; it is not a stretch to think they were bellowing some kind of war cry as they proceeded. The wind might have overpowered the noise of their stampede and calmed Israel's anxiety a bit.

Regardless of what they thought, the Egyptians did wait and wait for a while. Even with supernatural power, it took several hours, **all night**, for the wind to dry up the sea. This is the second time "**all night**" is mentioned in as many verses, which both answers and presents some questions about the narrative. First, this was all happening at night. While apparent, it is important to note because it impacts the experience dramatically for the Israelites. There is no way either the Israelites or the Egyptians slept a wink that night. For the Israelites, the imminent threat of the Egyptians, the anxiety about what God was doing, and the noise of the wind all contributed to a restless night. It also confirms a previous theory that they most likely could not see what was happening with the water. We speculated that, due to the enormous number of people, it is unlikely they could all witness the water being parted. Now, that theory is bolstered by the fact that it was dark out. Even if it was a full moon and fiery pillar, it would have been difficult to fully perceive and understand what was happening.

Further, exhaustion does not typically lend itself as an asset to strengthen faith. The Israelites were already terrified; they were already struggling to trust God. The time of day and lack of sleep were not helping their disposition. Have you heard of the "Mind after Midnight" hypothesis? It proposes and scientifically defends "that people are more likely to make bad decisions when they haven't had enough sleep, and they're awake when their circadian rhythms are telling them to be asleep."[74] This, unsurprisingly, confirms God's design for humanity—that we need rest. The Israelites, at least their adults, were not getting adequate rest that evening.

Hopefully, at least some of their young children were asleep. As a mother, my mind goes to everything the moms would have done to ensure their children got some sleep. Perhaps they bundled them up in a makeshift bed in a cart or something. I am sure other moms stood holding their little ones, trying to rock them to sleep. (I'm also sure they appreciated the natural "sound machine" created by the wind!) Moms do whatever they can to help little ones rest. Yes, it is because we love them, but we also know our lives will be much better in the morning if our children are well-rested. Leaving Egypt was already quite a disruption in routine; they had to establish a new routine as travelers. The added stress of being up all night was probably setting their nerves on edge that much more.

So why did God do this at **night**? The answer cannot be known, but I believe it is because the additional weakness of Israel shines a brighter spotlight on God's strength. He has made it clear that He was the One doing everything; their fatigue drains their energy and removes them from being consequential participants in this narrative. Israel was fully and completely dependent on God to save them; it was physically and emotionally impossible for them to do it on their own.

At some point in the night, God gave Moses confirmation that it was safe for the Israelites to move forward, and they did. They **went through the midst of the sea on the dry land, and the waters were like a wall to them on their right hand and on their left.** As we have noted before, God does not do things halfway. His sovereignty is seen in the smallest details, just like in the overarching narrative of the gospel throughout history. In this brief verse, we should notice one particular detail that would have made a world of difference—that they walked through **the sea on the dry land.**

While sounding rather obvious, the bottom of this sea had been wet for a very long time. The dampness likely would have penetrated far deeper than the mere surface of the muddy ground beneath it. It is one thing for the wind to dry up the water. It is a whole other matter for the wind to dry up the ground. Why does this matter? Because it would have been difficult at best, impossible at worst, for the Israelites to cross that large of a canyon between water through thick, wet sludge.

We live in the low country, and shortly after moving here, I had my first experience with something called pluff mud. Pluff mud is difficult to describe—it is like gooey sludge that can also act as quicksand. It is everywhere around here, and it is very difficult to discern it from just regular, non-sinking mud. You can be walking along certain beaches or marsh landscapes just fine, only for your next step to sink you into a foot-deep hole. And it is so hard to get out of. I almost lost a boot once from an unfortunate encounter with pluff mud. Pluff mud is impossible to walk through, at least with any kind of normal expectation of speed or grace.

I have no idea about the exact composition of the bottom of the sea the Israelites were walking through, but I am quite certain it would normally be a muddy disaster if only the water were removed. This would make rolling carts through it impossible and walking extremely difficult. For God to dry it out enough to not only cause the waters to recede but also to make the land completely dry is a miracle of noteworthy proportion. He was not only making their escape possible; He was making it dare I say, pleasant! While I am sure their feet were getting dirty, they were not getting *stuck*, and that must have given them a bounce in their steps of hasty retreat.

One of the most iconic images, at least in our minds, in all of Scripture is how **the waters were like a wall to them on their right hand and on their left** as the Israelites walked through. This parting of water was not like two puny waves conveniently making just enough room for the Israelites to leisurely stroll through. They were like walls on either side of them. Unfortunately, this is one instance where our English, modern-day minds are really at a disadvantage when reading a text like this. When we think about a wall, we typically think of something like a retaining wall—something between four to ten feet high. This is a gross misunderstanding of what walls were like back in ancient biblical times. When an ancient near Eastern person thought about a wall, they thought about a city wall—a huge fortress used for protecting them against enemies. Indeed, "the term used for 'wall' here, *homah*, connotes a very large wall—not a small stone wall or retaining wall but always a massively large (usually a city) wall, towering above the Israelites."[75]

While each city wall varied to some degree, scholars agree that these walls were massive. Some stones from the temple enclosure in Jerusalem still exist today and "measure thirty feet…long, eight feet…wide, and three and one-half feet…high, weighing over eighty tons…Josephus tells of stones in the temple of Solomon sixty feet…long."[76] These are just the *stones* used for the wall! If even remotely the same number of stones for those walls were used as bricks are used in walls today, it is legitimately hard to fathom how enormous these walls (and thereby these walls of water) were. The Israelites very well may have seemed like ants crawling in between these colossal walls of water.

Take a moment to sit and meditate on what such an experience would be like. Their thoughts were likely scattered in a million different directions, from fearing that the walls might come crashing down at any moment to experiencing the adrenaline-infused wonder that momentarily pushed aside their exhaustion. Were they able to see creatures swimming around in the walls of water? Did any of them reach out and run their hands along the walls as they walked by? While I might initially think they would feel the spray of water on their faces, it is doubtful, as any significant spray would have made the ground wet. Was the wind still blowing at full force, or did it subside a bit as they walked on? Were their livestock animals frightened, or did God miraculously keep them calm to ensure their progress? Were some of the faithful elderly among them moved to tears by the magnificent provision of God? Were they overwhelmed by the fact that they were able to live through such an extraordinary experience? Did any of them have the foresight to understand that they were living through one of the greatest moments in history?

So many thoughts, feelings, sights, and sounds must have overwhelmed their senses as they walked through this sea. How long did it take? The text allows for the possibility of several hours, which we will explore soon. The point here is that God has once again provided for His people. They were literally surrounded by walls of water so high that they probably could not see the tops, especially since it was dark out. God revealed both His omnipotence over every aspect of creation and the intimate protection of His people in a glorious display of power the world has scarcely witnessed since.

Exodus 14:23-31

> **Then the Egyptians took up the pursuit, and all Pharaoh's horses, his chariots and his horsemen went in after them into the midst of the sea. At the morning watch, the Lord looked down on the army of the Egyptians through the pillar of fire and cloud and brought the army of the Egyptians into confusion. He caused their chariot wheels to swerve, and He made them drive with difficulty; so the Egyptians said, "Let us flee from Israel, for the Lord is fighting for them against the Egyptians. (14:23-25)**

Before long, **the Egyptians took up the pursuit, and all Pharaoh's horses, his chariots and his horsemen went in after them into the midst of the sea.** Back to the timeline for a moment. I believe this whole experience happened in gradual phases and was a fluid timeline. While the wind is stated to have blown **all night**, it is obvious from reading the text that the Israelites did not wait until morning to begin crossing the sea. That leads me to believe that the wind started on one side, and as it dried out the ground, the Israelites followed. It also makes sense that as the Israelites moved forward, the pillar of cloud followed behind them. Thus, it was all a moving train, so to speak—the wind was the engine, blowing the water away and drying the land. Israel followed closely behind as the ground became dry as the second railcar. The cloud, third in the train, followed closely behind the last of the Israelites to keep the barrier between Egypt and Israel. Finally came the Egyptians as the caboose. It does not appear that the Egyptians had a singular big moment of decision to follow the Israelites into the sea. It is not as if the cloud lifted suddenly and completely, enabling them to finally chase after them. Rather, it was gradual. The cloud cleared up enough to allow the Egyptians to pursue Israel, but not at a rate they were able to catch up to and overtake them.

Regardless of speed, the Egyptians, including their horses, chariots, and horsemen, ended up **in the midst of the sea.** Then, **at the morning watch,** God took further action against them. Back in ancient times, nights were divided into three watches for military defense purposes and four when we get to New Testament times. The approximate time period of the **morning watch** would have been between the hours of 2 a.m. and sunrise.[77] This supports the "moving train" theory. The wind did blow all night, and all parties moved with it as it dried up the land enough for them to do so. But God was about to derail the caboose.

Sometime in the wee hours of the morning (but not yet at dawn – 14:27), **the Lord looked down on the army of the Egyptians through the pillar of fire and cloud and brought the army of the Egyptians into confusion.** I love teaching our girls big, theological terms because it allows us to explore big, theological concepts together. We learn about concepts like redemption and will spend days talking about how God redeemed His people throughout history and how He redeems us through Christ today. Three of my favorite theological characteristics to explore are God's omniscience, omnipotence, and omnipresence. We can almost get lost in the vastness of each, stretching our minds and strengthening our faith in the process.

At first glance, God looking **down on the army of the Egyptians** seems to suggest that He was otherwise occupied or not really paying attention to what was happening. This, of course, is entirely false; God sees and knows everything: "Indeed, even the very hairs of your head are all numbered" (Luke 12:7). Nothing escapes His notice, a concept that is difficult for our finite minds to understand. However, He also gives people and circumstances His special attention at times. How do these two concepts coexist? I like to think of it in terms of peripheral vision. As a mother, I have excellent peripheral vision. I can focus on a task and still be fully aware of what my children are doing at the same time. This is how I caught one of our daughters using her finger as a tissue the other day while I was reading to them, and I promptly ended that excavation. They try, but they have not fully explored the reaches of my peripheral vision!

In a much more supernatural, mind-bending way, God's peripheral vision is both flawless and limitless. He both sees and knows everything and also turns

His attention specifically to certain situations. God, then, did not look down to discover something new; He instead turned His special attention toward the Egyptians for the final blow He was about to deliver against them.

While not confined to time or space, God chose to look down through something that was present—**the pillar of fire and cloud**. We have seen how the pillar represented God's presence; therefore, it makes sense that He would choose it as the vantage point to **look down on the Egyptian army**. Using our moving train theory, the cloud was likely still positioned between the Egyptians and the Israelites, though not opaque enough to prevent the Egyptians from both seeing and pursuing the Israelites. It is possible that the Egyptians had gained some ground and were getting a bit too close to the Israelites. We know, through our familiarity with this narrative, that God ends up destroying the Egyptians. But before He does that, He thwarts their pursuit, presumably to give the Israelites enough time to finish crossing the sea.

God's tactic was to bring **the army of the Egyptians into confusion. He caused their chariot wheels to swerve and made them drive with difficulty.** The basic meaning of the word for **confusion** (*hamam*) here "seems to be 'to give attention to' in the negative sense, that is 'harass,' 'trouble,' often with the purpose of creating panic."[78] God uses this tactic several times through Scripture, which confirms it as a useful tool in holy wars.[79] The initial object of the confusion was the **chariot wheels**. It is no coincidence that a primary source of Egypt's confidence in battle becomes the object of their undoing. Chariots were a strong "symbol of military might and power" in ancient times.[80] Not every army possessed chariots, and it is no small detail previously noted (14:7) that Pharaoh had six hundred select chariots in addition to others. The Egyptian officers and commanders riding them undoubtedly felt certain of their victory riding in such status symbols. Instruments that seemed to be unconquerable became the lynchpin of their defeat.

God caused their **wheels to swerve, and He made them drive with difficulty**. Scholars speculate over exactly how this unfolded. Some say it was the soft ground of the sea bottom that would have caused these problems;[81] others think the wheels came off or were locked/jammed[82]. I think it is unlikely the ground caused the issues first because Israel undoubtedly had carts and wagons and were having no trouble getting across. Second, God makes it clear that He is the one who sent **confusion and difficulty**. Having trouble riding chariots across the soft ground is not hardly surprising and may not be indicative of supernatural intervention. For this reason, I also think that the wheels coming off or jamming, while certainly possible, still does not go quite far enough in giving God credit. Driving would be impossible without wheels or with locked ones, not just difficult, as the text states. The NASB translates it with the correct emphasis, then, that the wheels began **to swerve** as the direct result of God's hand against them. Some kind of uncontrollable swerving reinforces that God had sent confusion among them. It might be strange if their wheels started falling off, but it would be far more baffling to suddenly lose the ability to steer straight with no apparent environmental reason.

The pride of the Egyptian army was now the source of confusion and, as we see now, fear. God enabled them to immediately recognize the source of their chariot chaos, though—His hand: **"Let us flee from Israel, for the Lord is fighting for them against the Egyptians."** No meeting was needed to discuss what was happening and what they should do about it. The officers did not pause in the midst of the sea to ponder the perplexity of the situation. They figured out pretty quickly who was responsible because this was all too reminiscent of the plagues. They were not so far removed from the plagues, nor were their hearts so hard that they could not recognize God's hand when they saw it. When they did, their response was to **flee**. No one in any kind of right mind could do otherwise. And God finally allowed them to be in their right minds right when it was too late.

> **Then the Lord said to Moses, "Stretch out your hand over the sea so that the waters may come back over the Egyptians, over their chariots and their horsemen."**

So Moses stretched out his hand over the sea, and the sea returned to its normal state at daybreak, while the Egyptians were fleeing right into it; then the Lord overthrew the Egyptians in the midst of the sea. The waters returned and covered the chariots and the horsemen, even Pharaoh's entire army that had gone into the sea after them; not even one of them remained. (14:26-28)

Imagine this scene as if you were there as an Israelite. You are exhausted. You have been traveling for several days, which you have never done before, carrying all of your worldly possessions and not really having any idea exactly where you would end up or when you would get there. Just as your adrenaline wanes, your biggest enemy comes roaring back, which you assume means your certain death. Terrified, you realize the night has only just begun. Is God here? Does He really care? What is happening?

Then whispers of information start spreading through the crowd like a strange game of telephone. Something is happening – something big! But no one knows the details. The cloud pillar starts moving and positions itself between you and the Egyptians. Then, the deafening roar of wind, unlike anything you have ever heard before, fills the air. Someone yells, "the water is moving!" Another screams in fear, "we're going to die!" Amidst the chaos, some try to remain calm, encouraging others to do the same. You attempt to make sense of the situation, but the noise and darkness overwhelm your senses.

Suddenly, you are bumped forward. Disorientation turns into understanding as you realize the mass of people and belongings is moving forward—toward the sea! Positioned far back in the crowd, you couldn't see anything before, but now you are about to see what everyone has been talking about. It's your turn. Looking up, you see walls bigger than any Egyptian fortress you've ever seen. Where did they come from? Then it hits you – they are made of water! The wind had plowed a channel through the middle of the sea, causing the waters to tower above on both sides, leaving a dry walkway in between.

Then your heart freezes—you're supposed to walk through that channel! You must place your tiny, insignificant self in an even more vulnerable situation than with the Egyptians. Water could come crashing down at any moment, washing you away like a speck of dirt on a plate. But wait, is this God? Surely, He's performing another miracle on our behalf. Surely, this is a part of His rescue. Regardless, you don't really have a choice. Staying put means facing the Egyptians; moving forward means putting your faith in God and seeing what He has in store.

So you walk. And walk. Your eyes bulge in wonder as your gaze travels from left to right and back again. You rub your eyes, trying to wake yourself up in case this is all really a dream. After all, you are still very tired. Looking around, people seem to be processing it in various ways. Some, like you, seem dumbfounded. Others talk excitedly with their loved ones, chatting loudly over the roar of the wind and water. Then, you see tears dripping from the faces of others whose faith you've admired for years. They seem to understand something that you don't—that this moment is somehow transcendent. You want to be like them, you always have. So, you whisper a prayer in your heart asking God to give you that kind of faith—the kind of faith that sees and trusts in Him.

You make it to the other side with a refreshed heart despite fatigued feet. You move aside to make room for others, then head to a higher vantage point where you can watch and see what God will do. You know the Egyptians were following; would they make it all the way across? No one else is running, but even if they did, there was nowhere to go. Just empty wilderness ahead. It took all night, but predawn has come—the blues and purples of the night are turning to reds and oranges, preparing the way for the dawn. And there you are, your gaze transfixed on those fortresses of water just as the sun breaks free from the horizon…

This moment bore enormous historical, theological, and also personal ramifications in the lives of every person who participated in it. Moses and every

Israelite had made it across the sea safely; now they would look back and behold the final judgment against the Egyptians. God told Moses to **stretch out** his **hand over the sea so that the waters may come back over the Egyptians** and destroy them, along with **their chariots and horsemen.** Without hesitation, Moses complied, and **the sea returned to its normal state at daybreak.**

The rising of the sun brought the final descent of the Egyptians. Any fear the Israelites had regarding those walls of water was confirmed against their enemies as God broke His grip and allowed the walls to crash down on the Egyptians.

My sister was a competitive collegiate high diver, and there is much consideration that goes into that sport. The highest dives are off a 10-meter platform, roughly 33 feet above the water. While people can dive from higher, it is unwise to do so because if you do not know what you are doing, you risk serious injury or even death. Even knowing what you are doing can cause injury. My sister received many minor (and sometimes not so minor) injuries from hitting the water at just a slightly incorrect angle. Water is a force that should be treated with the utmost respect; its power and weight are shocking.

While the Egyptians were not diving into it, the water was diving onto them, and the pressure crushed them. The **waters returned and covered the chariots and the horsemen, even Pharaoh's entire army that had gone into the sea after them.** This further proves that the walls of water were no mere retaining walls. It is almost humorous how critics claim they were, suggesting that this part of the sea (wherever it was) was more like a creek. How could a small amount of water cover and kill the entire Egyptian army, over six hundred of their chariots, along with countless foot soldiers? It couldn't. As we have seen, these walls of water were massive, and when God let them go, the entire army was wiped out to the point that **not even one of them remained.**

But the sons of Israel walked on dry land through the midst of the sea, and the waters were like a wall to them on their right hand and on their left. Thus the Lord saved Israel that day from the hand of the Egyptians, and Israel saw the Egyptians dead on the seashore. When Israel saw the great power which the Lord had used against the Egyptians, the people feared the Lord, and they believed in the Lord and in His servant Moses. (14:29-31)

When we come to the end of a journey, it is wise to look back at its beginning. In this narrative, looking back on the plagues reveals both powerful truths and poetic justice. Each plague obliterated an aspect of Egyptian strength, from their natural resources to their health. The plagues were also an affront to their gods, as God showed His dominance over every created "god" the Egyptians worshiped.

We will not dive back into every plague, but rather focus on a particular thread running through the first, last, and then the sea here. The first plague involved God turning the Egyptian water into blood. The Nile, one of the most important sources of life sustenance for them, was turned into blood, along with all the other waters of Egypt—rivers, streams, pools, and all reservoirs, including water already gathered in wood and stone vessels (Exodus 7:19). Drinking, bathing, cleaning, watering plants...all of it became impossible without strenuous labor digging for water. They also had to deal with the stench, not just of the blood itself, but of all the fish that died because of it. It was quite literally a disaster; blood got on everything, and the Egyptians would have struggled to remove it from whatever it touched. Their source of life became a source and symbol of death.

The connection between that first plague and the last (God taking the lives of the Egyptian firstborns) was no accident. The water turning to blood was a formidable foreshadowing of what was to come because of their pride and stubbornness. Death bookends the plagues. But until studying our current passage now, I had never realized that the poetic justice did not stop with the plagues. God began His judgment by turning the Nile into unidentified blood; He ends by filling the water of the sea with the blood of the Egyptians. The first plague did not just foreshadow the tenth plague; it also presaged God's final judgment against them.

A couple of more parallels can be pursued. First, and yes, it is graphic, but **Israel saw the Egyptians dead on the seashore.** It is likely that before they reached the shore, the bodies of the Egyptian army floated similarly to the dead fish in the Nile during the first plague. While disturbing to contemplate and even more disturbing for the Israelites to witness, such an image serves as a profound reminder that God is the ultimate Judge and holds all of life in His hands. It certainly reminded Israel: **when Israel saw the great power the Lord had used against the Egyptians, the people feared the Lord.**

God's wrath is hardly a fun or popular topic to discuss. But ignoring it can lead to our demise and weakened faith. As Solomon wrote, "the fear of the Lord is the beginning of knowledge" (Proverbs 1:7). Those who do not fear God fail to understand His power, holiness, righteousness, or wrath. Witnessing the floating and then washed-up bodies of the Egyptians was sobering for the Israelites and prompted them to reflect on the wrath and righteousness of God. His justice is perfect, and He executed it against the Egyptians, just as He had declared. The fate of death that the Israelites had feared from the Egyptians was now one they witnessed against them; the Egyptians were dead and would never be a threat to Israel again.

Another contrasting parallel to the first plague is the image of water acting as a cleansing and purifying agent. While numerous examples are applicable in Scripture, a prominent one is found later in Exodus—water being the cleansing agent for the priests as they approached the altar. They were to wash both their hands and feet with it before ministering at the altar. So serious was this instruction that if they disobeyed, they would die (Exodus 30:18-21). In a similar way, God used water to cleanse Israel from the Egyptians, with the sea crashing down upon them. He wiped them out of Israel's life like water wipes away filth from our bodies. The opposite was true for the first plague—the Egyptians could not get clean from the water God had turned to blood. They desperately wanted and needed clean water, but none was to be found. The imagery is compelling: God sovereignly provides both the instruction and instruments through which we may be cleansed and withholds it from those who dishonor Him.

Lastly, a powerful connection can be seen between God swallowing the Egyptians into the depths of the sea just as He does our sins. Micah the prophet writes:

> He will again have compassion on us; He will tread our iniquities under foot. Yes, You will cast all their sins into the depths of the sea. (Micah 7:19)

Egypt was not the cause of Israel's sins, but it did fuel them as well as represent the slavery they had to their sin. As we discussed, the Israelites feared Egypt more than God on more than one occasion. This revealed a major lack of faith on their part, one they would unfortunately struggle with for the rest of their lives. But the more potent image here is what Egypt represented—slavery. Egypt enslaved Israel like our sins do today. As Jesus said,

> Truly, truly I say to you, everyone who commits sin is the slave of sin. (John 8:34)

We are each born into depravity, and it does not take long before we exercise it by willfully disobeying—all have sinned and fall short of the glory of God (Romans 3:23). Our youngest daughter is two years old right now, and let me tell you, she is in the full throes of exercising her depravity. She is testing every limit and pushing every button to see what we will allow, and she unleashes anger when she discovers that we do not put up with very much. We do the same in our sinful flesh. Even the most ardent rule followers are doing so with evil motives apart from Christ. We truly are dead in our sins and, even more terrifying, objects of His wrath (Romans 1:18; Ephesians 5:6).

That is one reason why God's grace in salvation is so astonishing! Through the gospel, we transform from objects of wrath into objects of His love. The gospel is:

> The good news of God's plan to rescue a spiritually dead, broken, condemned, and sin-enslaved people, offering forgiveness of sin, eternal life, and the restoration of peace with Him through the comprehensive and final sacrifice of Jesus Christ—who was born of a virgin, lived a sinless life, died on the cross, was buried, and rose again—bringing us to life in Him, adopting us into His loving family, and securing us in His glorious future.

Jesus took the punishment we deserved, and "He knew with His last breath, all our sin would go with it."[83] *That* sin—the sin that has consumed us and that we wrestle with on a daily (okay, hourly, and minute-by-minute) basis is no longer counted against us. We are no longer subject to its chains; we no longer bear eternal punishment for it. Yes, we experience earthly consequences as the result of our sin, but we are no longer objects of God's eternal wrath. Just like He swallowed up the Egyptians and they were no more, God casts our sins into the depths of the sea, and we bear no more of their eternal consequences. God obliterated the Egyptians like He obliterated our sin in the gospel. Both were wiped away, and neither would control the fates of their prior victims again.

The mention of God saving Israel **from the hand of the Egyptians** is no accident. We have seen strong hand imagery thus far in the narrative, and this reference drives the point home. No **hand** of an earthly enemy is any kind of match for the hand of the Heavenly God. Unfortunately, only two English translations capture the most literal translation of the original text. While God's **great power** is certainly being communicated, that phrase should actually be translated as "the great hand that Yahweh displayed against the Egyptians."[84] Readers are supposed to be hit in the face with the hand vs. hand imagery—how the Egyptians' hand was puny and handicapped in comparison to the hand of

God acting on behalf of Israel. God reigns, no created being is any match or formidable foe against His outstretched hand.

It took a while, but Israel finally **believed in the Lord and in His servant Moses.** The only other direct reference to Israel believing God or Moses thus far was way back in 4:31, "So the people believed, and when they heard that the Lord was concerned about the sons of Israel and that He had seen their affliction, then they bowed low and worshiped." That first expression of belief did not last long, probably only mere hours until Pharaoh rejected Moses' request and increased Israel's labor (5:21). The Israelites obeyed God's instructions through Moses throughout the unfolding of the plagues, but there is never an explicit mention of their belief expressed again until now.

After witnessing such a sobering massacre, they would be daft not to believe. Further, this whole experience confirmed and reinforced their belief **in His servant Moses.** Does this mean the Israelites held Moses in some kind of theistic light? That they thought him to be in some kind of god-like status? Not hardly. This simply means that they recognized the hand of God clearly on his life, and understood that Moses was the leader God had specifically and deliberately chosen to preside over them.

Summary

We come to the end of an era with the conclusion of this chapter, and the way God orchestrated it surpasses even the most creative imagination. We commenced this section with the beginning of Israel's journey: **God did not lead them by the way of the land of the Philistines, even though it was near**. By this point, Israel should have learned that attempting to confine God within a box is a perilous and fruitless exercise, and He skillfully evaded any such attempt on their part. They did not travel the way they expected and likely had no idea why. But God had His reasons, and He provided us with the main one: **the people might change their minds when they see war and return to Egypt.**

Why anyone would choose to go back to slavery seems incomprehensible to us. But we must remember that while the grass can appear greener on the other side, it can also resemble death. God knew that His people were vulnerable and ill-equipped to handle anything other than putting one foot in front of the other at the moment. They were not warriors; they were not even an established nation yet. If they witnessed war, whether observing the Philistines at war or Egyptian outposts, they would be tempted to give up and turn back. God did not want to take that chance, so He removed the possibility by having them take a peculiar route.

As the Israelites went **by the way of the wilderness to the Red Sea**, we are told that Moses brought something along with them—**the bones of Joseph**. Joseph was one of the most faith-filled men we read about in all of Scripture. In spite of achieving enormous success in Egypt, he knew that Egypt was never going to be his people's home, so he made them promise not to leave him there when they left. Moses made sure to keep that promise by bringing his bones along.

The Israelites concluded the next leg of their journey at **Etham**, a location now only left to speculation. But the destination was not as important as how God got them there. He **went before them in a pillar of cloud by day and in a pillar of fire by night to give them light** that never left the people. We are not told how big the pillar was, but it must have been substantial enough for upward of two million people to be guided by it. While only those directly in front needed to actually see it, others could play follow-the-leader a bit and stay on track.

I also believe that the visibility of the pillar, to some extent, depended on the faith of those observing it. As we saw later in the narrative, the Egyptians were not afraid of the pillar when it stood between them and Israel. That would have been peculiar if they saw it in its full glory because it certainly was no natural phenomenon. Rather, I believe that the clarity and size of the pillar directly corresponded to the "lens of faith" of the observers. In other words, some likely saw its full size and grandeur, while to others, it appeared more obscure. Regardless, God led them through the pillar, and they did not stay in Etham long.

In another unexpected twist of events, God instructed Moses to have Israel **turn back and camp… by the sea.** They had already deviated from the expected path, and now God directed them to turn back and enter a dead end by the sea. This would not have made sense to anyone, but once again, God had a plan. He knew that Pharaoh was regretting letting Israel go, so God would **harden Pharaoh's heart**, and he would **chase after them.** God was going to **be honored through Pharaoh and all his army, and the Egyptians** would know that He was God.

Sure enough, **Pharaoh and his servants had a change of heart** (compliments of God), and decided they wanted their slaves back. They certainly were not going to tiptoe up to them and ask them nicely to re-enter slavery. Instead, Pharaoh **made his chariot ready and took his people with him; and he took six hundred select chariots and all the other chariots of Egypt with officers over all of them.** They had dominated Israel with force for several hundred years and planned to do so once again.

Despite everything God had just done for them, **as Pharaoh drew near, the sons of Israel looked, and…they became very frightened.** While a point of legitimate concern, Israel decided to fear Pharaoh more than God. Again, this would have been understandable if they hadn't just witnessed ten plagues absolutely destroy Egypt over the last several months. But alas, they instantly grew terrified and **cried out to the Lord.**

In an impressive display of leadership, Moses told them not to fear but rather to **stand by and see the salvation of the Lord.** Moses had come a long way from the coward God first approached at the burning bush. God transformed him into the leader He created him to be. This not only gives us hope for Israel in their current cowardly state but also supplies us with lots of hope as well.

God then told Moses to **lift up** his staff, and stretch out his **hand over the sea and divide it** so the Israelites could walk through on dry land. Moses had witnessed more than he ever thought possible by this point, but I can imagine his eyes bulging once again at this directive. God was going to do what?! But God made it clear to Moses that He was going to get the honor for this final defeat, and it was going to be a spectacular one at that.

Before Moses stretched out his hand, God took action by moving the pillar of cloud from in front of Israel to behind them. The pillar **came between the camp of Egypt and the camp of Israel…and one did not come near the other all night.** God answered their prayer in a powerful way. Again, the Egyptians did not immediately flee, which makes me think God had hardened their hearts beyond the point of sanity. Or, according to my previous theory, they did not see the pillar in its full form. Perhaps it appeared more like a dense fog; they could not proceed because they could not see through it. Regardless, the pillar kept the Egyptians away so God could work the next part of His miraculous plan.

Obediently, **Moses stretched out his hand over the sea; and the Lord swept the sea back by a strong east wind all night and turned the sea into dry land, so the waters were divided**. The wind was miraculous. No ordinary wind could be that targeted and strong to dry up not only a huge sea, but the ground underneath it too. Israel began walking through the middle of the sea with sure steps, no doubt in awe over what they were doing and seeing.

At some point, the pillar moved again, and the **Egyptians took up pursuit.** It seemed as though they were getting a bit too close to the Israelites, so God **brought the army of the Egyptians into confusion. He caused their chariot wheels to swerve, and He made them drive with difficulty.** While the pillar was not enough to phase them, this was. The Egyptians recognized Who was behind their difficulties, freaked out, and started to **flee.**

Unfortunately for them, it was too late. God told Moses to stretch out his hand again, **and the sea returned to his normal state at daybreak.** Thus, **the**

Lord overthrew the Egyptians in the midst of the sea. The **entire army** had perished, **not even one of them remained.** Israel was finally free and safe from their greatest enemy for the last several centuries.

When Israel saw the great power which the Lord had used against the Egyptians, the people feared the Lord. They finally redefined and refocused their fear from great trepidation to great reverence to the One who alone deserves it.

GROUP STUDY

Introduction

The object of our fear controls our souls.

Fear is an unfortunate reality of life. We all fear something—the loss of a loved one, terminal illness, loss of work, a prodigal child, etc. While most fears live deep within the recesses of our minds, they occasionally emerge and take over our lives.

- What are you afraid of?
- Describe a time in your life when you were most afraid.
  - How invasive was your fear?

The Word

Israel had experienced a new birth into freedom, but they were fragile. Like any newborn, they were vulnerable and incapable of taking care of themselves. They needed to learn who God was and how to trust Him, and it began with following His lead even when it didn't make sense.

> **God did not lead them by the way of the land of the Philistines, even though it was near; for God said, "The people might change their minds when they see war, and return to Egypt." (Exodus 13:17)**

> **"Tell the sons of Israel to turn back and camp…by the sea. For Pharaoh will say of the sons of Israel, 'They are wandering aimlessly in the land; the wilderness has shut them in.' Thus I will harden Pharaoh's heart, and he will chase after them; and I will be honored through Pharaoh and all his army, and the Egyptians will know that I am the Lord." And they did so. (Exodus 14:2-4)**

- What did God know about the Israelites that they perhaps didn't even realize about themselves? (13:17)
- What did Pharaoh think about Israel's strange travel itinerary?
  - How was God going to use that against him?

- What was God's endgame with this plan?

While Moses knew what was going on behind the scenes, the Israelites didn't (there were far too many to communicate with in real-time without instant ways of communication). Their job was to trust and obey, which they did. But not for long.

> **As Pharaoh drew near, the sons of Israel looked, and behold, the Egyptians were marching after them, and they became very frightened; so the sons of Israel cried out to the Lord. (Exodus 14:10)**

It would be reasonable and respectable if this had not been their sole response. There's certainly nothing wrong with crying out to God when we are distressed; in fact, that's what we're supposed to do! But that's not the whole story:

> **Then they said to Moses, "Is it because there were no graves in Egypt that you have taken us away to die in the wilderness? Why have you dealt with us in this way, bringing us out of Egypt? Is this not the word we spoke to you in Egypt, saying, 'Leave us alone that we may serve the Egyptians'? For it would have been better for us to serve the Egyptians than to die in the wilderness." (Exodus 14:11-12)**

- What does Israel's response reveal about their trust and belief in God?
- Is their response surprising after what they just witnessed through the plagues? Why or why not?

Fortunately for Israel, their disappointing response to the threat against their freedom did not thwart God's plan.

> **Thus the Lord saved Israel that day from the hand of the Egyptians, and Israel saw the Egyptians dead on the seashore. When Israel saw the great power which the Lord had used against the Egyptians, the people feared the Lord, and they believed in the Lord, and in His servant Moses. (Exodus 14:30-31)**

- While the victory at the sea served to free Israel from Egypt once and for all, what else did it accomplish, especially regarding Israel's faith?
  - How did the object of their fear change?

Apply

> Have I not commanded you?
> Be strong and courageous!
> Do not tremble or be dismayed,
> for the Lord your God is with you wherever you go.
> Joshua 1:9

> When I am afraid, I will put my trust in You.
> In God, whose word I praise,
> In God I have put my trust; I shall not be afraid.
> What can mere man do to me?
> David, Psalm 56:3-4

Fear is a natural response to situations that threaten our joy and peace. Because we live in a fallen world, we will experience trials and suffering. But we have a choice when we face them, we can decide what the object of our fear will be. Will we hyper-focus on the threat and cave to anxiety? Or will we redirect our focus to God and experience peace in the midst of the trial? Israel chose to focus on Egypt, and the object of their fear didn't change until their circumstances did. But God desires more for us. He wants us to fear Him more than any circumstances in life.

Read these verses about what it means to fear God:

"You shall fear the Lord your God; you shall serve Him and cling to Him." (Deuteronomy 10:20)

"The fear of the Lord is to hate evil." (Proverbs 8:13a)

"Let all the earth fear the Lord; let all the inhabitants of the world stand in awe of Him." (Psalm 33:8)

"Do not fear those who kill the body but are unable to kill the soul; but rather fear Him who is able to destroy both soul and body in hell." (Matthew 10:28)

- How does fearing God differ from being afraid of things in this world?

We began this group study with this idea: the object of our fear controls our souls.

- What are some ways we can redirect our focus from fearing our circumstances to standing in awe of the One who controls them?
- How can we glean courage from John 16:33?

"These things I have spoken to you so that in Me you may have peace. In the world you have tribulation, but take courage; I have overcome the world." John 16:3

WEEK THREE

PRAISE

Exodus 15:1-15:21

PERSONAL BIBLE STUDY QUESTIONS

1. Who sang the first part of the song? (15:1)
2. Fill in the blanks: (15:2)

The Lord is my _____ and _____.

He has become my _____.

    a. In what ways has He been those things to you?

3. Verse 3 states, "The Lord is a warrior." Why was that particularly beneficial to Israel at that point?
4. What imagery do they use when describing what God did to Pharaoh? (15:4-5)
5. What's the significance of God's "right hand," especially in light of what He told Moses in Exodus 3:20? (15:6)
6. How do they describe how God piled up the waters? (15:8)
7. What did the enemy desire? (15:9)
8. How does verse 10 describe the Egyptians' demise?
9. Who else had heard what God had done for the Israelites? (15:14-15)
    a. What was their reaction to the news? (15:14-16)
10. What would God do with His people? (15:17)
11. Who took the timbrel in her hand and led the women out with dancing? (15:20)

COMMENTARY

Exodus 15:1-15:21

The Oxford Dictionary defines "praise" as a verb used to "express warm approbation of; to proclaim or commend the excellence or merits of; to speak highly of; to laud." We praise what we admire, especially if we have benefited from the one we are praising.

Consider a boss who praises his employees for a job well done. The employee has done something admirable, something that benefited the company. The employer, in turn, recognizes the accomplishment of his employee and goes out of his way to commend him for a job well done. This motivates the employee to continue doing good work and reaching for new goals, and everyone benefits from it.

We also praise people we admire and respect. Celebrities, professional athletes, business owners, social media influencers, and more hold our interest and are the objects of our praise. We follow them, talk about them, and are quick to praise them when the opportunity presents itself. These people may not have directly benefited our lives (they may not even know we exist!), but that does not stop us from thinking highly of them and praising them nonetheless. Praise is something we all do, and if we are honest, it is something we all love receiving.

But Christians have a slightly more intense definition of praise. Thanksgiving is thanking God for what He gives us, but praise is thanking God for who He is—for His character. How frequent is praise in our relationships with God? What does our praise for Him look like? Is it merely lip service as we sing in church on Sunday mornings? Is it less frequent than that? Do we reserve praise only for when He provides us with an extra blessing? Do we praise Him regardless of circumstances? Or do we take the time to praise Him at all?

God had just accomplished one of the most monumental victories the world has ever known by destroying the Egyptians and allowing His people to cross the sea safely. This story will be remembered forever, and the Israelites who witnessed it must have been absolutely beside themselves in awe of what they had just seen. They must have pinched themselves a lot on that walk through the sea and several times as they watched the Egyptian bodies wash up on the shore after being decimated by the walls of water. This was a huge moment that demanded a huge response, and to Israel's credit, that was exactly what they did.

Exodus 15:1-21

Then Moses and the sons of Israel sang this song to the Lord, and said, "I will sing to the Lord, for He is highly exalted; The horse and its rider He had hurled into the sea. (15:1)

I must begin this section with a confession: poetry and song lyrics are not my forte. Many scholars have researched this song to degrees far beyond my capabilities (and, if I am honest, my interest), and I am thankful for them. Arguments have been made for when this song was written, who wrote it, its main point, how it should be divided up into stanzas, and much more. However, our study will focus on content more than textual criticism and linguistic structure. We will touch on a couple of linguistic topics here and there but will spend the majority of our time on theology and applying it properly to our lives.

Immediately after witnessing the annihilation of the Egyptian army, **Moses and the sons of Israel sang this song to the Lord.** Despite some criticism about the origin of the song, the most straightforward reading and understanding is that Moses is its author. This song "may be the oldest piece of sustained poetry in the Hebrew Bible: a paean of praise to God, the biblical way of expressing gratitude."[85] The books of the Pentateuch (the first five books of the Old Testament) were written by Moses, likely near the end of his life. This song, however, was composed right after the crossing of the sea, some forty years prior to the rest of the book's penning, which is why it is commonly known as the "Song of the Sea."[86]

Most commentators assume this song was spontaneous, not composed over a long period of time with strict concentration and editing processes.[87] This makes sense because of its content and purpose—it is a song of praise and gratitude for what God has just done for them. Many of us can probably relate to this, at least somewhat. I have often become so overwhelmed with thanks for answered prayers, unexpected blessings, etc., that I will spontaneously start praying, and the prayers will turn into a song of some sort. Because I am not a talented songwriter and am often surrounded by young children, these "songs" are usually of the "speak and repeat" variety, but it works. We dance around the kitchen, in the car, or wherever we find ourselves consumed with extra bursts of praise, and we enjoy the dance/song/praise party immensely.

One example was when my husband got a promotion at work. We suspected he might get it, but you never really know with these things, so we had tempered our expectations a bit. When we got the call that he did get it, I immediately told the girls, and we started a praise and thanks party. We sang, prayed, and danced our way in circles around the house, thanking God for letting Daddy get the job and then asking that he would excel in it. We found ourselves doing our little song/dance/prayer spontaneously throughout the day and had a grand ol' time doing so.

Our little songs are hardly inspired (or remembered), but Moses' was, and his song became an instant hit. It was likely adopted immediately by the Israelite people and sung regularly from that point onward, becoming a part of their culture of worship.[88] One part of parenting guaranteed to bring tears to my eyes is when our littles worship—when I hear powerful words of truth sung in their sweet, little, off-key voices. Imagine what it must have been like for hundreds of thousands of people to join together in one accord and with one voice praising God for what He had done for them at the sea! The roar of the wind was replaced by the roar of voices lifting their praise to God as an offering of thanks. The rush of the waters crashing down transformed into the rush of breath gathered for continued lyrics and dancing. This song was not given a lot of thought upon its writing, but it would be the source of meditation for countless minds for years to come.

This song was sung **to the Lord,** but, as we will see, it was also sung about the Lord. Oftentimes, our songs of praise do the same, for we pop back and forth between directly addressing Him and reminding ourselves of truths about Him. Both are wonderful; both are valid. God is always pleased when His children meditate on and speak His truth, just as He is glad when we pray to Him directly.

> **"I will sing to the Lord, for He is highly exalted; The horse and its rider He had hurled into the sea." (15:1b)**

Rarely is it advisable to begin worship with "**I**," but here, it works well and reveals a couple of important points about the rest of the song. First, it reveals the first-hand vantage point of the singers with the content of their song.[89] This "**I**" undoubtedly refers to Moses first since he is the author of the song. But the Israelites would have adopted his words and internalized them in order to also use them as an offering of praise to the Lord. They, along with Moses, witnessed God rescue them from the Egyptians through the plagues and the parting of the sea. They saw with their own eyes the bodies of the Egyptians floating to the surface of the water and then drifting lifelessly to the shore. Every sense was utilized and affected by their deliverance from Egypt. Centuries later, the Apostle John would begin one of his letters similarly about Jesus—"What was from the beginning, what we have heard, what we have seen with our eyes, what we have looked at and touched with our hands…" (1 John 1:1). The Israelites were direct witnesses and were intimately involved in every aspect of the exodus.

Their direct involvement naturally produced direct praise. They were personally affected by the exodus and would offer personal praise to **the Lord** who orchestrated it. Despite being sung by a choir of hundreds of thousands of people, its lyrics and meaning were profoundly personal to each of them. It was a song they would each "own" individually. Each participant in the song would meditate on its words and join in its resonance personally; it was not merely a corporate exercise. In this way, joining in the "Song of the Sea" was akin to the Passover. Each Israelite had to participate in the Passover and intentionally comply with God's mandates to spare their firstborn. They all did so, but the act was initially a personal act of worship. The same is true for this song. It was a personal expression of gratitude and praise to God. Not every Israelite may have internalized it the same way; like any group of people, there was likely a broad spectrum of faith among them. But the focus of this song was personal—direct thanks from a specific singer to the one and only Lord.

To the Lord, each Israelite sang. While seemingly obvious, this point must not be overlooked because the entire narrative has been conveying a strong message—God, specifically Yahweh, the "I AM," is *the* only true God. No one else compares nor can stand against the God of Israel, the God who created the universe and sustains it with His hand. Egypt was one of, if not the most powerful nation in the world at that point, and God overthrew them using the very forces of nature they worshipped. They put their hope in the sun, but God made it clear He controls the sun and does whatever He wants with it. The same is true with water, creatures, health, pestilence, and life and death itself. **The Lord** rescued Israel, and it is **the Lord** they praise in this song.

The Israelites **will sing to the Lord, for He is highly exalted; the horse and its rider He has hurled into the sea.** The concept of exaltation is hardly new or unique in Scripture. In fact, "exaltation is one of the most significant and pervasive themes the Bible employs to portray the majesty and greatness of God and of Jesus Christ."[90] However, the specific word for **exalted** (*ga'a*) here is only used in five verses in the Old Testament. Only two of these reference God, and they are both found in this chapter of Exodus, here and in 15:21, when Miriam repeats this lyric. Both of these are double uses of the word, *ga'a ga'a*, which is translated **highly exalted**. God is not just exalted, He is exalted to the highest extent possible in creation and among His people.

In that specific moment, as they stood transfixed to the scene of destruction before them, Moses and the Israelites exalt the Lord most obviously because **the horse and its rider He has hurled into the sea.** There is no hidden meaning here; Moses is referencing the horses and riders of the Egyptian army. One commentator wisely notes that **highly exalted** "and Yahweh's act of casting horses and riders into the sea are intended to be contrasting phrases and to indicate Yahweh's rulership over both the heights and the depths."[91] Isn't that imagery beautiful? It reminds me of Psalm 139: 6-10:

> Such knowledge is too wonderful for me; It is too high, I cannot attain to it. Where can I go from Your Spirit? Or where can I flee from Your presence? If I ascend to heaven, You are there; If I make my bed in Sheol, behold, You are there. If I take the wings of the dawn, If I dwell in the remotest part of the sea, Even there Your hand will lead me, And Your right hand will lay hold of me.

God's presence and power are everywhere and without limit. He is exalted above the heavens just as His wrath is experienced in the depths of hell. To those who belong to Him, these truths bring great comfort and peace. But for those who refuse to submit to Him, like the Egyptians, they will discover His power and sovereignty one way or another.

The Lord is my strength and song, And He has become my salvation; This is my God, and I will praise Him; My father's God, and I will extol Him. (15:2)

Moses' thanks for God's actions turns to praise for His attributes, particularly how they relate to Moses (and the Israelites by extension). First, **the Lord is my strength and song.** While most Bibles translate this phrase similarly, in Hebrew, **song** (*zimrat*) "is a double entendre, for its stem can mean both 'to sing, play music,' and 'to be strong,'" so it could also be rendered "my strength and my might."[92]

Normally, we do not closely associate **strength** with **song**, but in God, they are inextricably linked. God is both our strength and the reason we sing. He is the source of our power and the origin of our praise. The more we meditate on His truth, the stronger our faith becomes and the more inspired we are to offer Him our praise. Notice, however, that it is not God's actions that are Moses' strength and song, but His person. Moses certainly thanks God for what He has accomplished on the Israelites' behalf, but he recognizes that his **strength** and **song** are derived from God Himself. We are far too often guilty of limiting our focus to God's actions, not His person and character. The results of God's hands are wonderful, but they should remain as a means to the end of ascribing worship and adoration to *Him*.

God is Moses' **strength and song, and He has become** his **salvation**. This phrase reveals a couple of powerful truths. First, salvation was a process for Moses, as it is for many of us. There is no mention of a specific moment in time when Moses began trusting God and believing in Him in a salvific way. When we were introduced to Moses at the burning bush, he was certainly no giant of faith. He made every excuse he could think of to avoid the call God was placing on his life. For quite some time after that, he was still unsure, kind of obeying God, but not completely, and certainly not with abandon. It seems that sometime early on in the plagues, his faith became real, and something began clicking for him. Faith began taking hold of his heart, and God subsequently became his **strength**, **song**, and **salvation**.

In addition to being a process, salvation for Moses and the Israelites was both physical as well as spiritual. While that seems obvious, we must realize that these are separate actions, and one does not necessarily lead to the other. The physical salvation of both Moses and the Israelites has been quite obvious in our narrative—they were physically delivered from slavery in Egypt. Spiritual salvation is personal, and while there are no specific records of personal declarations of faith amongst the Israelites, God certainly provided them with ample opportunity for it through events like the Passover.

Yet, one important observation should be noted: physical salvation, even by miraculous circumstances, is no guarantee of salvific faith. We are often tempted to think that if we witnessed a miracle, or if God did something miraculous in our lives, we would believe and dedicate our lives to Him, no questions asked. Unfortunately, that is not accurate. Many people have witnessed the hand of God directly and still refused to acknowledge His Lordship in their lives. The Egyptians are obviously the best example of that in our narrative. They were on the receiving end of God's wrath, and they still refused to bend the knee to God and turn to Him instead of clinging to their illusions of "gods." Additionally, it is doubtful that all the Israelites trusted in God in a salvific way at this point as well. They are amazed, no doubt. But as we will soon see, they have not fully trusted Him or made Him the Lord of their lives as Moses has.

Moses continues his personal declaration of faith: **This is my God, and I will praise Him; My father's God, and I will extol Him.** For centuries, many Israelites thought of God as their **father's God**, the God of their ancestors. Their familial lineage was remembered all the way back to Abraham, and even God introduced Himself to Moses as the God of his father, "the God of Abraham, the God of Isaac, and the God of Jacob" (Exodus 3:6). But salvation cannot be claimed on the basis of family lineage. Moses moved from knowing about God through his family tree to embracing Him personally—**this is my God**. While it is accurate to acknowledge God as the God of his fathers, to Moses, He was also *his* God, and Moses steadfastly declared that he would **praise** and **extol Him.**

Remarkably, this is the only time this Hebrew term for **praise** (*nava*) is used in the whole Old Testament. It means to beautify, show oneself beautiful, or adorn oneself with beauty. [93] Moses was not just exalting God as his superior and acknowledging His holiness, he was shining light on God's beauty or the manner in which God is holy. One commentator translates Moses' words here as "I will enshrine Him," capturing Moses' desire to preserve and treasure God's splendor in his own life. [94] A mark of a maturing Christian is their ability to see, meditate upon, and then desire to adorn God's beauty with their own lives. Moses has grown astronomically in his faith since the burning bush encounter, and his passion now is inspiring.

Moses seeks to adorn God's magnificence with his life, for he worships God personally and has a relationship with Him. Yet worship is also corporate and follows a strong line of heritage in the Israelites. In this way, Moses declares that he **will extol Him**. The term for **extol** (*rum*) here means "to be exalted" or "to be high."[95] It is used nearly 200 times throughout the Old Testament and has previously been used in Exodus. It was first used in Exodus 7:20, referring to how Aaron lifted (*rum)* his staff and struck the water in the Nile so that it turned to blood for the first plague. Similarly, it was used to describe the manner in which Israel left Egypt in 14:8—how they "were going out boldly" (*rum*). Lastly, it described the action of Moses, who lifted (*rum*) his staff up over the sea to divide it in Exodus 14:16. Each of these described a loftiness, either literally or in spirit. But now it is used to worship God—to lift *Him* high in the heart of Moses and other Israelites singing this song.

Also worth noting is Moses' commitment to continued worship: **I *will* extol Him** (emphasis added). While this song was spontaneous, its praise would remain a commitment on his behalf. This follows the pattern set forth in the Passover of setting aside intentional time to worship but also remaining committed to its continuation year after year. It is good, healthy, and pleasing to God when we worship, but doing so once or even occasionally is not enough. Worship realigns our hearts with God and exalts Him to His rightful place in our lives. We, as Christians, need to worship often, for we need to remind ourselves often of who God is and what He has done on our behalf. Moses was committed to keep lifting God up in his life; we are wise to do the same.

> **The Lord is a warrior, The Lord is His name. Pharaoh's chariots and his army He has cast into the sea; And the choicest of his officers are drowned in the Red Sea. The deeps cover them; They went down into the depths like a stone. (15:3-5)**

God is worthy of our praise for many reasons, and one top reason for Moses and the Israelites was the fact that **He was a warrior** on their behalf. War imagery, as well as literal references, have been evident in our narrative thus far: God fighting on Israel's behalf (14:14, 25) and the Egyptians coming after Israel in a literal battle array (14:6-9). As we have also observed, the Israelites were not warriors; they were not even minimally trained soldiers. They were former slaves with skill sets limited to those that would benefit their Egyptian masters. They were not capable of defending themselves militarily, even if they had the bravery to (which they did not). The Israelites were sitting ducks, waiting for the Egyptian dogs to pounce, but God stepped in and eliminated the threat. God remains undefeated as a Warrior—woe to those who find themselves as His enemies.

Lest there be any confusion about who Moses is talking about, he plainly states that **the Lord is His name**. The **Lord** used here is Jehovah, or Yahweh, which is the most common and formal name used by God to identify Himself both to Israel and the world. Yahweh means self-existent or eternal and communicates the holiness or "set-apartness" of God.[96] God cannot be compared to or confused with any idol; He created and sustained everything people would otherwise worship. He is *the* God, the one and only true God, worthy of the worship and adoration Moses and the Israelites attribute to Him in this song.

God's sovereignty was on display when He cast **Pharaoh's chariots and his army...into the sea**, and when **the choicest of his officers are drowned in the sea**. Again, we have a reference to the **chariots** and then **the choicest** of Pharaoh's army. These were the elite, the most thoroughly trained, and the most honored group in the Egyptian army. But the best Egypt had to offer was not even a ripple in the ocean of God's ability to overthrow them. One aspect of God that I love and find myself in awe of often is His creativity. He could have miraculously armed the Israelites to fight back and beat the Egyptians in a traditional warfare method. That would have been the most expected kind of victory. But God cannot be put in a box and often likes to prove it. Instead of fighting the Egyptians with swords and shields, He defeated them with water and **drowned** them **in the sea**.

God sometimes turns His created order on its head to remind us that it is His head to turn. The Egyptians regarded themselves quite loftily, God, in turn, had **the deeps cover them**. The word for **deeps** here (*t*ʰ*homot)* is the same word used during the creation account "to describe the primordial "deep" (*t*ʰ*hom).* In other words, the Red Sea is described in Exodus 1:5 in a manner reminiscent of the chaotic water that God tamed at creation. The Red Sea has become 'The Sea.'" [97] Several hundred years later, Jesus would also take command of water and calm raging seas (Luke 8:22-25). These actions not only showcase God's power, but also His consistency. God "is the same yesterday and today and forever;" it is hardly surprising that the God who created the sea is the same One who can use it to still accomplish His purposes (Hebrews 13:8).

It certainly should not have surprised the Egyptians at this point. Yet, they wore arrogance like a crown and puffed themselves up enough to believe they could be victorious over God. So God took their lofty selves and threw them **down into the depths like a stone.** As the Psalmist would later declare, "You save a humble people, but the haughty eyes You bring down" (Psalm 18:27, ESV). Further, it is quite ironic that the Egyptians who lived "in the land of dry sand and graves, should suffer a burial in the watery depths, but a fitting end" for people who made the Nile a watery grave for infants. [98] The imagery of heights and depths reveals that God's justice is both sufficient and poetic, and makes clear displays who reigns—God and God alone.

> **Your right hand, O Lord, is majestic in power, Your right hand, O Lord, shatters the enemy. And in the greatness of Your excellence You overthrow those who rise up against You; You send forth Your burning anger, and it consumes them as chaff. (15:6-7)**

In addition to the imagery of heights and depths, the symbolism of hands, specifically the **right hand** communicating power, is potent. God's **right hand…is majestic in power** and **shatters the enemy.** As we saw in the previous study, one's right hand, in the case of battle, "normally held the warrior's weapon and brought victory."[99] God's right hand never experienced loss or defeat. When He extends it, victory is sure, and justice will be complete.

Yet God's hand is not just a brute force of strength. To be **majestic** is to cause inspiring awe or reverence in the beholder, especially in relation to size, strength, power, or authority.[100] Rarely do we take time to stand in awe of things in today's culture and society at large. We always seem to be rushing from one task to the next; the practice of being still and the act of meditation are largely forgotten. Here, Moses is declaring that God's power is something worth meditating upon—something worthy of our awe and adoration. It is **majestic,** and to any keen observer, something far more compelling than merely a display of brute force. God's power is both limitless and beautiful, in total control, and delivered with utmost attention and purpose. His actions are not messy, nor are they arbitrary.

Overthrowing the Egyptians and shattering **the enemy** was not accomplished in an uncontrolled fit of rage or a tantrum. It was deliberate, and its ramifications reached far beyond the physical realm of this world. To be clear, God did **shatter** (*ra'as*) them. This word is used only twice in Scripture and carries with it the image of a brittle object being shattered completely.[101] But it was not as if God completely lost His temper, grabbed a pot like a toddler would, and threw it across the room in a fit of rage. His judgment against the Egyptians was far more calculated; He wanted the Israelites and the world to see that no one stands against Him and succeeds.

As Moses expresses next, **in the greatness of Your excellence, You overthrow those who rise up against You.** God's superiority and eminence are vast, and it is from this position that He will **overthrow those who rise up** against Him. God's enemies are like ants attempting to challenge the ocean. With one swift wave, they are no more. They never stood a chance.

While God's judgment is calculated and in control, He is not without emotion. He loves His people and considers Israel as His son. There is understandably, therefore, an emotional aspect to the justice He renders on their behalf. Moses notes that God sends forth His **burning anger, and it consumes them as chaff.** At first glance, this imagery may seem out of place since we have been reflecting upon the Egyptians' destruction in the sea. However, God's anger is drawn from the centuries Egypt mistreated His people.

One such instance was when Pharaoh withdrew straw from Israel's brick-making. The Egyptians had provided the Israelites with straw, but when Pharaoh grew angry about Moses' request for Israel to leave, he increased their labor by making Israel get their own straw. Thus, "the people scattered through all the land of Egypt to gather stubble (chaff) for straw" (Exodus 5:12). God, in "a striking, taunting piece of irony,"[102] gathered the Egyptians for destruction just as they had forced Israel to gather straw for brick-making. He brought them to the sea, mirroring how His people brought straw to their brick-making stations. He consumed them like the Egyptians wanted to consume the Israelites' hope. God protected His people from the Egyptians, but no one could protect the Egyptians from Him.

> **At the blast of Your nostrils the waters were piled up, The flowing waters stood up like a heap; The deeps were congealed in the heart of the sea. The enemy said, 'I will pursue, I will overtake, I will divide the spoil; My desire shall be gratified against them; I will draw out my sword, my hand will destroy them.' (15:8-9)**

One intriguing aspect of poetry is the imagery it employs in its descriptions. These verses obviously recount Israel's deliverance from Egypt at the Red Sea, but unlike the narrative we read in chapter 14, they use powerful poetic imagery to affirm the sovereignty of God. The east wind mentioned in chapter 14 now becomes **the blast of God's nostrils.** Some may be tempted to think this is some sort of discrepancy, but that is hardly the case. It is simply a personification of the events. Whereas in 14:21, the Lord "swept the sea back by a strong east wind all night," we now have a creative expression of the origin of that wind—God's breath. All it took was one strong exhale from God to overthrow an entire army.

As one commentator notes, "this is a powerful image, and we should not think that ancient writers were any less adept at using such imagery than we are. To call the wind a nostril blast is to say that the wind is *His*, His to command as easily as we breathe in and out."[103] The image of God's breath/nostrils takes us back to the creation account in Genesis 2:7 when "God formed man from the dust of the ground and breathed into his nostrils the breath of life; and man became a living being." The same God who created man's nostrils and breathed life into them also created wind from His nostrils, which took the lives of His enemies. So much poetic justice is displayed here, along with God's unquestionable sovereignty over every aspect of His creation.

At God's breath, **the waters were piled up, the flowing waters stood up like a heap,** and **the deeps were congealed in the heart of the sea.** As we have seen, the water was split and became like walls on the right and left of the Israelites as they passed through the sea (14:22). The imagery here heightens the imagination of both the singers and the readers for generations to come. God **piled up** the waters until they **stood up like a heap**, further confirming that this body of water was no mere stream. The walls of water resembled a mighty city's walls, acting as fortresses protecting God's people from destruction. Further, the ground **in the heart of the sea** was **congealed.** What had been submerged since creation was now uncovered and hardened to make a path for the Israelites to cross safely.

The enemy made their best attempt to follow. They **said, 'I will pursue, I will overtake, I will divide the spoil; my desire shall be gratified against them; I will draw out my sword, my hand will destroy them.'** We have no record of these exact words from the Egyptians, but the point has been previously communicated—the Egyptians sought to overpower and re-enslave the Israelites. Again, we may be tempted to see discrepancies between the narrative and the song, particularly with the inclusion of dividing the spoil and drawing out their swords to destroy them. The narrative made it clear that the Egyptians wanted only to make them slaves again, with no mention of plunder or killing. However, both plunder and killing would inevitably be part of overtaking the Israelites.

First, the Egyptians would most certainly have wanted to plunder the Israelites because much of Israel's wealth originally belonged to them. Remember, God had inclined the hearts of the Egyptians to give the Israelites "articles of silver and articles of gold, and clothing," resulting in the plunder of the Egyptians as the Israelites left Egypt (12:35-36). Israel had been slaves for hundreds of years and had not been able to amass significant riches, but God made sure they did not leave Egypt empty-handed. Some believe that the amount of wealth given was akin to what Israel would have been owed for all their years of service. While it is impossible to know for sure, it would not surprise me in the least, as God's justice is complete, and He consistently demonstrates how abundantly He provides for His people. Thus, in pursuing the Israelites, the Egyptians quite likely had a secondary motive of reclaiming their valuables.

Furthermore, killing is almost always a result of militant takeovers. In order to subdue the Israelites, the Egyptians likely had every intention of **drawing their swords** and **destroying them**. Now, they hardly intended to annihilate all of the Israelites since their primary goal was to recapture and re-enslave them. However, collateral damage is a reasonable expectation in any military operation. In all likelihood, the Egyptians expected some measure of resistance and would have had no problem making examples of anyone who rose up against them. This reference in the song, therefore, does not take too many poetic liberties; it is highly probable that this was all coursing through the minds of the Egyptians as they pursued Israel.

> **You blew with Your wind, the sea covered them; They sank like lead in the mighty waters. Who is like You among the gods, O Lord? Who is like You, majestic in holiness, Awesome in praises, working wonders? You stretched out Your right hand, The earth swallowed them. (15:10-12)**

No evil intentions of an enemy can thwart God's plan for and protection of His people. As in verse 8, we have another reference to the wind, indicating that God blew it, causing the sea to cover them. The same breath that had been referenced in parting the sea is responsible for its collapse back into normalcy. In the previous narrative, it was Moses' outstretched hand (at God's command) that loosed the towers of water, allowing them to crush the Egyptians beneath. However, now we learn that the more specific cause was a shift in the wind that God had created. Moses' outstretched hand was the action God used to turn the wind. This makes sense because as we have previously concluded, the wind had to have been blowing continuously to keep the water parted, and the land dry beneath it. However, in mere seconds, God shifts the wind. Instead of flowing *through* the middle of the sea to keep it open, it flows *toward* the middle of the sea on both sides to allow the water to crash down again. The force of this must not be overlooked. Walls of water that high would have been powerful enough on their own to destroy anything in their path simply by being let down. But here, it seems as though God did not just release the water; He blew it with extra force, causing the Egyptians to sink **like lead in the mighty waters**.

We may once again be tempted to think that there is a discrepancy since we read about the bodies sinking when we previously read that the Egyptian bodies were seen "dead on the seashore" (14:30). However, there are several reasonable conclusions that can explain both assertions. Most obviously, neither account declares that *all* the Egyptians either sank or washed up on the shore. With an army that size, it is probable that there were hundreds of bodies that did both—floated to the shore and got stuck somehow at the bottom of the sea. The chariots and weaponry certainly would have sunk to the bottom after the initial mayhem of water being unleashed. It would hardly be surprising to find out that some bodies got stuck with them. Thus, no discrepancy exists; the carnage of the Egyptian army was vast.

I love the cause-and-effect, back-and-forth focus within this song. Moses focuses on God and praises Him for who He is and what He has done, then talks about what He has done, then praises Him again, then recounts again what God has done, and so on. It is such a healthy and potent reminder that we are to do the same. When we recall the goodness, holiness, and power of God, He will bring examples to our minds of each attribute, both from Scripture and our own experiences. Mentally reliving those experiences naturally causes us to praise Him again for His countless amazing attributes, and so the praise cycle continues.

Moses shifts back to praise: "**Who is like You among the gods, O Lord? Who is like You, majestic in holiness, awesome in praises, working wonders?**" Let's begin from a helicopter perspective. These questions are obviously rhetorical. Moses and everyone listening know that there is no one **among the gods** who is like the God, no one **majestic in holiness, awesome in praises, working wonders**. No other being can even be compared to God because He is infinitely beyond any created being. Certainly, no other genuine gods exist. The reference here and elsewhere throughout Scripture is to aspects of creation that people have worshiped in the place of God—misdirected objects of adoration and praise. Only the God of the Bible is a God at all; none can compare to Him.

Yet for the sake of thoroughness and as an adornment to his adoration, Moses articulates some attributes of God at the forefront of his mind. First, He is **majestic in holiness**. The word for **majestic** here is the same as in verse 6, and carries the idea of awe-inspiring greatness. In verse 6, it was used to qualify God's power; here, it is used to highlight God's **holiness**. As discussed in our first volume and briefly here, holiness is one of, if not the most predominant themes in the book of Exodus. God is constantly setting people and objects apart throughout this whole book, ultimately showcasing His own holiness and how He is set apart distinctly and powerfully as Creator from His creation. Moses' praise in this song is right on point for the theme of Exodus—there is no one like God, no one **majestic in holiness, awesome in praises**, or **working wonders**. God alone is God, set apart entirely from His creation simply by being "I AM."

Powerful worship occurs when we realize, like Moses, that God is one to be feared. The term **awesome** here (*yare*) carries with it the idea of fear and holy reverence. We first saw this term with the midwives in chapter 1—"the midwives feared (*yare*) God" (1:21). Though Pharaoh was a powerful threat, the midwives feared God more than the king of Egypt and pledged their allegiance and actions to Him above any other. We also saw this term used of Moses after he killed the Egyptian and was afraid (*yare*) he had been discovered, so he fled (2:14). Moses was then afraid (*yare*) to look at God when he encountered Him at the burning bush (3:6). Some of the Egyptians feared (*yare*) the word of the Lord. They took cover when He said He would send hail, but Moses knew that Pharaoh did not yet fear (*yare*) the Lord after that plague (9:20, 30). The Israelites were very afraid (*yare*) when they saw the Egyptians pursuing them, and Moses instructed them not to fear (*yare*) because they would soon see God's salvation on their behalf (14:10, 13). Finally, when the Israelites witnessed the Egyptians' doom, they feared (*yare*) the Lord and believed Moses.

Some may be under the mistaken impression that fearing the Lord is a bad thing, that God is somehow mean for requiring the fear of His people. Quite the opposite is true, actually. It is by sheer grace and mercy that God allows us to see Him with any kind of accuracy. When we see God even remotely for who He is, our eyes not only open to the reality of who He is, but the reality of who we are as well. Fear is the only appropriate response to seeing holiness because it is then we remember and realize our gross lack thereof.

A couple of years ago, my husband and I started hearing scuffling noises in our attic at night after putting our girls to bed. We made several attempts to identify the creatures causing the disturbance, but to no avail. The moment we turned on a light, nothing was visible. After having several "experts" visit over the next several weeks, we discovered three things: marsh rats had taken up residence in our attic, very few people knew how to effectively eliminate them, and finding those who did was a costly process. Rats are nasty creatures, but they are cunning. One might fall for the peanut-butter-in-the-trap trick, but that's about it. All their companions would observe the unfortunate rat and avoid the traps. Rats are also prolific breeders and multiply astonishingly rapidly (I'll spare you the details). Several months and thousands of dollars later, we rid the attic of rats and replaced everything their disgusting, wretched selves touched.

I share this not to gross you out but to make a point. In the spiritual realm, we are the rats. We are darkness-dwelling little fiends who hate light and scamper at alarming rates when any light is visible. Our sin is pervasive and incredibly difficult to get rid of. We cannot take a magic pill, check off to-do lists, or go to enough confessions to rid ourselves of the sin that consumes us. Therefore, when we, as sinners, get a glimpse of the holiness of God, the natural and only response is terror. We flee because we cannot stand the light. It is literally painful, and we are so accustomed to darkness that we cannot understand it. So we cower and run away in fear.

We do not fear God because He is mean; we fear God because we are awful, and His perfection is painful to our sin-dulled senses. His holiness is shocking for those who dwell in darkness, which is all of us prior to accepting Christ as our Savior. He is also terrifying because we know that we deserve to be the objects of His holy wrath. "The wages of sin is death," and "it is a terrifying thing to fall into the hands of the living God" (Romans 6:23; Hebrews 10:31). Seeing God's holiness is spine-chilling for those who know what they are looking at, but it is also the beginning of faith for those who cast their gaze upon Him in repentance. Pharaoh and the Egyptians witnessed the hand of God at work and refused to believe; the result was being the objects of His wrath and much-deserved destruction.

When Moses says God is **awesome in praises**, he is saying that God is worthy of our utmost fear and reverence because His worthiness is so beyond ours. This phrase has also been translated as "awesome in glorious deeds" (ESV), "awesome in glory" (NIV), "fearful in praises" (KJV, NET, ASV, YLT, HNV), and "awesome in splendor" (NLT). Because of what He has done for the Israelites most specifically, God is worthy to be feared. Indeed, the Israelites feared Him when they saw what He did to the Egyptians; it is a normal, healthy response to fear someone who can execute that kind of justice on that large of a scale.

God worked many **wonders** on the Israelites' behalf through all the plagues and then at the sea. He **stretched out** His **right hand**, and **the earth swallowed** the Egyptians. Repetition is a staple in songs and poetry, as we see another reference to God's **right hand**, communicating His unmatched power. Another repetitive yet uniquely curious statement is how the Egyptians were swallowed up. While the term for **earth** (*'eres*) is most often used to describe "land," it also "sometimes has the meaning 'underworld' or 'hell,' as it almost surely does here."[104] Thus, Moses did not suddenly forget or make a mistake in asserting that land covered up the Egyptians when it was clearly the sea. Rather, he is likely referring to death. Because of their unrepentant sin against God and His people, the Egyptians were swallowed up by death.

> **In Your lovingkindess You have led the people whom You have redeemed, In Your strength You have guided them to Your holy habitation. (15:13)**

Unfortunately, many people believe that the God of the Old Testament is somehow different than the God of the New Testament and/or Jesus. They claim that in the Old Testament, God was mean, wrathful, angry, and bent on judgment, while Jesus was merciful, kind, and meek. This misconception, and frankly, egregious error, is derived from a misunderstanding of God's character and is combated here within Moses' song. Moses has described how God's wrath was poured out on the Egyptians, yet here also declares God's **lovingkindness** toward His people.

It was because of God's **lovingkindness** that He **led the people whom** He had **redeemed**, not because of some callous adherence to justice. God's

lovingkindess is referenced often throughout the Old Testament, over 250 times. It carries with it a strong sense of loyalty and has also been translated as "unfailing love" (NIV), "steadfast love" (ESV), "faithful love" (CSB), and "loyal love" (NET). God did not love Israel because they deserved it (far from it), He loved them because they were His chosen people. Exacting vengeance on the guilty people who had enslaved them for hundreds of years is hardly harsh or unfair; it is a strong display of love and loyalty for His people.

Another familiar (and powerful) concept throughout Scripture is that of redemption. Redemption means to save, avenge, acquire by purchase, and reclaim as one's own. God **redeemed** Israel from the Egyptians. He saved them, avenged them, reclaimed them as His own (as opposed to Egypt's), and "purchased" them by exacting vengeance on their former captives. The Exodus is the most powerful display of redemption that God provides us with until Christ, and one crucial aspect to understand is that redemption is costly.

> At the Exodus the Lord redeemed Israel at the expense of Egypt. Since it was a case either that Israel perish at Egypt's hand or that Egypt perish in order that Israel go free, the Lord did not hesitate, nor, says Isaiah, would he ever hesitate to pay whatever price Israel's redemption demanded: *at all costs* he will redeem his people for himself. [105]

Both the Exodus and the cross were costly beyond what any human is capable of paying. Just like Israel could not redeem themselves from Egypt, neither can we ever hope to redeem ourselves from sin. It is simply too pervasive; a body without a pulse cannot bring itself back to life. We (like Israel) need a God who is not only capable of redeeming us but has the desire to do so. We need a God who is not only all-powerful but also all-loving. And that is exactly who God is. God is not only capable of paying our debt of sin, He wants to and has done so by giving His Son to die in our place. In the Exodus narrative, death came to the firstborn sons, lambs, and the Egyptian army to redeem Israel both from Egypt and their own sins. In the gospel, Jesus willingly took their place so that we, the people God has mercifully set His affections toward, can be united with Him. Like Israel, we are the objects of God's lovingkindness and redemption if we will only accept Christ's sacrifice and invite Him to be the Lord in our lives.

The song, until this point, has primarily focused on God and His power against Egypt. However, in these verses, we see a slight shift toward Israel and the journey they will now embark upon toward the promised land. God's strength not only delivered them from Egypt, but will guide them to His holy habitation. Throughout the journey out of Egypt and through the sea, God led Israel with a pillar of cloud and fire. Israel never had to question if God was with them. They simply had to look forward to see the pillar and be reassured that He was there and guiding them toward their new home—the long-awaited promised land.

The term for **guided** here, *nahal*:

> ...originates in the vocabulary of shepherding and denotes leading the sheep to a watering place. Its use here thus evokes the idea of God's tender, loving care for His people—His "flock"—whom he leads from slavery to freedom and guides through the wilderness, while supplying all their needs. [106]

Again, God loves Israel. He has a strong affection for them, and at every step of their journey thus far, He has intentionally led them in the way He knows is best for them. Even when they did not understand it, like when He took them the long way and then led them back to the sea, He knew what He was doing and what was best for His "sheep." The imagery of shepherding is hardly foreign to us; we discussed it in the first volume since that was the profession Moses pursued after fleeing Egypt and ending up in the land of Midian. It is also a constant metaphor used throughout Scripture to describe the relationship between God and His people. Even Jesus used it to describe Himself:

I am the good shepherd; the good shepherd lays down His life for the sheep. He who is a hired hand, and not a shepherd, who is not the owner of the sheep, sees the wolf coming, and leaves the sheep and flees, and the wolf snatches them and scatters them. He flees because he is a hired hand and is not concerned about the sheep. I am the good shepherd, and I know My own and My own know Me, even as the Father knows Me and I know the Father; and I lay down My life for the sheep. (John 10:11-15)

Jesus, the perfect example of a shepherd, cares deeply about the sheep within His flock and guides them on the right path. Guiding sheep, in this metaphor, is both physical and spiritual. Israel certainly needed to be led physically—they had no idea where they were going. They were homeless, defenseless, and incapable of establishing a permanent residence for themselves. But they were also lost spiritually. They, like Moses, needed to internalize and personally own the faith of their fathers. They had been obedient thus far for the most part, but obedience is not always confirmation of genuine faith (as we will see soon enough).

In the same way, Christ leads us in more than one way. The primary way is spiritual as He guides us to the gospel and then further into it as we grow as His disciples. He also leads us physically and emotionally as He teaches us to lean on His Word and trust it over and above our whims. We can each be thankful for God's guidance into the promised land of our faith, the gospel, and ultimately, eternity with Him in heaven.

The manner in which God **guided** the Israelites is certainly important, but equally crucial is the destination, prompting us to identify the **holy habitation** mentioned in these verses. Traditionally, it is understood as the promised land, but other suggestions include Mount Sinai and the Temple on Mount Zion. [107] I propose a broader interpretation. It seems plausible that God's **holy habitation** is anywhere He specifically focuses His presence (as opposed to His constant omnipresence). For Israel, God was leading them to their own land where He would reside in the temple, but His special (or manifest) presence was evident every step of the way. He resided within the pillar of cloud and fire, then Mount Sinai, and then in the tabernacle before reaching the promised land. Thus, it seems as though this reference is two-fold: first, **God's holy habitation** is wherever God reveals Himself with a greater manifestation of His presence, and second, it has an inherent future reference to the promised land, and ultimately, heaven with Him.

This imagery extends into the New Testament and the church through Christ. God guides us into the gospel through Jesus and indwells us with His Holy Spirit, leading us into righteousness and sanctification. His presence is with us everywhere, but it is also specially concentrated when two or more of His people gather together (Matthew 18:20), and we will eventually be in His unhindered presence in heaven. Thus, God's holy habitation should not be viewed narrowly, as His presence hardly has a narrow focus. He is leading the Israelites (and us thousands of years later) to Him both immediately and in the future, temporarily and then eternally.

> **The peoples have heard, they tremble; Anguish has gripped the inhabitants of Philistia. Then the chiefs of Edom were dismayed; The leaders of Moab, trembling grips them, All the inhabitants of Canaan have melted away. (15:14-15)**

We encounter another shift in focus with this stanza of the song. Moses has praised God and recounted His mighty works against the Egyptians at the sea, and he has also praised Him for leading the Israelites toward Him with utmost lovingkindness. Now he shifts his focus outward to other people groups and nations. The Egyptians and the Israelites were not the only ones who had heard about the wonders of God's hand. While the speed of news distribution was slower compared to today's internet era, information did spread in the ancient world, albeit gradually.

The people have heard; they tremble at what God had done on behalf of the Israelites. Again, the plagues took months to unfold. They did not hit all at once, and it is likely that as they were happening, news began to spread to surrounding nations. We read about the "mixed multitude" who traveled out of Egypt with the Israelites back in 12:38; transients, residential aliens, and tradesmen were common back then and were likely the primary source of news traveling between people groups. And they were probably all too eager to spread the word about the miracles they had seen or heard about in Egypt. God was hardly subtle in the plagues, and while His primary purpose was to redeem His people from the Egyptians, a second and very real purpose was to reveal Himself to the world and identify Himself with the Israelites. Unsurprisingly, it worked. People all over **heard** and **they tremble**[d] at the news of what Israel's God has done for them.

First, we read about **the inhabitants of Philistia,** who had been **gripped** by **anguish**. **Philistia** is likely mentioned first because they were the closest and most formidable enemy to the Israelites. [108] The book of Judges documents numerous encounters between the Israelites and the Philistines. Israel repeatedly failed to conquer all the land of the Philistines, largely due to their own actions, and the Philistines remained a formidable adversary throughout the generations of the Judges. At this time, however, **the inhabitants of Philistia** were deeply fearful of the God of the Israelites.

The word for **anguish** (*hil*) is only used seven times in the Old Testament and incurs a strong sense of pain and agony. In fact, in five of its seven mentions it is used to describe the pain associated with childbirth. [109] As a woman who has given birth four times, three of those times without an epidural, let me tell you, it is excruciating. It is actually quite shocking that someone can endure that kind of pain and live to tell about it. I can also say without exaggeration that in the midst of those final moments, I doubted I would live through it! Childbirth is an **anguish** like I have never experienced before and have no plan to experience again.

Yes, there is immense physical pain, but it is also emotionally exhausting. Unless you are one of the rare, fortunate ones blessed with short labor, you struggle intensely for hours, doing anything and everything imaginable just to gain an ounce of comfort. My labor with our fourth daughter was awful. Normally, contractions ebb and flow, peak, and release. Not with her. I never got relief from contractions after about 5 centimeters of dilation. It was a constant peak, then another peak, followed by a smaller peak, then Mount Everest, and back again. The physical pain was unrelenting, but it didn't take long for me to lose it emotionally either. There's only so much stamina to draw from; even the most disciplined, prepared people have a breaking point.

Our "reward" for enduring such misery during contractions is increased pain so intense that it's hard to breathe. By the end of it, you are a disheveled mess of tears, sweat, hormones, and a burning desire to just get that kid out! This is the kind of anguish used to compare what the Philistines were experiencing when they heard about the God of the Israelites and His mighty wonders. Like a laboring mother, they were not in a good place. And God was afflicting them without even having to lift a finger against them.

Philistia was not the only people group anxious about their new rival. **The chiefs of Edom were dismayed** as well. The Edomites were the descendants of Esau, Jacob's twin brother. Despite being family, they were never super friendly with the Israelites, though that is not terribly surprising considering the friction experienced by Esau and Jacob originally. They eventually became stark enemies and would encounter each other in battle several times.

At this point, however, they had heard about how the God of the Israelites decimated Egypt and **were dismayed.** This term carries with it the idea of being afraid and "usually expresses an emotion of one who is confronted with something unexpected, threatening or disastrous."[110] God was certainly unexpected, at least in the sense that He had not acted on behalf of Israel for hundreds of years. He was also quite threatening and disastrous for anyone who stood in His way, which would include the Edomites.

The leaders of Moab had a similar reaction as **trembling grips them** because of God. At this point in history, neither Edom nor Moab was a fully established nation with strict borders or kings. [111] They, like Israel, were a unique people, but were emerging as nations and were "undergoing a continuing process of settlement rather than fully settled and politically established as nations at the time of the Exodus." [112] However, they were not naive; they were hearing reports of Israel's God and had an appropriate response of fear. The **leaders of Moab** (and the rest of their people, by responsible deduction) were gripped with **trembling**. Another word for **trembling** is quaking, and that was exactly what their demeanor was—quaking in fear at the reports they were hearing.

It should be noted that neither Edom nor Moab was directly a part of the promised land, "but access to the land required passage through those countries." [113] God was striking fear in the hearts of not only those who would eventually be conquered but even the people groups Israel would have to interact with to get there. Just as He parted the sea, God was parting the way for the Israelites to reach to the promised land. He was removing certain obstacles out of the way and clearing the path for His people to walk through on dry, easy-to-be-crossed land.

Lastly, we read **all the inhabitants of Canaan**, and how they **have melted away** in their fear. **Canaan** is a broad term representing a geographical region, largely where the Israelites were going to conquer as a part of their promised land. Edom, Moab, and now Canaan were the geographical order the Israelites would eventually encounter on their way to the promised land. [114] They would have to pass through Edom first, then Moab, before continuing to their destination of Canaan. The Canaanites descended from Canaan, Ham's son and Noah's grandson, and this name "was one of the old names for Palestine, the land of the Canaanites dispossessed by the Israelites." [115]

The current **inhabitants** of Israel's future land **melted away** at the news of what God had done for His people. The phrase **melted away** is fairly straightforward, meaning to melt, dissolve, dissipate, or faint. The Canaanites became weak to the point of "falling apart" out of fear of God. Most interesting about this phrase is that a Canaanite spoke it several decades later when Joshua was leading the conquest against the inhabitants of the promised land. When Moses died and Joshua assumed command, his first order of business was to send spies throughout the land, especially Jericho (Joshua 2:1). In Jericho, the two spies met a harlot, Rahab, who saved their lives from the king of Jericho. Rahab hid them on her roof, and when she came to inform them that it was safe, she said:

> I know that the Lord has given you the land, and that the terror of you has fallen on us, and that all the inhabitants of the land have **melted away** before you. For we have heard how the Lord dried up the water of the Red Sea before you when you came out of Egypt...when we heard it, our hearts melted and no courage remained in any man any longer because of you; for the Lord your God, He is God in heaven above and on earth beneath. (Joshua 2:9-10, emphasis added)

Fear of God struck the hearts of the Canaanites, setting the stage for further acts of victory of God on behalf of His people.

At this point, a couple of questions arise. If this song was composed right after the parting of the sea, how did other nations find out so quickly? Furthermore, how did Moses know what they were thinking at that point? Several explanations have been offered, but two are most probable. First, it is possible that while the bulk of this song was written immediately after the parting of the sea, some words were added and/or changed as the years passed, and knowledge of its aftermath became more readily available. Moses did not write the book of Exodus (or the rest of the Pentateuch) until likely the end of his life, so it is quite possible that when he did, he wrote down the most current version of the song that was still sung in Israel's corporate worship.

It is also possible that Moses sang those exact words right after the sea rescue, and that the words were prophetic. He was certainly a prophet who communicated God's message to His people, and God revealed future events to him before they unfolded. It would not be surprising at all for Moses to declare these words, knowing they were not true yet, but believing they would be fulfilled one day. Moses, then, would be praising God in advance for His continued work of blessing and provision for His people.

Regardless of the exact explanation, whether it was a later updated version or prophetic in nature, we can rest assured that there *is* an explanation, and that this is not some glaring discrepancy or error in Scripture. The people surrounding and inhabiting the promised land were indeed fearful of what they had heard about God:

> **Terror and dread fall upon them; By the greatness of Your arm they are motionless as stone; Until Your people pass over, O Lord, Until the people pass over whom You have purchased. (15:16)**

Moses repeats that **terror and dread fall upon them**; no one stands erect when God displays His immense power. In that regard, we once again read about **the greatness** of God's **arm**, which is an extension of the hand imagery that has saturated the narrative thus far. When God extends His arm of judgment against someone, they fall either in fear or death. Moses declares that the result of either renders God's enemies **motionless as stone**. Just as the Egyptians "went down into the depths like a stone" (15:5) when the sea crashed over them, Moses prays that the future enemies of Israel will become **motionless as a stone** out of terror and, ultimately, death as Israel conquers them.

The request is for the enemies to remain frozen in fear **until Your people pass over, O Lord, until the people pass over whom You have purchased.** The term for **pass over** here can also be translated as "cross over," which clearly resembles how the Israelites crossed over the sea; "both are works of God." [116] Moses is anticipating a successful **pass over** into the promised land, yet another example of how God provides for the people He has **purchased.**

Purchased (*qana*) is a unique term that can also be translated as "created." While some people struggle in choosing which one is the best fit in this specific context, one commentator wisely notes:

> "It is a false dilemma to think that we must choose between these meanings. They each convey God's creation in history of a people by redeeming them from slavery to give them their identity...the feat involves redemption for the purpose of recreating/owning as a special possession...the theme of God's creation of a new people and Yahweh's redemption of this people have been twin themes running through Exodus."[117]

God both creates and redeems a people for Himself, and neither of these feats could have been accomplished by Israel on their own. The same is true for us. We were both created and redeemed by God in and through Jesus Christ. Just as it would be impossible for us to create ourselves, it is impossible for us to redeem ourselves from sin and be declared righteous before God. Without God's direct and divine intervention for us, we would not exist, nor would we have hope.

Furthermore, God was far from finished creating with the completion of the creation account in Genesis.[118] Every baby is a new creation, just as every seed that matures into a plant or tree. God created a people for Himself in Israel long after the creation of the universe, and He formed the church after Jesus' ascension through His Holy Spirit. He continues to create new life with every person who surrenders their heart and life to Christ, which is expressed in redemption, the other aspect of *qana*. "Therefore, if anyone is in Christ, they are a new creature; the old things have passed away; behold, new things have come" (2 Corinthians 5:17).

Through Israel, God shows us that He is both the Author and Savior of His people; He makes us new. God will guide us securely through the gospel into a new life in Him, just as He guided His people to cross over to their new land and through the sea.

You will bring them and plant them in the mountain of Your inheritance, The place, O Lord, which You have made for Your dwelling, The sanctuary, O Lord, which Your hands have established. The Lord shall reign forever and ever. (15:17-18)

In the last verse, we made a shift from Israel's enemies back to God and His relationship with Israel, and that continues here. God **will bring them and plant them in the mountain of** His **inheritance.** While poetry is not my strength, I do love and appreciate dramatic imagery like we see here with Israel being planted. God picked them up and out of Egypt with the intent to plant them elsewhere—a new place where they would grow and flourish beyond what they ever could have dreamed possible. Indeed, God "will continue to move his people until their goal is reached and he replants them in the land of Canaan— as he planted his first human pair in the garden of Eden." [119] Adam and Eve were planted in the garden for a specific purpose, just like Israel would be planted in their new land for a purpose, to radiate God's light and truth to the world.

The **mountain of Your inheritance** refers to "Canaan, specifically, the hill country and Jerusalem, Mount Zion, for there Yahweh will plant his people...and establish his temple." [120] Mountains are integral parts of many biblical narratives, especially portraying encounters with God. The imagery is fitting, of course, because being high on a mountain resonates with a part of our soul that longs to reach up to God, who is often associated with height:

> The Lord is high above all nations; His glory is above the heavens. Who is like the Lord our God, Who is enthroned on high, Who humbles Himself to behold The things that are in heaven and in the earth? (Psalm 113:4-6)

Before getting to their final destination, Israel will make a stop on Mount Sinai (as we will soon see in our narrative), where God will plant the seeds of His law with them. In the wilderness, Israel will get a glimpse of what awaits the future of their nation—how they will be established and dwell on "high" with God as their King.

As we noted in our discussion of 15:14-15, God is omnipresent; He is everywhere at all times. The idea of a dwelling place for Him, therefore, is curious. How does a God who is omnipresent dwell anywhere specifically? Such a dwelling refers to a special concentration of His presence. **The place, O Lord, which You have made for Your dwelling, the sanctuary, O Lord, which Your hands have established** is ripe with meaning and foreshadow. Most obviously, the **sanctuary** will come to mean His tabernacle, and then His temple in Israel. During the days of the tabernacle, King David would become disturbed over the fact that he dwelt "in a house of cedar, but the ark of God dwells within tent curtains" (2 Samuel 7:2). He wanted to build God a house fitting for His presence, but God did not want David to, and His response was compelling:

> I have been with you wherever you have gone and have cut off all your enemies from before you; and I will make you a great name, like the names of the great men who are on the earth. I will also appoint a place for My people Israel and *will plant them*, that they may live in their own place and not be disturbed again, nor will the wicked afflict them any more as formerly. (2 Samuel 2:9-10, emphasis added)

While David certainly had good intentions, God had better plans. He had been leading His people every step of the way and once again stated that He would **plant them** where He desired. God allowed His presence to be tangibly represented among His people—the pillar would be replaced with the ark of the covenant. But the key point here is that God was the One in control, not His people. "Israel will be planted in *His* land; He does not come along with them into *their* land."[121] His sanctuary is and will always be one that His hands have established. Just as He established Israel as His own people, He would also be responsible for establishing His lasting presence among His people.

Once again, we see a powerful allusion to the coming of the Holy Spirit after Christ's ascension. We cannot control or coerce the Spirit of God into our lives. His presence, like God's presence among Israel, cannot be manipulated or contained. It is a gift, and one that we far too often misunderstand, ignore, or take for granted:

> Do you not know that you are a temple of God and that the Spirit of God dwells in you? (1 Corinthians 3:16).

> Or what agreement has the temple of God with idols? For we are the temple of the living God; just as God said, "I will dwell in them and walk among them; and I will be their God, and they shall be My people." (2 Corinthians 6:16)

When we accept Christ as our Savior, He seals us with His Spirit (Ephesians 1:13). He never leaves us. But His presence does not guarantee His blessing. His habitation does not automatically procure our transformation. Just like Israel could not control God's presence in their lives, so we cannot control His presence in ours. He dwells within us, but is not a magic genie accommodating our every request. Rather, His presence is to be admired, cherished, and elevated in our minds, hearts, and lives. As John the Baptist said, "He must increase...I must decrease" (John 3:30).

God establishes His presence among His people when and how He wants to do so. Just as His right hand displayed His unmatched power over the world's fiercest opponents, so His hand will establish His sanctuary the way He desires. He is in control, and He **shall reign forever and ever.**

One of my favorite aspects of the name "I AM" (what God called Himself when talking to Moses) is its eternality. God always has been and always will be; He is the Alpha and Omega, the beginning and the end. He is infinite and never had a beginning, nor will He ever have an end. It is impossible for us to exhaust that truth because we are finite people limited to time and space. But it is beneficial to ponder from time to time, because it reminds us of God's holiness and how He alone is worthy of our worship.

Because our culture often muddles the meaning of words, a phrase like God **shall reign forever and ever** sounds more like the ending of a fairy tale instead of the articulation of a powerful truth. We cannot fathom forever, so we chalk it up to the same stuff "Neverland" is made of. When we do this, we are robbed of so much truth the Spirit can use to transform our lives.

Let's begin by diving into it within its immediate context. Reminding Israel of the eternality of God's reign is how Moses concludes his song of praise. Parting words are powerful; some would argue that they are the most important part of any speech, song, or book. The final thought is most likely what the listeners will take with them, so it needs to be strong. Moses could have ended the song with many other aspects of praise, but concentrating on God's never-ending reign reveals his commitment to remind the Israelites that God is their future, He is in control, and no one can thwart His rule.

Aligning themselves with God was not just a wise battle strategy; it was life-giving. The Author of life is also its sustainer, and those who place their faith in God will have eternal life with Him **forever and ever**. The ramifications of this truth are impossible to contain or explain fully here. But for a brief moment, let's bask in the truth of eternal life:

> For He must reign until He has put all His enemies under His feet. The last enemy that will be abolished is death…Now I say this brethren, that flesh and blood cannot inherit the kingdom of God; nor does the perishable inherit the imperishable…For this perishable must put on the imperishable, and this mortal will have put on immortality, then will come about the saying that is written, "Death is swallowed up in victory. O death, where is your victory? O death, where is your sting?" The sting of death is sin, and the power of sin is the law, but thanks be to God, who gives us the victory through our Lord Jesus Christ. (1 Corinthians 15:25-26, 50, 53-57).

I am currently in an ongoing conversation with a young woman struggling deeply with homosexuality. She is sweet, beautiful, kind, and considerate, and until we began conversing, she thought she was a Christian. Just yesterday, I was able to share the gospel with her and help her to understand what it means to be a Christian and yes, what it will cost her to profess faith in Christ. I refuse to give her false hope that God will magically zap those desires from her immediately upon conversion (though I earnestly pray He does). But I am committed to sharing the truth that life in Christ is so much better than any pleasure we gain in death.

The crux of Christianity is Jesus and His resurrection. It is that we have been raised from death to life in Christ, and our eternal life with Him is secure through Christ's sacrifice and the Holy Spirit's sealing.

Eternity is real and exists in one of two places: heaven or hell. We will either reside with God forever and ever or burn in agony with Satan for the same. But make no mistake: it is a choice. The work of salvation is God's alone, but accepting it and embracing the gospel in our life from that point forward is a response we are required to give. God alone saved the Israelites from the Egyptians. He pummeled Egypt with the plagues and then crushed their army at the sea. Israel made no contribution to their salvation yet had a choice in how they responded to it. At this moment, they were making the right choice—praising Him for His salvation and the fact that His reign will last **forever and ever**.

With that, the song concludes and we have a brief interlude of commentary before Miriam takes the stage:

> **For the horses of Pharaoh with his chariots and his horsemen went into the sea, and the Lord brought back the waters of the sea on them, but the sons of Israel walked on dry land through the midst of the sea. (15:19)**

These verses serve as "a brief prose summary of the occasion for the celebration closes the composition and reconnects it with verse 1."[122] It seems a rather straightforward reminder of why Moses sang the song, to celebrate God's victory over **the horses of Pharaoh with his chariots and his horsemen**. Some scholars believe that this means *only* the chariots and horses were the ones to pursue Israel into the sea, while the rest of the army must have stayed behind at the edge of the sea.[123] There is simply no evidence that this is true. Numerous mentions of Pharaoh's entire army are included in the preceding narrative, and 14:28 makes it clear that "the waters returned and covered the chariots and the horsemen, *even Pharaoh's entire army that had gone into the sea* after them; not even one of them remained (emphasis added)." It is possible that some of the army remained behind in Egypt, perhaps injured or recovering soldiers, some lesser generals, or those who needed to remain to keep the cities secure. But based on previous details in the narrative, there is no reason to believe that only the horsemen and chariots were the ones to be killed in the sea.

Why, then, does this verse only mention the horsemen and chariots? It is likely because these were the strongest and most praised members of Pharaoh's army. The destruction of regular foot soldiers is not as great of an accomplishment. Foot soldiers, while undoubtedly trained and equipped well with armory, were not nearly as formidable in their status. Every nation had foot soldiers, but not every nation had horsemen and chariots, especially six hundred of them. Further, God had told Moses that He would "be honored through Pharaoh and all his army, through his chariots and his horsemen" (14:17). Overthrowing the most prestigious warriors was the note God wanted to end on with Egypt. The charioteers and horsemen were used for victory, and everyone knew it. But God would have the final word, overthrowing them **into the sea** while **the sons of Israel walked on dry land through the midst of the sea.**

> **Miriam the prophetess, Aaron's sister, took the timbrel in her hand, and all the women went out after her with timbrels and with dancing. Miriam answered them, "Sing to the Lord, for He is highly exalted; The horse and his rider He has hurled into the sea." (15:20-21)**

With that reminder of God's victory, we now arrive at the fairly controversial introduction of Miriam and her song. Some scholars and laypeople alike have become rather prickly about it for a number of reasons, but mainly because it seems to be "another instance of letting a less talented man upstage a more talented woman."[124] Her song is only one verse while her brother's is over fifteen. Further, they believe her verse was first, and male editors later down the road moved it to behind Moses'. Arguments continue, but they will not be articulated here.

This is hardly the time to present a full biblical synopsis on womanhood and the proper worldview we should adopt from it. However, because it has become such an issue and the fact that I am a woman, it seems appropriate to address it briefly while commenting on the verses themselves.

We were introduced to Miriam back in the second chapter of Exodus, though only as Moses' sister. Now we learn her name. She is also identified as a **prophetess**, which was rare but not unheard of. Other named prophetesses were Deborah (Judges 4:4), Huldah (2 Chronicles 34:22), and Noadiah (Nehemiah 6:14). Miriam may have been one of the first in Israel, but it is doubtful her status was questioned or undermined at the time since we read no hint of it in the text.

However, many people have arisen over the years who have called Miriam's role as a **prophetess** into question because they do not believe that women should hold any position of leadership. To clarify, we are not explicitly told that she held an official position of leadership, but we are told in these verses that she led the women; it is certainly not a stretch to believe that she fulfilled some kind of leadership role in Israel. Herein lies one of the mucky aspects this text brings out—the raging controversy of what women are permitted to do within the leadership of God's people.

For the record, I am a conservative, complementarian woman who believes God's overall design for humanity embodies male headship. However, as Scripture clearly indicates several times throughout its pages, this does not mean that women are never permitted to hold any positions of leadership. To assert that claim is ludicrous, foolish, and an irresponsible interpretation of Scripture. One of the basic tenets of hermeneutics is that we are subject to the authority of Scripture; Scripture is not subject to our authority. We therefore have to submit ourselves to its truth, regardless of whether or not it fits within our personal biases and opinions. Women, like Miriam, held several prominent roles throughout biblical history, and it is a fact that needs to be accepted.

Miriam's specific role was as a prophetess. Prophets and prophetesses were men and women God communicated through. Since the Bible was not written yet, especially this early on, there was no written word of God. Communication from God came through various means—dreaming, visions, casting lots, and prophets. Being a prophet was a serious calling with grave consequences if the prophet did not speak exactly what God had communicated. Later, God would declare:

> But the prophet who speaks a word presumptuously in My name which I have not commanded him to speak, or which he speaks in the name of other gods, that prophet shall die. (Deuteronomy 18:20)

Death was the result of a false prophecy; that is how seriously God takes His Word. Thus, Miriam, like both of her brothers, Aaron and Moses, held an esteemed office and calling. God used each of them to speak His words to Israel, and they presumably complied. We have no specific record of any of Miriam's prophecies, but we know from this title and a later event that God held her position to a high standard.

Later, when the Israelites were in the wilderness, Moses married a Cushite woman, and apparently, neither Miriam nor Aaron were fond of the union. Yet instead of praying about it or perhaps seeking to understand Moses' thoughts and intentions with a private, humble conversation, Miriam and Aaron spoke against Moses with jealousy. The Lord heard it and punished Miriam by inflicting severe leprosy upon her for a week (Numbers 12:1-15). Thus, while Miriam certainly held a prominent position in Israel, especially among women, she did not always live up to her calling.

She was a leader, but she was also always in subjection to another human leader, namely, Moses. By this point, it was an established and accepted fact that God had chosen Moses to lead His people. We do not know if Miriam arose to leadership based on familial proximity to Moses, or if she had already been known as a strong woman of faith beforehand. But we do know that while Miriam may have had an influential role, she was not in the most influential role (neither did Aaron or any of the elders either, by the way). I do not write that to be controversial or claim women are somehow lesser than their male counterparts. Again, I am a woman and love being one! Rather, male headship is a beautiful gift designed by God. Women should not be threatened by it. God uses women just as powerfully as He does men in the roles (both influential and submissive) that He has called us to.

In addition to being a **prophetess**, Miriam is also referred to as *Aaron's sister*. The most likely reason she is referred to as Aaron's sister instead of Moses' sister is that it was standard practice for "a younger daughter to be known as the sister of the first-born male in the family," which was Aaron.[125] Moses was certainly the most well-known member of the family, but Aaron was still the oldest and received the rights and privileges associated with that title.

Once identified, we are told that Miriam **took the timbrel in her hand, and all the women went out after her with timbrels and with dancing.** The **timbrel** "is most likely the portable frame drum, a percussion instrument constructed of two parallel membranes stretched over a loop or frame. It was apparently used exclusively by a special class of female musicians."[126] It stands to reason that Miriam was at least somewhat familiar with playing the timbrel, as she did not hesitate in taking it **in her hand.** The **timbrel** has been mentioned once before in Scripture, in Genesis 31:27, when Laban caught up with Jacob, who had fled because Laban had refused to let him and his family go: "Why did you flee secretly and deceive me, and did not tell me so that I might have sent you away with joy and with songs, with timbrel and with lyre..." The timbrel, then, is certainly associated with celebrations, quite fitting for this song of worship at the sea.

Equipped with her instrument, Miriam led **all the women** who **went out after her with timbrels and with dancing.** As alluded to previously, this action

155

suggests that she was seen in some kind of leadership role, at least (or especially) among women, since they followed her. **Dancing** is not a very common reference in Scripture, but it was a common practice in ancient times. Only twice do we read about it in Exodus, here and later in 32:19, when the Israelites sin grievously against God—dancing in the worship of an idol. It also seems to have been performed mostly by women, which may be one of the reasons David's wife, Michal, "despised him in her heart" after seeing David dance in worship with the ark of the covenant (2 Samuel 6:16). Regardless, dancing was associated with praise and celebration, which is certainly what Israel is doing after the sea.

Miriam answered them, "Sing to the Lord, for He is highly exalted; the horse and his rider He has hurled into the sea." Now, we arrive at the second controversial part of this section, namely the timeline of when it unfolded. The two words that are challenging to determine are **answered,** and then Miriam's command to **sing**. At first glance, it would seem as though Miriam's song is a response to Moses' because otherwise, who is the "**them**" she is answering? But then, as many seem to believe, it is possible that her song was first because of her imperative statement to **"Sing to the Lord,"** when Moses' song begins with **"I will sing to the Lord."**

Those who believe that Miriam was the originator of the song get prickly about its placement after Moses' in the text because they believe it should have come before. In response, I would encourage fellow women (and indirectly, men) to approach such matters with humility and refrain from getting offended. Fixating on a seemingly small, and frankly, insignificant matter, and attributing it to gender oppression may indicate deeper underlying issues that require introspection and spiritual counsel. If such matters trigger discomfort, a deeper exploration of the Word, prayer, and seeking godly counsel can be beneficial.

Instances of offense seem to be on the rise in today's world, with gender and race emerging as prominent topics. Over the past century, women have been actively involved in movements seeking gender equality on various fronts. While this is not the space for an exhaustive analysis of these movements and worldviews, it is worth addressing one aspect concerning Scripture.

Simply put, getting offended by Scripture is a good thing. If we believe that Scripture is the inerrant, infallible, inspired, and living Word of God, and embrace its authority in our lives as believers in Christ, we are guaranteed to get offended by it. Why? Because truth is offensive to our sin-infested hearts and minds. The Holy Spirit's role includes addressing and convicting us of our sins. Proper hermeneutics is crucial to ensure accurate interpretation, but if we find ourselves disliking what we read, it is not the Scripture that needs altering; it is our hearts.

The author of Hebrews states that "the word of God is living and active and sharper than any two-edged sword, and piercing as far as the division of soul and spirit, of both joints and marrow, and able to judge the thoughts and intentions of the heart" (Hebrews 4:12). Scripture was not and is not meant to be a squishy pillow for us to hug when we need to feel better about ourselves. It exists to make us better—to make us more like Jesus—and that process is not always pleasant. Of course, when we achieve victory over specific sins through the power of the Holy Spirit, there is no greater feeling in the world! But the process in getting there is tough and not for the faint of heart.

We come to the cross filthy, covered in the mud of sin with layers so deep they seem impenetrable and are for anyone but Christ. At the cross, Jesus declares us clean and establishes our righteousness, and from that point on, we spend our lives partnering with His Spirit to wash away the caked-on crust of sin we have grown so accustomed to, so our outer man can start resembling the inner man He has created through our redemption. Washing off and peeling back those layers is not comfortable; sometimes, it feels like a pressure washer on raw skin. But that is part of the process, that is how God uses Scripture to cleanse our hearts and minds.

When we get irritable about something we read, we must do two things: 1) make sure we are interpreting it correctly, and then 2) submit to the truth and ask God to conform us to it. Regarding our specific passage, ultimately it does not matter if Miriam was the original author of the song. What does matter and is worth noting, however, is that Miriam is mentioned—and named. If you read the first volume of this study, you will remember that women were not exactly esteemed in ancient times. But God valued women (obviously, He created them!) and held them in high regard, especially over and beyond other cultures. Remember, all throughout Exodus, we read about God setting Himself, people, and situations apart. The first chapter strongly juxtaposed Pharaoh/king/man against the Hebrew midwives/lowly/women. Pharaoh is portrayed in a negative light in every regard; the lowly midwives are esteemed highly, and in quite the shock, are actually named (Shiphrah and Puah).

Using Miriam's name in our passage is a way of not only formally recognizing her but esteeming her like God did with the midwives to begin the book. In other words, this first section of Exodus "begins and ends by highlighting the significant role of women. They are both saviors and singers, midwives and minstrels."[127] Far from demeaning women by putting Miriam's song at the end, God is highlighting her contribution and using her to promote an even stronger contrast between the army of Pharaoh and a simple Israelite woman. God opposes the proud, extends grace to the humble, and vividly illustrates that His thoughts and ways transcend human understanding (James 4:6; Isaiah 55:8). Thus, there is no need for offense. God strategically placed Miriam's role in the celebration.

Two final thoughts should be noted regarding the verse she sang. First, instead of a back-and-forth, echo-style song between the men and the women that many assume it was, it is possible that it was more of a duet. One commentator explains, "when the community joins together for the common songs and celebration, there is a strong sense of solidarity…Moses leads the brothers and Miriam leads the sisters…mutual complementarity functions as a key model for the unity and efficiency of the entire community."[128] While it is impossible to know exactly how it was sung, both men and women sang it together, which was a beautiful picture of the unity God desires for His people.

The last noteworthy observation is that although only one small lyric is recorded, it is likely that Miriam and the women sang the entire song with the men. One midrash (an ancient Jewish commentary on the Torah) explains it as such, and it does make a lot of sense. While theologically insignificant whether the women sang the whole or part, the coherence of the story suggests that the women sang the entire song in unison with the men.

Summary

Much debate surrounds various aspects of the song of Moses and Miriam, but we should never get so bogged down in the algae that we miss the purpose and theological significance of the ocean. First and foremost, it was a song of praise and thanksgiving for what God had done for them at the sea, which, of course, was the final culmination of what He had done for them in the previous months to free them. Taking specific, dedicated, and even spontaneous time to praise God is not only commendable but necessary in the lives of believers. Worship recenters our perspectives and realigns our hearts with God's. It puts Him back in His rightful place on the throne of our hearts as we beg Him to increase so we may decrease (John 3:30). It also allows us to enter His spiritual reality instead of remaining stunted by the physical realm.

Worship allows us to see reality for what it is—to look beyond the temporal and gaze upon the eternal. That is what this song did for the Israelites. It allowed them to celebrate an event that may have happened in the physical realm, but afforded them the opportunity to see into the spiritual realm, understanding that God had redeemed them. They sang about how **the horse and its rider He had hurled into the sea**. This was a physical reality repeated numerous times throughout the song (vs. 4-5, 10, 12, 21). God literally destroyed Israel's enemies using physical, natural means (water), but the victory was far beyond what they could touch, see, and hear. Physical circumstances were merely the launching point from which Israel could jump more fully into the truth and understanding of God. He is **my strength and song and has become my salvation**. Only He is the Redeemer and Victor in our lives; only He can accomplish His eternal purpose through temporal circumstances:

> Yours, O Lord, is the greatness and the power and the glory and the victory and the majesty, indeed everything that is in the heavens and the earth; Yours is the dominion, O Lord, and You exalt Yourself as head over all. (1 Chronicles 29:11)

As Moses sang, **"Who is like You, majestic in holiness, awesome in praises, working wonders?"** Through this song, we are reminded of these powerful truths in our lives. Sometimes, God accomplishes miraculous victories in the lives of His children—total remission from cancer, swerving a vehicle just in time to avoid a fatal collision, an unexpected promotion that eases so many financial burdens, the return of a prodigal child, the freedom from an addiction, or the healing of a deeply battle-scarred marriage. These victories are sweet and should be celebrated with intentional worship, much like the Israelites did with this song, both in the present, triumphant moment and then for generations to come.

Sometimes, however, we do not experience miraculous victories on this side of heaven. Like the several generations of Israelites who were born and then died in slavery in Egypt, we may have to cling to God's promise of what will come— the reality of heaven that awaits us even when our earthly circumstances are so bleak. The enemy wants nothing more than to keep us blinded by our pain that we lose sight of the relief, joy, and peace we have in Him. We may never experience the day of freedom on this earth, but we can cling to the hope He offers and celebrate right alongside those who do.

Now faith is the reassurance of things hoped for, the conviction of things not seen. For by it the men of old gained approval. By faith we understand that the worlds were prepared by the word of God, so that what is seen was not made out of things which are visible…And without faith it is impossible to please Him, for he who comes to God must believe that He is and that He is a rewarder of those who seek Him…All these [Abel, Enoch, Noah, Abraham, and Sarah] died in faith, without receiving the promises, but having seen them and having welcomed them from a distance, and having confessed that they were strangers and exiles on the earth…but as it is, they desire a better country, that is, a heavenly one. Therefore God is not ashamed to be called their God; for He has prepared a city for them. (Hebrews 11:1-3, 6, 13, 16)

Like the Israelites, we must place our faith in God's Word, not in temporal circumstances. Whether or not we experience tremendous victories as they did, we can be assured that our victory in Christ has come in salvation and will come in totality when we see Him face to face one day. We must submit to His providence in our lives, confident that for His people, He **will bring them and plant them in the mountain of** [His] **inheritance.** His presence is what we long for, and He is worth clinging to. **He is highly exalted**, and worth celebrating and praising regardless of circumstances.

GROUP STUDY

Introduction

Praise Him for His worthiness, not just His benevolence.

Thanksgiving is thanking God for what He gives us; praise is thanking God for who He is. Both thanking and praising God are a healthy and wonderful aspect of our faith that should regularly be exercised in our lives. We've all had times of extra blessing in our lives that give us wonderful reasons to break out in spontaneous praise to Him.

- Share a time in your life when praising God was easy and overflowed from your heart.

The Word

Israel was finally free. Not only had they left Egypt, but God had drawn their enemies out and crushed them with implausibly high walls of water after safely delivering His people to the other side of the sea. Israel recognized their deliverance and responded with gratitude, praising God from whom all blessings flow.

> **I will sing to the Lord, for He is highly exalted; the horse and its rider He has hurled into the sea. The Lord is my strength and song, and He has become my salvation; this is my God, and I will praise Him; my father's God, and I will extol Him. (Exodus 15:1-2)**

- What is the first reason why Moses and the Israelites were praising God in this song?
  - Why is that significant (as opposed to praising Him first for what He'd done for them?)

- How many times is the word "my" used in these short verses?

  - What does that reveal about the nature of their praise?

Israel's song of worship was both corporate and intensely personal. It focused on God's character while also highlighting what He had done for them.

One beautiful aspect of songs and poetry is the imagery they invoke, and this one is no exception:

> **The Lord is a warrior; the Lord is His name. (Exodus 15:3)**

> **Your right hand, O Lord, is majestic in power, Your right hand, O Lord, shatters the enemy. (Exodus 15:6)**

> **At the blast of Your nostrils the waters were piled up. (Exodus 15:8a)**

> **You blew with Your wing, the sea covered them; they sank like lead in the mighty waters. (Exodus 15:10)**

> **You will bring them [His people] and plant them in the mountain of Your inheritance. (Exodus 15:17)**

- What is your favorite use of imagery in these verses?

  o What does it reveal about God?

- How do these imagery examples increase our understanding of God?

Apply

> I will bless the Lord at all times;
> His praise shall continually be in my mouth.
> David, Psalm 34:1

> Let the word of Christ richly dwell within you,
> with all wisdom teaching and admonishing one another
> with psalms and hymns and spiritual songs,
> singing with thankfulness in your hearts to God.
> The Apostle Paul, Colossians 3:16

Praising God, especially through song, is a beautiful and impactful way to worship. Moses and the Israelites sang to God, first praising Him for who He is and secondly because of what He'd done for them.

- What attributes of God have been particularly praiseworthy in your life and faith lately?

- What are some things He has done for you—both in the gospel and then personally in your life?

While praising God is important, it's not always easy. We don't always experience "victory at the sea" moments. Sometimes, we find ourselves in the midst of the sea for years—knowing the enemy is close behind, feeling scared and unsure of what will happen. But even in those challenging times, we can still praise Him. His character remains constant regardless of circumstances, and He is still worthy of our worship.

- What attributes of God can you cling to when you're still "in the midst of the sea" in your life?
  - What habits can you incorporate into your daily life that will allow you to focus on His character and truth more than on your circumstances?
- How can you encourage someone else who may currently be "in the midst of the sea"?

Doth not all nature around me praise God? If I were silent, I would be an exception to the universe. Doth not the thunder praise Him as it rolls like drums in the march of the God of armies? Do not the mountains praise Him when the woods upon their summits wave in adoration? Doth not the lightning write His name in letters of fire? Hath not the whole earth a voice? And shall I, can I, silent be? – Charles Spurgeon

WEEK FOUR

The Grumble Tumble

Exodus 15:22-16:8

PERSONAL BIBLE STUDY QUESTIONS

1. Where did Moses lead Israel after the Red Sea? (15:22)
2. What problem did they run into three days into the wilderness? (15:22)
3. Where did they end up? (15:23)
   a. Why was it named that? (15:23)
4. How did Israel respond to that problem? (15:24)
5. What did God want Moses to do? (15:25)
6. Read the proposition God made for Israel. (15:26)
   a. What was He inviting them to do?
   b. If they did those things, what would He do for them?
7. Where did Israel camp next? (15:27)
   a. What was there?
   b. How did that place differ from the one they just left?
8. Where did they go after that? (16:1)
   a. When did they do so? (16:1)
9. What did they do when they arrived? (16:2)
   a. Why did they do that? (16:3)
10. How does God respond? (16:4-5)
11. Even though the Israelites directed their grumbling to Moses and Aaron, who were they really grumbling against? (16:8)
    a. In what ways is this applicable to your life?

COMMENTARY

Exodus 15:22–16:8

"Pop-pop! Pop-pop!" echoed our adorable yet slightly mischievous two-year-old as we pulled into the allergist's parking lot for my weekly allergy shots. She eagerly anticipated her "pop-pop," a lollipop that the sweet nurses started giving them even though I was the one receiving the shots. The irony isn't lost on me.

Since we don't keep candy in the house, getting a lollipop is a real treat for them. The only issue is that Jessli just turned two, so it's not exactly the safest thing for her to eat unsupervised. She tends to bite off the entire top part, leaving only the hard candy ball in her mouth. Not an ideal situation. To manage this, I allow her to lick the lollipop while I get my shots and during our walk back to the car. However, as soon as I buckle her in, I take the lollipop away.

Her response makes it seem like I'm torturing her. Her excited bursts of "pop-pop, pop-pop!" as we arrived have morphed into mournful sobs of "pooooopp-pop, pooooopp-pop!" as we leave. The lollipop consumes her thoughts and actions, and being two, she cannot comprehend that I'm potentially saving her life by taking it from her.

Typical toddler.

When things go their way, they are sunshine and rainbows—full of giggles, silly banter, and joy. But the second their joy is threatened in any way—the millisecond they feel slighted—it's game over. The loving parent is instantly transformed into their mortal enemy, and they completely lose touch with reality.

Regrettably, Israel knew exactly what it was like to be a spiritual toddler. Their peak of praise in the last chapter did not last long, and they soon found themselves in a tough situation where God took away their "pop-pop" (in this case, easy access to food and water). While admittedly a more dire circumstance than Jessli's lollipop, their reaction reveals the same lack of trust and gratitude. The God who had just received their praise would now receive their scorn.

Exodus 15:22–27

> **Then Moses led Israel from the Red Sea, and they went out into the wilderness of Shur; and they went three days in the wilderness and found no water. When they came to Marah, they could not drink the waters of Marah, for they were bitter; therefore it was named Marah. So the people grumbled at Moses, saying, "What shall we drink?" (15:22-24)**

The previous chapter concluded with Israel's triumphant song of praise at the sea. Israel had just watched God annihilate the Egyptian army, and the bodies of soldiers and their horses had not yet swelled with death when Israel praised Him. It was a spiritual high that they had not experienced as a nation before, and God rightfully got the glory for it.

If only it would have lasted.

With Egypt finally put in their past, **Moses led Israel from the Red Sea, and they went out into the wilderness of Shur.** While unremarkable in English, the original Hebrew of the beginning of this verse is curious and deliberately draws "attention to Moses by describing how he leads out the people."[129] It is not merely a general statement about Israel continuing their journey led by Moses as he follows God. Some scholars actually believe "that Moses had to compel the people to move on because they were preoccupied with collecting the spoils of the drowned Egyptians."[130] It is impossible to know that for sure, but it is not out of the question. The Egyptians had voluntarily given Israel much of their wealth before they left Egypt, but there was no explicit mention of Israel having any weapons or other necessities for war. We will soon read that they went to battle, which leads us to believe they were equipped at least somewhat militarily. This assertion is certainly possible. The Egyptians' bodies had washed up on the seashore, presumably along with much of their armory. The Israelites could have easily confiscated it after their song of praise.

Whether they were busy looting Egyptian corpses or merely frozen at the sight of the carnage, the Israelites needed some prodding to continue their journey. The Red Sea was meant to be the final chapter of their slavery, not their story.

So Moses leads them away from the sea and **into the wilderness of Shur.** They finally make to the goal they originally told Pharaoh about in 5:1, "Thus says the Lord, the God of Israel, 'Let My people go that they may celebrate a feast to Me in the wilderness.'" They have made it to the wilderness, which is one step closer to the Promised Land. This **wilderness of Shur** "is a vast, rugged, and sparsely populated wilderness region in the northern Sinai."[131] As one would expect, the wilderness was not an amusement park populated with people. It was barren and not superbly sustainable for life, so no one lived there.

In order to reach the lush territory of their new home, they needed to pass through the desolate region of the wilderness. God had His reasons why. One may be that the Israelites needed to learn how to be satisfied in God before getting to a place that would satisfy them physically and economically. Or maybe the lack of distractions in the wilderness would enable them to focus more fully on God as they learned how to follow Him in their newfound freedom. Regardless of the reasons, God intentionally led them into the wilderness. He had lessons to teach them, and the instruction began quickly.

After traveling **three days into the wilderness**, they found **no water.** Their first difficulty in the wilderness carries the theme of water, which we have seen in both the first plague and the victory at sea. Water sustains life, so its absence was a serious problem for Israel, especially because there were so many of them— both people and enormous amounts of livestock. A small group of travelers might be able to find sustain themselves with smaller water sources, but providing for hundreds of thousands of people was no simple task in the wilderness. They carried some water with them as they traveled, but could not go too long between refilling their supplies.

Pressing on, they arrived at **Marah but could not drink the waters of Marah, for they were bitter; therefore, it was named Marah.** This sentence reads a bit awkwardly because it is difficult to tell at what point this location received its name. The Israelites actually named it Marah when they arrived at this point and discovered that the water was not fit to drink. It presumably did not have a name until now; it was just a random, anonymous place in the wilderness. Thus, when Moses wrote about this episode decades later, it was natural for him to use its name so readers would recognize the location he was referring to before providing clarification about its name and origin.

As the text reveals, **Marah** (*mara*) means "bitter." This reminds us of how Egypt had made life bitter for the Israelites (1:14), and also the bitter herbs that were eaten at the Passover to represent it (12:8).[132] Another familiar and contextually fitting use of this Hebrew word is in the book of Ruth. When Naomi, Ruth's mother-in-law, returned to Bethlehem after losing her husband and two sons, she was greeted by the women of the city. But she told them not to call her Naomi, which means "pleasant," but rather Mara, "for the Almighty has dealt very bitterly" (*marar*) with her (Ruth 1:20).

Bitterness was both a literal and spiritual disposition for Naomi and the Israelites. The Israelites finally found water and were excited to drink their fill and stock up for the next leg of their journey. It was understandably disappointing when they tasted the water and realized that it was revolting. This kind of water "is often clear so that it looks potable but in fact contains large percentages of dissolved mineral salts that render it undrinkable."[133] It is apparently quite a common discovery in desert springs, but perhaps Israel did not know that since it was their first experience in the wilderness.[134] Regardless, their excitement over finding water was soon replaced with rank disappointment. The water resembled death more than life.

This physical discovery led to a spiritual decision for Israel: would they respond in faith or in fear? Would their spirits resemble the bitter water, or would they remember that God controls all water, as He displayed with the first plague and at the sea?

Unfortunately, they fail their first test of faith. Instead of remembering and dwelling upon the truth, they let their emotions and physical circumstances dictate their reaction. Instead of praising God for His power and asking Him to provide, **the people grumbled at Moses, saying, "What shall we drink?"** The question by itself may have seemed reasonable and could have been asked with a tone of respect. But the verb **"grumbled"** reveals the tone of whining, reminding us of their response when they saw the Egyptians coming after them at the sea. They were accusing God, not trusting Him. They were attacking Him, not appealing to Him as their Savior. This reaction may not have been one of fear like at the sea, but it revealed the same disbelief in God.

Such a reaction is also exceedingly childish. Israel, while large in number, was an infant in its existence as an independent nation and was just now learning how to depend on God as their King. Reactions like this one at Marah reveal their immaturity and adolescent perspective. Despite having experienced the hand of God accomplishing miracle after miracle on their behalf, Israel was still an immature child in faith—grumbling against Him (via Moses) at the first roadblock they encountered.

> **Then he cried out to the Lord, and the Lord showed him a tree; and he threw it into the waters, and the waters became sweet. (15:25a)**

Moses promptly took their request and **cried out to the Lord** on their behalf. The verb **"cried out"** (*sa'aq*) is familiar to our narrative; we have seen it five times thus far in Exodus.[135] The last two instances were in the previous chapter when Israel cried out (*sa'aq*) to God as the Egyptians approached (14:10) and when God asked Moses why he was crying out (*sa'aq*) to Him (14:15). To cry out to God meant to acknowledge their need and beg for God's intervention.

Moses knew he could not do anything to save Israel from their current, or any other, predicament of having no water. It had not been his power that changed the Nile to blood, took the lives of the Egyptian firstborn, or parted and subsequently crashed the sea. Moses was the conduit, the instrument through which the power of the divine worked. He knew God was the only One who could help, and his cry testifies to that fact.

God responded by showing **him a tree**, which Moses then **threw... into the waters, and the waters became sweet**. These brief words present a conundrum in scholarly circles because so much information seems to be missing or ambiguous. First, the word "tree" can be translated in numerous ways, including "piece of wood" (NIV, NLT) and "log" (ESV). It is doubtful that Moses uprooted an entire tree by himself unless it was an adolescent one. That said, we are simply not told what kind of object this was, other than it being made of wood. Some even suggest it could have been a reference to wooden charcoal, made from Acacia trees common in that part of Arabia, which were "useful for desalinating water." [136]

Theories about the wood abound, as well as the way it was used. Three main theories surrounding the latter are suggested. First, this whole action was primarily a metaphor representing the "tree of life" as the Word of God. According to this theory, the "tree of life" (or Word of God) cleansed the water as it does our souls. Just as we need water to live, so we need the truth of God's Word for our souls to live. This view is supported by the fact that the root word for **showed** (when **the Lord showed him a tree**) is the same root word from which the word Torah (the law, "instruction") comes from. [137] Advocates of this view also claim that "the origin and development of Israel's law begins here," [138] and "to be deprived of its spiritual sustenance for three days is life-threatening," as was the Israelites' lack of water. [139]

Another interpretive theory "is that God instructed Moses practically in how to deal with the situation" by telling Moses how to use the wood to purify the waters. [140] In other words, there was no miracle. This view sees a distinction between a miracle and an instructive teaching. According to these advocates, a miracle is when God does something completely contrary to nature, like with the plagues and sea parting. Instructive teaching, contrarily, means showing/instructing Moses how to solve a problem; in this case, using Acacia wood to make the water acceptable for drinking.[141]

A final theory is the most literal translation—God told Moses to throw a wooden object into the water, and his obedience rendered the water clean and suitable for drinking. According to this interpretation, "Moses' faith in being willing to do what God commanded him, without understanding why or how it would work, is what is implicitly commended here."[142] Proper hermeneutics demands that we interpret the text literally unless the context or literary genre demands otherwise. Thus, this interpretation is the most hermeneutically sound. While the others are interesting and may stimulate theological and apologetic exercises, the most probable and responsible interpretation is that God told Moses to throw the wood into the water, he obeyed, and the water became clean.

The focus here, and always, should remain on God and what we can learn from His faithful (or not-so-faithful) servants. In this case, Moses' obedience is juxtaposed with Israel's whining; his trust to Israel's doubt. God responds to Moses and supplies Israel's needs. They needed water to live, so God transformed the contaminated water into water that was sustainable for life.

It is also a beautiful representation of what God has done for them thus far. He turned the bitter circumstances of slavery into sweet freedom and fellowship with Him. This action at Marah also reverses the first plague. While God turned the "sweet" waters of the Nile into a bitter one of blood for the Egyptians, now He reverses it to provide for Israel, whom He loves. God has been with and for Israel every step of the way; the time has come for them to recognize it and respond to Him in trust and obedience.

As we have seen, the literal, grammatical, and historical method of interpretation does not restrict readers; it actually frees us to draw truth from passages and apply them to our lives. But we must remember the crucial distinction between interpretation and application. Our job is to read the text within its context and draw out theological principles from it. We are never permitted to force our opinions or exercise unwarranted creativity on passages in an attempt to discover some kind of hidden meaning. We are to glean the theological principles from a portion of Scripture, then apply those principles to our lives today.

One principle evident in this brief narrative is that of trust. Moses serves as the positive example, while Israel represents the negative. Moses turned to the Lord for help, trusting that He would provide. In contrast, Israel grumbled against Moses, and God by extension. Moses, in faith, pleaded with God to save them, demonstrating a matured trust. The Israelites turned against Him with a spoiled air of entitlement. Another principle is Moses' obedience. God instructed him to throw wood into the bitter waters, and Moses did so, which further confirms his growth in faith. Did it make sense to Moses? Did Moses fully understand why God wanted him to do that? No and no. But it did not matter. Moses trusted in God's omniscience beyond his limited understanding and chose to walk in obedience.

These theological principles of trust and obedience are ones we can learn from and apply in numerous ways today. When a child is making awful decisions, it is easy to complain, get frustrated, lose your temper, and solely focus on behavioral modification. Trusting and obeying God, however, means storming His Throne for that child as often as possible, praying with him/her, extending grace and love in tangible ways, remaining consistent in discipline, and being patient in responses. When you experience tension with your spouse, it is easy to get defensive, harbor bitterness, retaliate with snarky comments, withhold physical affection, and more. But trusting and obeying God means patiently loving, forgiving, praying for, encouraging, and speaking kindly to your spouse even when undeserved.

So many more examples exist, but the point is that trusting and obeying God means doing things His way even when we do not feel like it. Israel was facing a legitimately difficult and scary situation, but they took the easy and sinful way out, not the disciplined and righteous course of action. Instead of trusting God and living out their freedom, they turned against Him and put back on the chains of defeat and distrust. Moses, however, trusted and obeyed God despite his fears. He did not allow the anger, frustration, and ungratefulness of the Israelites to plant seeds of bitterness in his heart toward God. The choice is always ours: will we turn against God or lean into Him when times get tough?

> **There He made for them a statute and regulation, and there He tested them. And He said, "If you will give earnest heed to the voice of the Lord your God, and do what is right in His sight, and give ear to His commandments, and keep all His statutes, I will put none of the diseases on you which I have put on the Egyptians; for I, the Lord, am your healer." (15:25b-26)**

Like every other event thus far in the Exodus narrative, God not only knew this would happen, He orchestrated it. He **tested them**, knew Israel would fail, and knew it would be a good opportunity to make **a statute and regulation** for them that would carry on throughout the rest of their lives as His people. **Statute and regulation** can also be translated as an ordinance and ruling/judgment,[143] or a fixed rule.[144]

Before addressing the ordinance, we should note that there is some debate concerning the subject of God's words here. While most assume it is the general population of Israel, others believe God is addressing Moses specifically because in Hebrew, the pronouns in verse 26 are in the singular and male form. Advocates of this view believe that "given his special status, he [Moses] is distinguished from the rest of the Israelites and tested regarding his obedience to God."[145] Just as Abraham was tested in his obedience, so now it is Moses' turn as Israel's leader, or so the reasoning goes.[146] While it is certainly possible that God was speaking primarily to Moses, it is still safe to conclude that all of Israel is being addressed as well. Both Moses and Israel were tested at Marah (vs

25); it stands to reason that God's response to that testing includes all of Israel, not just Moses.

God explains His ruling for His people: **"If you will give earnest heed to the voice of the Lord your God, and do what is right in His sight, and give ear to His commandments, and keep all His statutes, I will put none of the diseases on you which I have put on the Egyptians; for I, the Lord, am your healer."** The use of the word **if** reveals that God was providing Israel with a choice. Rather than issuing a direct command for obedience, God communicated His rules to Israel, and left them with the decision of whether or not to comply.

I grew up in an independent Baptist church that leaned towards the Arminian camp and was also somewhat legalistic. Free will was preached far more than predestination, and actually, the only memories I have of any mention of predestination were negative (as in, theologically misguided). As I grew in my faith and learned more about Scripture, I developed theological leanings as a Reformed Baptist—predestination is a biblical fact, but then, so is our choice to obey or disobey. I share this because God allows us to live in a strange tension under several aspects of theology. Both God's total sovereignty and our ability to make decisions exist. It is impossible to know how those two things exist simultaneously, just as it is impossible to know how Jesus can be fully God and fully man at the same time. But both are true, and our passage reveals it.

God orchestrated a test for Israel, knowing that they would fail. He let them fail and then presented a proposition: He would instruct them on how to live, and they would decide whether to follow it or not. **If** they choose to obey, they will be blessed; if not, they will face punishment and hardship. It is a straightforward decree, but God clarified what it entailed. First, obeying God begins with listening to Him—If Israel **will give earnest heed to the voice of the Lord your God.**

This instruction is intensely practical and reminiscent of what Paul would later write to the Roman church:

> How then shall they call on Him in whom they have not believed? And how shall they believe in Him of whom they have not heard? And how shall they hear without a preacher? And how shall they preach unless they are sent?...so then faith comes by hearing, and hearing by the word of God. (Romans 10:14-15a, 17)

We cannot know anything unless we first hear (or read) about it. Information must be presented to our senses before it is transformed into knowledge, and later, into faith. It is no surprise, then, that God begins His proposal with instruction to listen. And not just casual listening, but to **give earnest heed** to God. They were not to run around like toddlers on a playground with Dad's voice just one of the numerous other noises clamoring for their attention. Rather, they were to sit like students on the first day of school—soaking in every word of their teacher so they would know what to expect for the year to come.

As with everything else in life, it is not just the act of listening that is important, but the object of our listening. We are bombarded with voices all day, every day. Whom we choose to listen to matters, and it matters more than we realize. Israel was called **to listen to the voice of the Lord** over and beyond anything or anyone else in the world. They had listened to the voice of Egypt for generations; now, they needed to train themselves to listen to God's voice. They needed to redirect their attention, focus, and ears from their slavery to their Savior.

One of my favorite passages in all of Scripture conveys this truth in a powerful way. After an enormous victory at Mount Carmel over the prophets of Baal (not unlike God's victory over Egypt in our narrative), Elijah falls into a bout of depression spurred on by fear of Jezebel. He ends up alone in a cave when "the word of the Lord came to him" (1 Kings 19:9). God told him:

"Go forth and stand on the mountain before the Lord." And behold, the Lord was passing by! And a great and strong wind was rending the mountains and breaking in pieces the rocks before the Lord; but the Lord was not in the wind. And after the wind an earthquake, but the Lord was not in the earthquake. After the earthquake a fire, but the Lord was not in the fire; and after the fire a **sound** of a gentle blowing. (1 Kings 19:11-12, emphasis added)

The word for **sound** (*qol*) is the same one as **voice** (*qol*) used in our passage, and came after fierce displays of wind, an earthquake, and a fire. In our passage, God had just shown Himself powerfully to Egypt using forces of nature at His will. But now, after those had passed and that victory had been won, God speaks gently to His people as He did to Elijah. While He is omnipotent and speaks through mighty, supernatural acts, He also knows we are weak, frail, and easily overwhelmed. Thus, He comes to us and, in this case, speaks through Moses to remind His people of their need to listen to His voice.

Yet listening is not an independent act. We can listen intently to someone all day long, but if we never take action, it is all for naught. That is why God includes the next part of His instruction: Israel must listen, then **do what is right in His sight, give ear to His commandments, and keep all His statutes**. Listening, when conducted properly, begets obedience. Israel needed to **do what was right in His sight.**

This seems obvious, but it is shockingly misunderstood and erroneously applied in our culture today. We far too often do what Israel will continue to do as their journey unfolds: "every man did what was right in his own eyes," which inevitably led to doing what was "evil in the sight of the Lord" (Judges 17:6; 3:7). When we use any barometer of obedience other than the **voice of the Lord**, we set ourselves up for failure because only He is the way, the truth, and life (John 14:6). We listen so we know how to act, and act in accordance with what God deems is right, not what we do.

Further, God tells Israel to **give ear to His commandments**. This might be confusing because God has not actually gone on record giving Israel His commandments yet (that is coming up in a few chapters). The most obvious and appropriate explanation is that God had given Israel at least some commands before now, and that the impending Ten Words (commandments) were a formal expression and solidification of the instruction given informally over the generations preceding this time. "After all, are we to think that the command to honor one's parents or the prohibitions against stealing, murder, or adultery are unheard of before Sinai?" [147] No, it is far more likely that God had provided them with basic rules and regulations over the years. They were expected to **give ear to His commandments** and were held accountable to them, even if those commands were articulated originally for the family of Israel, not yet for their nation.

After doing **what is right in His sight** and giving **ear to His commandments**, Israel was also supposed to **keep all His statutes**. To **keep** (*samar*) means to preserve, guard, or to watch. This word is used hundreds of times throughout the Old Testament, the first of which was way back in Genesis 2:15, describing how God put Adam in the "garden of Eden to cultivate it and keep [*samar*] it." Just as Adam would keep, preserve, and protect the garden, so the Israelites were supposed to keep, preserve, and protect God's **statutes** in their lives and hearts. The idea of keeping carries a weight of priority—we keep close to what we value. Israel was to value God's commands and preserve them in their lives because they (both the commands and Israelites) were His. God was their Leader and King; submitting to His laws was (and is) a privilege for His subjects. We, like Israel, do not *have* to be led by God, we *get* to be led by Him, and it is with such a perspective that we should **keep all His statutes.**

One last note before moving on to the last part of verse 26. God specifically says to **keep *all* His statutes.** As followers of Christ, we are not at liberty to pick and choose what we believe about the Bible. It is all or nothing, and if it is not all, it is nothing. There is no in-between, partial ground, or fluctuation in our pursuit and understanding of theological truths. Neither is there room for half-hearted or uncommitted obedience to His truth once learned. Being a Christian is not merely adding another line to our resumes or an asset to our portfolio. It is a new life—one dedicated to and transformed by the Holy Spirit, made possible through the sacrifice of Jesus Christ, and with the goal of bringing glory to God. God is challenging His people to **keep all His statutes** so they can avoid dire and unwanted consequences.

In this particular case, the consequence of not listening to and obeying God's commands was to be inflicted with the diseases God put on the Egyptians. If Israel would obey, He would **"put none of the diseases on you which I have put on the Egyptians; for I, the Lord, am your healer."** The exact nature of **the diseases** referenced here is unknown, but it likely refers to the diseases inflicted upon the Egyptians during the plagues, since these were still so fresh in the Israelites' minds. [148] These two diseases were the severe pestilence that killed the Egyptian livestock and the plague of boils inflicted upon the Egyptian people. Remember, Israel was traveling with an exorbitant amount of cattle and livestock; disease among them would be crippling to Israel's budding economy. Boils, more obviously, would be a terrible affliction to the Israelites as well.

While this may seem grim and harsh of God, there are a couple of truths we need to remember. First, sin has consequences; second, God loves us enough to discipline us. My husband and I are in the throes of raising four young daughters, and one not-so-pleasant aspect of parenting is discipline. Even more challenging is the constant effort to frame discipline within the context of the gospel. The goal of discipline (from God to us and us to our children) is restoration. It is to purge sin and re-establish peace within a relationship so it can flourish. This process is difficult, especially since sin is so rampant and manifests itself in more ways than we can count. God, the perfect parent, punishes sin because He wants to rid us of it and allow our relationships with Him to deepen. For Israel (and us), that meant listening to and obeying His commands. Anything other than that was disobedience and sin against Him, which would result in consequences (in this case, diseases).

Unfortunately, we as children often fail to look beyond punishment to the purpose of it. We view God as mean, uncompassionate, harsh, and unfair instead of as a loving Father who guides, corrects, and purges His children from sin so they can enjoy life with Him more fully. To use another example, consider a mechanic restoring a car. He has a vision for this car and knows everything that needs to be done to get it there. While the car technically has all its parts, some are old, rusted, or do not work at all anymore. So, he painstakingly removes the bad parts one at a time and replaces them with new ones that will enable the car to operate. While hardly a perfect metaphor, consider what would happen if the car were alive and threw a fit every time the mechanic tried to remove one of its parts. Instead of trusting the mechanic to make it new, the car fights him, thinks he is unfair, and refuses to cooperate. It is comfortable with the parts it knows—rusted, not functional, and collecting dust—and refuses to trust the one who can restore and remake it to a glory it cannot fathom.

Consequences hurt. They are uncomfortable and never fun. But they are necessary and beautiful evidence that God loves us enough to painstakingly remove the dung piles of sin that have crept into our hearts one shovelful at a time. God would inflict diseases on His people if they refused to listen and obey Him. He would temporarily cause them pain to set them on a path of eternal healing. Another example is setting a broken bone. Their sin and disobedience were like a broken bone—painful and crippling to their lives. God would punish them for their sin (or reset the bone), which would bring even more pain temporarily. But He always had their eternal benefit in mind. His goal was to get their attention and turn them back to Him, their **Healer.**

Just as God can use diseases to inflict punishment upon His people, He can also cure His people from any and all ailments. Job 5:17 says, "He inflicts pain, and gives relief; He wounds and His hands also heal." God is sovereign over all, and later, He sends Jesus as the Ultimate Healer of our souls— "He was pierced through for our transgressions, He was crushed for our iniquities; the chastening for our well-being fell upon Him, and by His scourging we are healed" (Isaiah 53:5). Healing Israel of their diseases serves as a greater reminder of our spiritual state: we are ailing sinners in need of an unfailing Healer. Outward infirmities mirror deeply spiritual ones in need of the healing attention only the cross and resurrection can bring. God heals physically, but more importantly, spiritually heals those who accept Christ as their Lord.

Then they came to Elim where there were twelve springs of water and seventy date palms, and they camped there beside the waters. (15:27)

After God provided Israel with instruction, we learn that they continued traveling, this time **to Elim. Elim** was "a wooded, freshwater oasis, generally identified with Wadi Gharandel." [149] This new campsite must have been a breath of fresh air for the Israelites. It had plenty of water (**twelve springs** worth) suitable for drinking and **seventy date palms** to provide a bit of shade. After their recent trial at Marah, **Elim** was a lovely reprieve where they could rest, hydrate, and refresh before heading to their next destination.

Coming to **Elim** after Marah is no accident and has a deeper interpretation, according to Pink:

> When we are walking in fellowship with Christ and the principle of His cross is faithfully applied to our daily life, not only is the bitterness of suffering for His sake sweetened, but we enter into the pure joys which God has provided for His own, even down here. "Elim" speaks, then, of the satisfaction which God gives to those who are walking with Him in obedience. [150]

Elim reminded the Israelites how good it is to willingly follow and obey the Lord. Not every circumstance in every stage of life will be lovely; in fact, Christ promises tribulation and trials to His followers (John 16:33). But even amidst those trials, we can rest in the knowledge that God has overcome the world, and we belong to Him. When we do experience seasons of calm and circumstantial blessing, we can savor them that much more, knowing they are a taste of what's to come for us in eternity with Him.

In the span of only six verses, Israel encountered many lessons. They needed some nudging from Moses to leave the Red Sea and went three days into the wilderness when they faced the roadblock of undrinkable water. The water at Marah was bitter, and instead of turning to God for help, they turned against Moses and grumbled about it. Moses, however, turned to God, listened to His instructions about throwing wood into the water, and obeyed. Unsurprisingly, the water became sweet, and God used this trial to teach them that things would go well for them if they listened and obeyed. If they did not, they would be punished, but only until restoration could once again take place. Their next destination was a wonderful oasis, a fitting reflection of the peace and refreshment that we have when we walk according to God's word.

Exodus 16:1-8

> **Then they set out from Elim, and all the congregation of the sons of Israel came to the wilderness of Sin, which is between Elim and Sinai, on the fifteenth day of the second month after their departure from the land of Egypt. (16:1)**

After being refreshed in Elim, Israel set out. Lest there be any doubt, Moses clarified that **all the congregation of the sons of Israel** set out; they did not separate into groups, nor did some of them abandon their people. God was keeping His people united, and while it is not elaborated on here, it is important to remember. Unity is crucial, especially when wandering through a wilderness experiencing freedom for the first time in their lives. Israel may not have prioritized unity, but they lived it out, and it is an understated blessing in this narrative.

Soon, they all **came to the wilderness of Sin, which is between Elim and Sinai**. At first glance, we may be tempted to think that **the wilderness of Sin** represented some kind of evil or perhaps was akin to a Sodom and Gomorrah type atmosphere where people habitually and flagrantly sinned. Thankfully, that is not true. The name **Sin** is simply "a transliteration of the Hebr. word *sin*, a designation that resembles the name 'Sinai'... [it] bears no relation to the English word 'sin.'"[151] This wilderness was located on the east coast of the Red Sea, and it is likely that the Israelites were "following rather consistently the old road that ran southward along the eastern side of the Red Sea that the Egyptians had used for mining commerce."[152] In other words, God was leading them along a known ancient path. Despite being a **wilderness**, it was not untraveled, wild territory. It was admittedly unknown to the Israelites, but it stands to reason that there was some kind of marked "road" that they were following; they were not just trekking through endless sand dunes or raw land.

Israel arrived at **the wilderness of Sin... on the fifteenth day of the second month after their departure from the land of Egypt.** A bit of ambiguity exists regarding the exact amount of time that had elapsed until this point, but the most probable translation is that one month had passed since they left Egypt. This conclusion is drawn from the fact that "the Israelites left Egypt on the fifteenth day of the first month of the year (the day after the full-moon night when the tenth plague/Passover occurred."[153]

> **The whole congregation of the sons of Israel grumbled against Moses and Aaron in the wilderness. The sons of Israel said to them, "Would that we had died by the Lord's hand in the land of Egypt, when we sat by the pots of meat, when we ate bread to the full; for you have brought us out into this wilderness to kill this whole assembly with hunger." (16:2-3)**

Unfortunately, a bit of time on the road did not inspire Israel to lean more fully on the Lord. Whereas Elim was a place of rest and restoration, the wilderness of Sin was one of trial and failure: **the whole congregation of the sons of Israel grumbled against Moses and Aaron in the wilderness.** We immediately notice the repeated mention of **the whole congregation**, which is the same word in Hebrew (*kol*) as "all" in the preceding first. All of Israel traveled together, which is a lovely expression of unity, but unfortunately, all would turn against the Lord once more in a disobedient, distrusting, rebellious front.

Another repeated word (and action) is **grumbled.** Just like Israel grumbled against Moses because the water at Marah was bitter, the people now grumbled again because of a lack of food. This time, the grumbling was against both Moses and Aaron, which is not noteworthy other than to remind us that Aaron was still seen as a prominent leader in Israel. Perhaps after a month of traveling, he had settled into a more visible role of leadership among the people, which is why they now accused both him and Moses instead of just Moses as before. Regardless, both Moses and his brother were in the proverbial hot seat, and they both became recipients of Israel's crankiness.

While the first reference of grumbling was mildly recounted, this one more fully expresses the dire state of their hearts: **"Would that we had died by the Lord's hand in the land of Egypt, when we sat by the pots of meat, when we ate bread to the full; for you have brought us out into this wilderness to kill this whole assembly with hunger."**

With this complaint, we encounter the same refrain of pessimism that the Israelites used against Moses when they saw the Egyptians coming after them at the sea. Once again, Israel says that they would have been better off dying in Egypt than facing their current troubling circumstance. This time, it was because they did not have food. In their minds, they would have been better off being killed **by the Lord's hand** in Egypt surrounded by ample food than to die in the wilderness by starvation. There is a lot to unpack in this punchy verse, so let's dig in.

Israel's response seems quite dramatic, and in some ways, it is. But in other ways, we can better understand their circumstances and gain a bit of insight into how they were feeling. Just like when they watched the Egyptians come at them in full force, hunger and starvation were very real and potent threats. While they exaggerated the Egyptians' intentions (assuming they were coming to kill them instead of re-enslaving them), starvation was not that much of a stretch. They had been gone for a month and had likely used up all the food reserves they had originally brought with them from Egypt. One commentator notes that everyone was likely affected to some degree by hunger at that point:

> As the Israelites saw themselves, their families, and their flocks growing thinner and as they saw day after day no likely source of food in the wilderness in which they were traveling, it became obvious to them that they were going to die unless something dramatic happened to reverse their plight. [154]

Being concerned about having enough food for millions of people and livestock was a legitimate point of alarm. The threat to their well-being and lives was real. However, just like with both the Egyptians' resurgence and the waters at Marah, while Israel had reason to be concerned, they did not have a reason to be mutinous against Moses, Aaron, and most importantly, God. They reacted to their circumstances, they did not respond with the truth they should have known well enough by this point. God had just told them to listen to His voice and do what is right in His sight; complaining to the point of wishing they were dead hardly follows that instruction.

It is curious how they said they would rather have died **by the Lord's hand in the land of Egypt**. The **Lord's hand** as an agent of death could refer to natural causes, the assumption being that they would have lived normal lives and died of old age, not have their lives cut short by starvation. [155] The **Lord's hand** could also refer to the plagues God inflicted on Egypt, particularly that of killing the first born, which was swift, as opposed to starvation, which is slow and tormenting. [156] Regardless of specific reference, the underlying accusation is that God used His hand numerous times against the Egyptians on their behalf; now it appeared that they were going to die in the wilderness by the *lack* of His hand intervening on their behalf. Did they actually, literally wish they had died in Egypt? Of course not. But as one scholar notes, "they made a comparison in their complaint between the simplicity of dying where they were and the absurdity of going to all the trouble they had gone to in the past month and then dying anyway."[157]

This perspective reveals that Israel both contemplated God's role in their lives and intentionally failed to believe His promises. Some people argue that the Israelites primarily took issue with Moses as their leader and were not really blaming or accusing God of anything. The opposite is proved with this text. Israel knew that God was their leader and in control of their destiny, but instead of trusting Him and asking for His help, they turned against Him and accused Him preemptively of their death. Moses and Aaron were His representatives; by going to them, Israel knew their message would be communicated to God.

Israel's pining for Egypt was grounded in the fact that they at least always had food there. Their lives may have been miserable as they did backbreaking work all day every day, got beaten for even the smallest infraction, and went to bed with pained and fatigued bodies; but at least they **sat by the pots of meat, and ate bread to the full**. They may not have had much else, but at least they had plenty of food in Egypt! Or so their thinking went. No doubt they were salivating over the memory of their former **pots of meat** and **bread**, but Israel had yet to learn one crucial lesson: that God is the Bread of Life. Instead of pining for Egypt's food, Israel should have pined after God and trusted Him to provide.

I do wonder if Israel had been seeking the Lord—if they had been singing praises to Him as they walked, reminiscing about all He had done in Egypt on their behalf, and excitedly recounting all His works with each other along the way—if they had been doing all those things, would they have ended up with this attitude at this point? Starvation did not happen overnight; they had been slowly running out of food since they left Egypt. Why did they wait until the breaking point to talk to God about it?

It seems as though their faith depleted with every serving of food. As they watched their supplies dwindle, their trust in God went with it. Instead of praising Him for His provision at every meal, they grumbled, doubted, and questioned Him in their hearts (and maybe with each other). This habit of complaining came to a head when the crisis could no longer be contained. The grumbling of their hearts exploded out as accusations against God. As Jesus said, "The things that proceed out of the mouth come from the heart, and those defile the man" (Matthew 15:18). We speak what we think, and it appears as though the Israelites had been thinking faithless thoughts instead of letting their eyes look to the Lord and their gaze be fixed straight ahead of them (Proverbs 4:35).

Instead of keeping their eyes on the Lord and their hearts tuned to His promises, Israel lashed out with the crux of their accusation: **"for you have brought us out into this wilderness to kill this whole assembly with hunger."** Not only does this accusation show a complete lack of faith, but it also demonstrates a lack of basic logic. It is lunacy to think that God orchestrated and carried out the plagues over the course of numerous months, and planned and executed the final defeat of the Egyptians at the sea only to have Israel die in the desert from starvation. God has revealed His brilliance and sovereignty in every detail of the narrative, most of which Israel was privy to. It is nonsensical dubiousness to entertain this idea, much less believe it to the point of verbally accusing Him of it. This proves the point that Israel had been sulking in distrusting thoughts for quite some time; their dissidence had been building up in their hearts until it left no room for truth and logic.

One lesson we constantly teach our daughters (and remind ourselves of) is taking every thought captive—nipping lies in the bud so they do not grow and push out the truth in our minds:

> For though we walk in the flesh, we do not war according to the flesh, for the weapons of our warfare are not of the flesh, but divinely powerful for the destruction of fortresses. We are destroying speculations and every lofty thing raised up against the knowledge of God, and we are taking every thought captive to the obedience of Christ. (2 Corinthians 10:3-5)

If Israel had done this from the beginning, if they had taken every thought captive and destroyed erroneous speculations about God caused by fear and hunger, they could have avoided so much angst and bitterness. They could have enjoyed fellowship with God as He wanted them to, and this whole episode could have been avoided. They may have faced a lack of food, but their response to it could have expressed faith and trust in God, and no doubt been rewarded by Him.

Fortunately, God abounds in mercy and showers His people with unmerited favor:

> **Then the Lord said to Moses, "Behold, I will rain bread from heaven for you; and the people shall go out and gather a day's portion every day, that I may test them, whether or not they will walk in My instruction. On the sixth day, when they prepare what they bring in, it will be twice as much as they gather daily. So Moses and Aaron said to all the sons of Israel, "At evening you will know that the Lord has brought you out of the land of Egypt; and in the morning you will see the glory of the Lord, for He hears your grumblings against the Lord; and what are we, that you grumble against us?" Moses said, "This will happen when the Lord gives you meat to eat in the evening, and bread to the full in the morning; for the Lord hears your grumbling which you grumble against Him. And what are we? Your grumblings are not against us but against the Lord." (16:4-8)**

Instead of punishing Israel for their irreverent and sinful behavior, God responds with grace and kindness. Grace is an unmerited favor—receiving something that we do not deserve. Israel deserved discipline but received grace instead. God told Moses, **"Behold, I will rain bread from heaven for you."** Their physical needs would be met, for God would provide them with bread. However, meeting that need would be far from ordinary and would reveal a much deeper spiritual truth: that God is the Bread of Life.

Bread would be provided not by happening upon some random field of wheat from which they could harvest it, but from heaven itself. By doing this, God would remind them day in and day out that He was the Source of life and the only One capable of supplying all their needs. This action is a powerful foreshadowing of Jesus' coming. While the bread from heaven would take away their hunger, Jesus would come to take away the sins of the world (1 John 3:5). Jesus would later say:

> "For the bread of God is that which comes down out of heaven, and gives life to the world...I am the bread of life; he who comes to Me will not hunger, and he who believes in Me will never thirst...I am the living bread that came down out of heaven; if anyone eats of this bread, he will live forever; and the bread also which I will give for the life of the world is My flesh." John 6:33,35, 51.

Israel's bread would satisfy their physical hunger, but Jesus would satisfy the spiritual hunger and depravity of countless souls. He, like Israel's bread, would come down from heaven as a gift straight from God. Just as Israel's bread would provide them nourishment, Jesus would provide sustenance and life for all who partook of His sacrifice by making Him the Lord of their lives. With this response to Israel, God was not only promising a remedy for their current situation but foreshadowing a resolution to the much bigger and more dire problem of sin and death in the world.

In recognizing that God's provision of both bread and salvation comes from heaven, we must also acknowledge its miraculous nature. Despite some commentators attempting to dismiss the supernatural aspect of the bread by claiming that it could be found on certain trees in the wilderness, that reasoning is insufficient. Such claims "fail to explain how it grew in winter as well as summer; how it was obtainable in every part of the wilderness, no matter where Israel's camp was pitched; or how [it was sufficient] to feed upwards of two million souls for almost forty years!"[158] God did not direct Israel to bread that already existed; He sent bread from heaven itself in the exact quantity needed to provide for His people.

Even though God's provision came at no cost to the recipient, it still required a response. God would provide bread for His people, but the people still had to **go out and gather a day's portion every day**. Bread would not just appear on their plates ready for consumption; the people needed to put forth the effort of gathering it daily. It is similar to receiving a wrapped gift. The recipient needs to put forth the effort of unwrapping and opening the gift, and then putting it to use.

A similar situation would occur with the widow of Zarephath years later. God instructed the prophet Elijah to go to Zarephath, and when he did, he met a widow and requested water and bread from her. Solemnly, she replied that she had no bread, only a handful of flour and a tiny bit of oil left that she was about to make as a last meal for her and her son to eat before they died of starvation (due to the widespread famine in the land). Elijah told her to make the bread but serve him first, and her obedience would result in God's blessing: "the bowl of flour shall not be exhausted, nor shall the jar of oil be empty, until the day that the Lord sends rain on the face of the earth" (1 Kings 17:14). And so it was. God filled the bowl of flour and jar of oil every day, providing what they needed to survive. The widow still needed to put forth effort to make the bread, but she did so with joy, trusting and thanking God for providing day in and day out.

Neither Israel nor the widow did anything to earn the gift God gave them, but they did need to take action in order to receive it. For Israel, God designed this process as a **test** to see **whether or not they will walk** according to God's **instruction.** Their test involved obedience, yes, to actually collect the bread, but also regarding how much to gather. God tells them that **on the sixth day, when they prepare what they bring in, it will be twice as much as they gather daily.** The text will go into more detail about this shortly, but for now, it is sufficient to note that God was establishing His commandment of Sabbath rest among His people. On the sixth day, He would provide what they needed to last two days, so they could rest and not have to gather the bread on the Sabbath every week.

Unlike the rest of Israel, Moses and Aaron were listening to God. After receiving His instruction, they told **all the sons of Israel, "At evening you will know that the Lord has brought you out of the land of Egypt; and in the morning you will see the glory of the Lord, for He hears your grumblings against the Lord; and what are we, that you grumble against us?"** Twice daily, the Israelites would be reminded of God's sovereignty and His glory. But it is not just a flippant reminder. Moses and Aaron say the Israelites **will know** that God has **brought** them **out of the land of Egypt**. The word **know** (*yada*) has been used numerous times in our study thus far, often referencing how God will cause people (both Egyptian and Israelite alike) to **know** that He alone is the Lord (6:7; 7:5, 17; 8:10, 22; 9:14; 10:2; 14:4, 18). This kind of knowledge is not a guess or wishful thinking, it is not a dream or hypothesis. It is sure and certain because it is founded upon the God of the universe.

God's provision for the Israelites was miraculous proof that reminded them He was in control. He brought them **out of the land of Egypt** through ten plagues and the monumental parting of the sea. He led them by the pillar of cloud by day and fire by night. He had never left them, nor had He turned a deaf ear to their needs (despite the manner in which His people indirectly approached Him about it). Their continued provision would give them every reason to allow their knowledge of the Lord to sink down to their hearts and into the deepest fibers of their beings.

Intellectual assent would have every opportunity to transform into active faith, especially when morning came and they would **see the glory of the Lord**. This is actually the first time we see the term **glory** (*kabod*) in the Exodus narrative. This term is "derived from the Hebrew concept of 'weight, heaviness, worthiness,' the term 'glory' in a doctrinal sense is used of God in (Ps 19:1 and (63:2), speaking of the heaviness, awesomeness, or intrinsic worth of God's being."[159] God's provision of food would reflect Himself—it would not be tiny, fleeting, unsubstantial scraps of food that were barely enough to keep the Israelites alive. It would be exactly what they needed, and this method of providing for them would prove that God alone knew exactly what they needed.

Despite God's continued miraculous provision and divine intervention for His people, the Israelites still did not trust God, and they thought they knew better than Him. Well, God reminded them through Moses and Aaron that **He hears your grumblings against the Lord**. Even though they did not deserve to have His ear, He listened to them and confirmed that their **grumblings** were indeed against Himself. Some scholars argue that the Israelites were only upset with and grumbling **against** Moses and Aaron as their human leaders, but the text clearly denies that with statements like this. The Israelites may have taken their complaints to Moses and Aaron, but their real complaint was against God, not them.

Furthermore, is it not ironic that God was willing to listen to a bunch of ungrateful, undeserving whiners when these ungrateful, undeserving whiners had refused to listen to Him? He had just told Israel at Marah that they needed to heed His voice and give ear to His commandments. Just days later, they were neither listening to nor obeying Him. They were grumbling, and Moses and Aaron made it clear that it was an affront **against the Lord.**

Moses and Aaron reminded the people that they were but human leaders following the Lord, with no authority of their own. By asking, **"What are we, that you grumble against us?"** they were reminding the people that they were servants following the Lord, as Israel should have been. It literally made no sense for the Israelites to grumble against Moses and Aaron, for they were doing nothing of their own initiative. As the Apostle Paul would later write, "be imitators of me, just as I also am of Christ" (1 Corinthians 11:1). Moses and Aaron were walking in obedience; the Israelites should have been following their lead, not despising their example.

At this point, Moses took over the communication and repeated much of what both he and Aaron had said in the previous verses, with one new addition: the mention of meat. God would give them **meat to eat in the evening and bread to the full in the morning.** The bread has been mentioned and will continue to be referenced in this chapter, but we are now specifically told that meat would also be given. This inclusion mirrors the Israelites' complaint in verse 3 about how they "sat by the pots of meat…[and] ate bread to the full" while in Egypt. Meat and bread were in abundance while they were slaves, so God (through Moses and Aaron) promised to provide them with a special portion of meat that evening.

The verse ends with another reminder that God both heard the Israelites' grumbling and that the Israelites were wasting their time whining to Moses and Aaron. Moses flat out states, **"Your grumblings are not against us but against the Lord."** Oh, how many skirmishes could be avoided if we shared this perspective? If we are living for the Lord—pursuing and walking in obedience to His commandments—there will be times when we experience persecution in one way or another. Every day, it seems as though our culture in America is becoming more and more averse to Christianity, and hatred is spewed at us anytime we speak out against the evils of this world. But we must always remember that it is not us that they are mad at; it is the One living in us.

Remember how Jesus called and converted the apostle Paul:

> As he was traveling, it happened that he was approaching Damascus, and suddenly a light from heaven flashed around him; and he fell to the ground and heard a voice saying to him, "Saul, Saul, why are you persecuting Me?" And he said, "Who are You, Lord?" And He said, "I am Jesus whom you are persecuting." (Acts 9:3-5)

Paul never personally persecuted Jesus; Jesus had already died, risen again, and ascended back into heaven when this encounter occurred. So why did Jesus say that? Because by persecuting Christians—people who followed Him—Paul was persecuting Jesus. The Christians were not acting on their own authority or according to their own ideologies but were rather following Jesus and His truth. The same holds true for Moses and Aaron here. Even though it seemed like it, the Israelites were not taking issue with them personally, but with whom they represented.

Summary

Israel has much to learn about God and what it means to place their faith in Him. This section began when **Moses led Israel from the sea**, likely with a bit of urging, as the Hebrew text seems to suggest. Perhaps they were collecting some of the Egyptians' weaponry, or perhaps they were still awestruck by what they had witnessed. Regardless, they were moving slowly, but Moses got them going once again.

They pressed on and **went three days into the wilderness** when they encountered their first problem as a totally freed people: they **found no water**. As they arrived at **Marah**, they came upon water but could not drink it because it was **bitter**. This posed a significant problem because they were approximately two million strong, in addition to countless livestock; they needed water (and a lot of it) to survive.

Unfortunately, Israel did not respond well to this test of faith. Instead of trusting the Lord, **the people grumbled**. Moses reverently took their concerns to the Lord, who in turn **showed him a tree, and he threw it into the waters, and the waters became sweet**. God had already performed numerous miracles involving water in our narrative. Moses was saved from the waters of the Nile that Pharaoh intended for death. God turned the water in Egypt into blood, changing it from a source of life to a source of death in the first plague. God again used water as an agent of death and destruction in both the hail plague and when the sea consumed the Egyptian army after His people had crossed safely to the other side. Turning bitter water sweet using a tree was not a difficult task for God, but Israel needed to be reminded of His power and their relationship to Him.

It was at Marah that God **made for them a statute and regulation**. He basically gave the Israelites an ultimatum: if they would **give earnest heed to the voice of the Lord…and do what is right in His sight, and give ear to His commandments, and keep all His statutes,** then God would **put none of the diseases on** them as He did on the Egyptians. God offered them salvation out of sheer grace; they did nothing to deserve it and nothing to earn it. However, they would need to respond with trust and obedience if they were going to live as His people. He was not going to force them, but He was going to expect them to if they wanted to continue living as the recipients of His blessings.

After Marah, **they came to Elim, where there were twelve springs of water and seventy date palms, and they camped there beside the waters**. God led them to a beautiful oasis of rest and refreshment after their failed trial. He allowed them a time to be restored—to gather energy before the next phase of their journey.

We are not told how long they camped at Elim, but after that, they packed up and **arrived at the wilderness of Sin**, one month after they left Egypt. Unfortunately, their first act in the wilderness was not to give thanks and praise to God for leading them. Instead, **the whole congregation of Israel grumbled against Moses and Aaron in the wilderness** because they ran out of food. Instead of praising God for His previous provision and asking Him for it again, they allowed their faith and trust in Him to diminish along with their food supply. Thus, when they reached the point of hunger, they lashed out against Moses and Aaron, sarcastically claiming that they should have just died by the Lord's hand in Egypt where at least they had food, instead of being brought into the wilderness to die there. Talk about a tantrum.

Instead of lashing out against their foolishness, God responded with utmost grace. Rather than raining down fire and brimstone in an act of merited judgment, He promised to **rain bread from heaven** as a test to see if Israel would finally walk in obedience to Him. Despite numerous chances to obey and trust Him, they had failed more often than not. He was giving them yet another chance to do the right thing and watch another miraculous provision unfold.

Moses and Aaron made it clear that they were simply following God's lead. The people's **grumblings** were not against Moses and Aaron **but against the Lord**. Israel needed to shape up and pay attention to what God was about to do—miraculously provide them with supernatural bread straight from heaven. Hopefully, they would get the hint that they needed Him for more than just physical bread. Hopefully, they would begin to realize that He was the only way to nourish their souls as well.

GROUP STUDY

Introduction

To grumble is to tumble—we trip as our faith stumbles.

Grumbling and whining accomplishes nothing except weakened faith and a hardened heart. It's difficult not to do, though, especially when encountering trials, setbacks, and pain.

- Share a time in your life when you found yourself grumbling and complaining.
  - What were you grumbling about?
- Was it a legitimate concern?
- How did it impact your faith?

The Word

Israel walked away from a spiritual high when they left the sea. But rather than keeping their gazes elevated on their Savior, they started looking down at their circumstances. And they didn't like what they saw.

> **When they came to Marah, they could not drink the waters of Marah, for they were bitter...so the people grumbled at Moses. (Exodus 15:23-24)**

- Why was this problem a legitimate concern?
- Why was their response not appropriate?
  - What should they have done instead?

God graciously did not punish them for their childish tantrum, but rather provided water and articulated a challenge of faith for them:

> **"If you will give earnest heed to the voice of the Lord your God, and do what is right in His sight, and give ear to His commandments, and keep all His statutes, I will put none of the diseases on you which I have put on the Egyptians; for I, the Lord, am your healer." (Exodus 15:26)**

- What were the four things God required of Israel?

- What would happen if they didn't meet those requirements?

You'd think Israel's faith would be bolstered again after experiencing another miraculous provision from the Lord. But unfortunately, just days later, they stumble again:

> **The whole congregation of the sons of Israel grumbled against Moses and Aaron...the sons of Israel said to them, "Would that we had died by the Lord's hand in the land of Egypt, when we sat by the pots of meat, when we ate bread to the full; for you have brought us out into the wilderness to kill this whole assembly with hunger." (Exodus 16:2-3)**

- What were they grumbling about now?
  o Was this a legitimate concern?
- What did their reaction to these circumstances reveal about their faith?

Apply

> Blessed is the man who trusts in the Lord
> And whose trust is in the Lord.
> The Lord, Jeremiah 17:7

> For we walk by faith, not by sight.
> The Apostle Paul, 2 Corinthians 5:7

Israel was very immature in their faith. Like toddlers, they could only see what was right in front of them. Their faith mirrored their circumstances—when things were good, their faith was strong. But as soon as they faced a trial, their faith stumbled and failed.

- Take a minute to think about your faith. How circumstantial is it? Does it stand through trials, or does it crumble at the first sign of something going wrong?

Read the following passages and discuss the following questions:

Consider it all joy, my brethren, when you encounter various trials, knowing that the testing of your faith produces endurance. And let endurance have its perfect result, so that you may be perfect and complete, lacking in nothing. (James 1:2-4)

In this you greatly rejoice, even though now for a little while, if necessary, you have been distressed by various trials, so that the proof of your faith, being more precious than gold which is perishable, even though tested by fire, may be found to result in praise and glory and honor at the revelation of Jesus Christ; and though you have not seen Him, you love Him, and though you do not see Him now, but believe in Him, you greatly rejoice with joy inexpressible and full of glory, obtaining as the outcome of your faith the salvation of your souls. (1 Peter 1:6-9)

- What are the differences between these perspectives and Israel's?
- What are the benefits of standing firm and faithful when we encounter trials in faith?

While it's challenging to read about Israel's failures at Marah and in the wilderness of Sin, it's also comforting. God's love, grace, and continued opportunities for them to follow Him reflect a similar pattern in our lives through Christ. No matter how many times we fail, He loves us unconditionally and yearns to strengthen our faith so we can become more like Him.

- What practical ways can you stand firm in faith the next time you encounter difficult circumstances?

WEEK FIVE

GRACE UPON GRACE

Exodus 16:9-16:36

PERSONAL BIBLE STUDY QUESTIONS

1. What did Moses and Aaron tell the congregation of Israel to do first? (16:9)

2. What appeared as Aaron spoke? (16:10)

3. What did God hear? (16:12)

4. What meat was provided for them at twilight? (16:12)

5. After they were full, what would the Israelites "know"? (16:12)

6. What came and covered the camp that evening? (16:13)

7. What appeared the next morning? (16:13)

a. What happened when it evaporated? (16:14)

8. What was the Israelites' reaction when they saw it? (16:15)

9. How much "bread" was Israel supposed to gather? (16:16)

   a. Did they obey? (16:17)

10. Were they supposed to store it overnight? (16:19)

11. Did they listen? (16:20)

    a. What happened because of it? (16:20)

    b. What was Moses' reaction? (16:20)

12. What would happen when the sun grew hot? (16:21)

13. What special provisions needed to be observed for the Sabbath regarding their collection of food? (16:22-26)

    a. Did they listen and obey? (16:27)

14. What did Israel name the bread? (16:31)

15. What was to be kept throughout their generations? (16:33)

16. How long did God provide it for Israel? (16:35)

COMMENTARY

Exodus 16:9-16:36

Each of us shares attributes with God. We are, after all, made in His image and receive spiritual gifts when we accept Christ as our Savior. Some of us are remarkable peacemakers, reflecting and magnifying the peace of God in and through our lives. Others, like me, are teachers and advocates of truth. Lying, even in jest, feels like nails on the chalkboard of my heart. God is truth, and I love sharing that with Him.

While we all share some attributes with God, we are not like Him in *every* way. None of us are balanced in our spiritual gifts and attributes; our scales tend to lean more towards one side than another. I am a truth and justice-oriented person, which means my grace and mercy gauge often leans towards empty. For instance, when I hear about a woman getting mugged at 2 a.m. in a back alley in downtown Savannah, my initial reaction is to question why she was there alone at that time of night in the first place. Putting yourself in that situation seems like you're just asking for something bad to happen. While not entirely true, this illustrates that compassion is secondary in the way my brain is wired.

Unfortunately, the same tendency applies to grace. There are some people and situations that tug on my heartstrings and receive grace that I would never normally offer. But to my shame, they are rare. Grace is something I struggle with personally, and I also struggle to understand it in God. I have the hardest time fathoming why He extends grace to people at all. We are just awful! We constantly sin against Him. Even the most devout Christians acknowledge the depths of their depravity, and it is terrifying how dark our hearts are. How could He offer us grace? Why would He care enough to sacrifice Christ?

As I have mentioned, my husband and I have four young daughters. We can all be thankful that I am not God for countless reasons, but mainly because

I would never willingly give one of them up to die for someone else's sin and outright guilt. We are not unjustly accused. We are not victims of a cosmic justice system, wrongly blamed on trumped-up charges. We are guiltier than we realize and deserve every second of eternity in hell.

But God.

But God is gracious and, in an act that seems absolutely absurd, gave His Son to die for us. He not only had mercy on us (not giving us the punishment we deserve—hell), but He was unfathomably gracious (giving us what we do not deserve—a new life with Him). I do not understand why and probably never will this side of heaven. But I am so thankful for it.

Israel had already experienced striking displays of grace in their journey thus far, and they did not respond well to them, as we saw in the last chapter. Nevertheless, God kept pouring it out over them. He kept providing for them despite their guilt, and my prayer is that our "grace and mercy gauges" are filled up a bit more after exploring this next passage.

Exodus 16:9-21

> **Then Moses said to Aaron, "Say to all the congregation of the sons of Israel, "Come near before the Lord, for He has heard your grumblings." It came about as Aaron spoke to the whole congregation of the sons of Israel, that they looked toward the wilderness, and behold, the glory of the Lord appeared in the cloud. And the Lord spoke to Moses, saying, "I have heard the grumblings of the sons of Israel; speak to them, saying, 'At twilight you shall eat meat, and in the morning you shall be filled with bread; and you shall know that I am the Lord your God.'" (16:9-12)**

The last section concluded with Moses telling the people what God would do for them and reminding them that their grumbling was not really against him and Aaron, but rather against God. Israel had failed once again in their faith, choosing to view God through their circumstances instead of viewing their circumstances through their faith in God. They had run out of food and were throwing a tantrum about it. In my "truth and justice" opinion, they deserved to be abandoned in the wilderness for their behavior. Fortunately, God had other plans.

Aaron once again takes on the role as the spokesman to Israel. Moses wanted him to address Israel, and we are not told why. Maybe Moses was flustered and angered by Israel's behavior and just wanted some distance. Perhaps he was just tired, or maybe he was falling back into the rhythm God established at the burning bush—using Aaron as Moses' mouthpiece. If you recall from the first volume, when Moses was afraid of God's call on his life to free Israel from Egypt, one of his excuses was his concern about speaking to the Israelites (the theory is that he had some kind of speech impediment). God graciously gave him an out and told him that his brother, Aaron, would be his spokesperson: "You are to speak to him and put the words in his mouth; and I, even I, will be with your mouth and his mouth, and I will teach you what you are to do" (Exodus 4:15). While Aaron would be the one uttering the words, the words originated with God and had been spoken first to Moses, resembling a prophetic game of telephone.

Moses told Aaron to tell Israel to **come near before the Lord, for He has heard your grumblings.** One commentator notes that this "may contain as much irony as seriousness," and I happen to agree. [160] Someone would have had to be deaf not to hear their whining. It must have been reminiscent of the tantrums that our two-year-old, Jessli, throws on occasion. While we put a swift end to them, no one can deny hearing her in the meantime. How such small lungs and vocal cords are capable of that much sound is truly a mystery. Israel's whining came from hundreds of thousands of people all at once; it had to have been loud. God certainly heard them and now beckoned them to **come near before** Him. This terminology will later be traditionally reserved for people to approach the Lord through the Ark of the Covenant, Tabernacle, or altar; but for now, it references the cloud through which His presence has been most prominently displayed.[161]

Though obvious, coming **near before the Lord** required both movement and intention. Just like the gift of the bread would require Israel's effort to collect it, so too coming before Him required their intentional movement toward the cloud. They needed to get off their behinds, out of their tents, and collectively gather before the Lord to hear what His response to their grumblings would be.

As Aaron continued speaking **to the whole congregation of the sons of Israel, they looked toward the wilderness, and behold, the glory of the Lord appeared in the cloud**. Until this time, the cloud had represented God—a miraculous pillar that led the Israelites from location to location and protected them from their enemies. It also was something that God looked through and used to bring the Egyptian army into confusion (14:24). So, while the cloud was a visible expression of God's presence, it had not represented His appearance until now.

While the Israelites were looking **toward the wilderness... the glory of the Lord appeared in the cloud**. The first mention of God's **glory** was just three verses prior—how the Israelites would "see the glory of the Lord" in the morning when they beheld His provision of food. They were told that they were going to see His **glory**, but it is only now that they actually see it displayed for the first time. To be sure, they had seen of evidence of God's glory before (His weightiness and worthiness) during the plagues and at the sea. But this is the first time they are collectively witnessing a theophany-type glimpse of God's glory, and it was manifested **in the cloud.**

We are not told specifically what His **glory** looked like **in the cloud**, or how it differentiated in appearance from a normal cloud. But later in Exodus, we will be told of another time that God's glory "rested on Mount Sinai," which looked "like a consuming fire on the mountain top" (Exodus 24:16-17). It could have also contained some elements of a strong storm, for when God would "come down on Mount Sinai in the sight of all the people" later in our narrative, we learn that "there were thunder and lightning flashes and a thick cloud upon the mountain and a very loud trumpet sound" (Exodus 19:11,16). So God's glory here in the cloud could have been some combination of a more intense cloud formation with the inclusion of fire and/or storm elements. We do not know exactly how it differed from the cloud that led them by day, but we do know that something about it changed, and that change was obvious and undeniably God's glory to all who looked.

Despite God revealing His glory to the whole congregation of Israel, He still only **spoke to Moses**. The reason for this is not articulated. Perhaps (and likely) the people were simply not ready to hear Him; they were not mature enough in their faith to either discern His voice or hear it. Later on, when Israel looked at God's glory on the mountain, they were terrified and would tell Moses, "Speak to us yourself, and we will listen; but let not God speak to us, or we will die" (Exodus 20:19). It stands to reason, then, that Israel was neither ready nor capable of listening to God directly at this point. Even if they did not realize it yet, Israel needed a human intercessor and prophet to speak to them on God's behalf.

God told Moses once again that He **heard the grumblings of the sons of Israel**. This is the fifth reference to Israel's **grumblings** in nearly as many verses. These references squash any temptation we have to feel pity for the Israelites and think they were not being all that bad. While they had reason to be concerned, they had no valid reason to doubt, question, or grumble against the Lord. They grumbled, presumably loud and often, and God acknowledged that He received the message.

Then He tells Moses to **speak to them, saying, "At twilight you shall eat meat, and in the morning you shall be filled with bread; and you shall know that I am the Lord your God."** While this instruction seems unnecessarily repetitive, it serves several purposes. First, "it addresses directly the people's implied criticism that YHWH is uninterested in them." [162] By repeating His response, God is confirming yet again that He not only sees and hears His people, but also cares enough to take action on their behalf. Further, this reiterates the point "that the Israelites shall know…that Yahweh is trying to establish with all of His actions, and now also with His words of guidance and instruction, His assertation that 'I am Yahweh your God.'"[163] God is no longer a passed down belief of their ancestors. He is their God personally, and they are both capable and expected to know that firsthand.

God providing the Israelites with both meat and bread also reveals the comprehensiveness of His provision, particularly in regard to time. They would go to sleep that evening fully satisfied by the provision of meat and would begin each day thereafter with His blessing of bread to give them energy and stamina throughout the day. While the meat would be a one-time provision, bread would be given constantly and continuously, a rhythmic reminder of His mercy, provision, omnipotence, and love for them as His children. He would not force them to love Him back (just like He does not force us to), but He provided them with more than enough irrefutable proof of not only His existence but also His affection toward them.

By telling them what He was going to do beforehand, God was also making it clear where their provision was coming from. The meat and bread were no more coincidences than the plagues were against the Egyptians. God articulated numerous times how He was going to provide, so there was no doubt about the provisions' origin. Israel would **know** beyond a shadow of a doubt that God is who He claims to be.

> **So it came about at evening that the quails came up and covered the camp and in the morning there was a layer of dew around the camp. When the layer of dew evaporated, behold, on the surface of the wilderness there was a fine flake-like thing, fine as the frost on the ground. When the sons of Israel saw it, they said to one another, "What is it?" For they did not know what it was. And Moses said to them, "It is the bread which the Lord has given to you to eat." (16:13-15)**

Everything seems more dramatic at night. My dad always used to tell us that nothing good ever happens after midnight, and while I do not entirely agree (lots of babies are born after midnight, for example), I understand what he meant. Emotions run higher in the evenings, and everything seems more dramatic at night than it does when morning comes. I cannot tell you how many awful nights of sleep I have had consumed by those "2am moments"—waking up worrying, thinking, and consumed with something that mattered very little during the light of day. We so easily get worked up in the evening, only to regret it when the sun breaks over the horizon.

While speculative, it seems fitting that God provided meat that night to calm the nerves of His people so they could avoid another frenzied evening of anxiety. Nerves had been on edge for days, and another night of waiting for provision could have wreaked far more havoc on their already frazzled hearts. So God provided first at night. He made it so **that the quails came up and covered the camp**.

> [Quails] migrate in vast flocks from central Europe to Africa in the autumn and return in the spring. They are small in size and make the long and tiring journey in stages. Flying low and landing exhausted, they are easily captured with nets or by hand...The tender meat of the baby quail is regarded as a great delicacy. It requires no oil for cooking and is speedily prepared over a hot flame. [164]

Israel received their meat without having to work very hard for it and ate to their fill that evening. Stress and anxieties were eased as they lay down to rest with full bellies. Further, it is likely they were able to rest better with full bellies than not. If you have ever tried to go to sleep while you are hungry, you know it is not always easy, and sleep is not always restful. I struggled with anorexia for years, and one of the side effects was insomnia. It is so difficult to sleep well when your body is not nourished. Israel had been running low on food for at least several days. Perhaps they had rationed it out to make it last longer, eating less and less every day. Regardless, it is likely they had not had fully satisfied bellies for a bit, so the gift of a good night's sleep on full bellies would have been an extra blessing indeed.

As promised, the next **morning, there was a layer of dew around the camp. When the layer of dew evaporated, behold, on the surface of the wilderness, there was a fine flake-like thing, as fine as the frost on the ground**. Quail may have been explained as purely a natural happenstance, but this bread was unequivocally supernatural. Dew was a naturally occurring phenomenon in the desert, just like it is in many other parts of the world; however, what became visible **when the layer of dew evaporated** had never been seen before.

On the ground was found **a fine flake-like thing, fine as the frost**. A more accurate and literal translation would be, "There on the surface of the wilderness was a crisp substance, thin like frost on the ground," so think less flakes and more like sheets. [165] It is difficult for us to get a comprehensive understanding of what it was like because we have nothing similar to compare it to. Though to be fair, neither did Israel. This was new and miraculous, to the point that **when the sons of Israel saw it, they said to one another, "What is it?" For they did not know what it was.**

Despite seeing it and presumably touching, smelling, and handling it, they had no idea **what it was**. It is a bit humorous picturing hundreds of thousands of people looking at this substance, scratching their heads, and then turning to each other, asking if anyone knew what they were looking at. None of their peers did, of course, because it had never been seen before, which amplifies the miraculous nature of God's provision for them. Credit could be given to no one (and certainly nothing) else because it literally had never existed before now. God became Creator again, just as He did in the Garden of Eden, providing food that His people neither planted nor toiled over in order to consume.

None of the congregation of Israel knew what it was, but their leader did. Moses recognized it and said, **"It is the bread which the Lord has given to you to eat."** The text does not explicitly say this either way, but it seems as though Moses recognized the bread for what it was. He had no need for God to tell him directly. Unlike the millions of other people standing all around him, seeing the same thing he was, Moses viewed the strange flake-like thing through a lens of faith. His spirit recognized the miracle because he had been looking for it with expectation.

Moses' spiritual sight here brings us back to our earlier theory about those who could see the cloud with heightened capacity as it came between the Egyptians and Israelites in 14:19-20. The pillar of cloud that miraculously provided light at night moved from in front of the Israelites to behind them in order to protect them from the Egyptians, which it did all night. Yet, since the Egyptians did not run away in terror, we posed the theory that perhaps the cloud's visibility matched the faith of those who were viewing it. Perhaps it appeared more as a dense fog to the Egyptians—an impediment to their pursuit, to be sure, but not something that would cause them to give up altogether. They were blind to the truth of what it was because they did not have a lens of faith through which they could see the reality of the situation. In a similar manner, it seems that Moses is the only one exercising his lens of faith, for he is the only one said to have recognized this bread for what it was—**bread which the Lord has given to you to eat**.

As a brief application point: which camp do you find yourself in? Do you align more with the Egyptians and Israelites who saw their circumstances with physical eyes and missed the spiritual entirely? Or do you align more with Moses, having developed the habit of putting on a lens of faith so you can recognize miraculous provision when you see it? Do you recognize the miracle, or do you need someone to explain it to you? I am not saying that we should read the hand of God into every minute detail of our lives—that front-row parking spot that opened up just as we drove up, an oddly shaped apple that could possibly bear a resemblance to the stone rolled away from Jesus' tomb, etc. But I am convinced that we miss many a blessing because our eyes are so tuned into this world that we neglect the spiritual one. With both the pillar of cloud and the provision of bread, Moses recognized them for what they were.

And if you have ever recognized God's provision before, you know in part what he must have experienced: a bolster of faith, joy, gratitude, and a strengthened peace, knowing He loves us and is powerful enough to provide in unmatched ways.

After identifying the **bread**, Moses continued instructing the Israelites per God's command:

> **"This is what the Lord has commanded, 'Gather of it every man as much as he should eat; you shall take an omer apiece according to the number of persons each of you has in his tent.'" The sons of Israel did so, and some gathered much and some little. When they measured it with an omer, he who had gathered much had no excess, and he who had gathered little had no lack; every man gathered as much as he should eat. (16:16-18)**

In the last few verses, we have seen God tell Israel what He was going to do, specifically, how He was going to provide for them. But He also instructed them about how they were to respond to His provision. Their numerous incidents of grumbling proved that Israel could not be trusted to respond with any measure of faith or appropriate action, so God gave them clear, step by step instructions on how they were supposed to gather and measure His provision of bread.

To be fair, this was a new substance. Israel could not reasonably know what to do with it. But therein lies a strong point: Israel wanted what they were used to eating in Egypt; God was giving them something totally different to prove Himself as their only source of life and sustenance.[166] God did not give them exactly what they wanted precisely because what they wanted was diametrically opposed to Him. They wanted the comfort of familiarity, even if it came with slavery. God wanted their trust and what was best for them, which meant stripping them of every "comfort" of their past as He formed them as a people for Himself. God was doing far more than meeting a physical need; He was giving them an opportunity to change their desires to match His. He was teaching them how to mature in their faith, which is something they desperately needed.

If they had been faithful and maturely expressed trust in God until this point, God's provision and instruction would read more like gentle guidance here as opposed to a toddler-level explanation of how it was going to work. As we have to remind our daughters, "If you act like a baby, you are going to be treated like one." These verses read similarly. God is telling immature, selfish children exactly what to do and how to act. No, He was not going to give them exactly what they wanted. He was going to answer their need how He wanted to, and they needed to follow His instruction to the letter if they wanted to receive it.

His instruction was simple, yet clear, **"Gather of it every man as much as he should eat; you shall take an omer apiece according to the number of persons each of you has in his tent."** As we have referenced before, God's provision was not enjoyed without effort on humanity's part. God gave them bread miraculously on the ground of the wilderness, but the Israelites had to take action in order to **gather** it. It did not take much effort, but it did take some; they needed to reach out and receive the blessing they had been given.

By all accounts, the terms **man**, **he**, and **his** tent are expressions referring to the general population, not necessarily males specifically. Scripture often refers to or uses male pronouns to represent humanity in general; it is not an affront to females, it is simply the way most of history has communicated. Thus, this verse could easily be translated as, "Each one is to gather as much as he needs. Take an omer for each person you have in your tent." [167] A responsible family member was to collect **as much as he should eat**, as well as **an omer apiece** for each person living with them.

It all sounds quite straightforward until we probe into what an **omer** is, because scholars can only offer educated guesses. Later in verse 36, we will read that "an omer is a tenth of an ephah," but that is the only other time the word **omer** is used as a measuring device in the whole Old Testament. An ephah "was a dry measure frequently mentioned in the Bible. It seems to have been the name of a vessel—a meaning it still had in Zechariah 5:6-10, where it was large enough to contain a person."[168] So a tenth of an ephah would obviously be much smaller, but still significant. It is impossible to know exactly how much an **omer** is, but the reasonable hypothesis of many Bible translations and some scholars is that it was approximately two quarts.[169] Ultimately, it seems to have been a particularly sized bowl/vessel that was common in that day, but has since been lost.

Whatever the exact measurement, Israel knew what it was, and God knew it would be sufficient for each of them per day. Each person was to have an omer's worth collected for him/her for every day (except the day before the Sabbath), and it would be exactly the amount they needed. It is curious that God implemented a measuring system at all. Why wouldn't He just tell them to go out and pick up as much as they wanted? I believe it was an instruction designed to curb their immaturity and prevent conflict. If collecting this food was a "free for all," and people could get as much as they wanted, it would inevitably become a competition. The fastest and strongest would get out there and collect more than they needed, forcing those with less physical stamina to go further and collect less than they needed. By implementing a measuring system, God was leveling the playing field, so to speak. He wanted unity and love to be among His people, eliminating even the possibility of competition from the start.

Further, having a measuring system, especially one that distributed the same amount to everyone equally, reveals God's continued miraculous provision. A strong, robust thirty-year old man eats much more than a four-year-old little girl. But God makes no distinction, which again contradicts what Israel thought they needed. They wanted the food they were used to eating in Egypt; God provided them with a mystery bread they had never seen before. They would naturally collect different amounts depending on age, gender, and/or physical condition; but God said to collect the exact same amount for each person every day. God was making it clear that He alone was their Provider and Sustainer. He was stripping them of their ability to control their circumstances, forcing them to recognize His control over them. It is silly that He had to do that at this point after all they have witnessed of Him in Egypt and thus far in their journey, but alas, it was necessary. Israel had much to learn about God, and by implementing systems like this, He was helping them do so, even if they had yet to recognize it.

To their credit, Israel obeyed God's instruction: **the sons of Israel did so, and some gathered much and some little.** At first, Israel had no idea what they were doing and had no reasonable way to know how much this strange bread would translate into an omer's worth. So they collected what they each thought they should—**some gathered much and some little**. We can give them the benefit of the doubt here, and not assume that those who **gathered much** did so with any ill intent or greedy countenance. It is likely they really just did not have any idea.

But we immediately discover that it did not matter because God leveled the playing field once again: **when they measured it with an omer, he who had gathered much had no excess, and he who had gathered little had no lack; every man gathered as much as he should eat.** This was a miracle within a miracle. God provided this mystery bread, which is miraculous, then tells people to gather and measure it so they only ended up with an omer's worth for each person. We were just told that people did *not* gather the exact same amounts— **some gathered much and some little**, so by all accounts, when they came back to measure it with their omers, there should have been some people discarding a bit while others would need to go out and get a bit more. But that is not what happened. Somehow, God miraculously evened out the amount they each collected before they even got back to their tents to measure it! When they did, the amount they had was exactly what they needed—**he who had gathered much had no excess, and he who had gathered little had no lack; every man gathered as much as he should eat.**

By doing this, "God ensures that everyone receives an ample supply, but discourages those who try to take more than their allocation."[170] This was yet another exercise of trust, even if the Israelites did not yet realize it. They needed to learn how to trust and rely upon God alone to provide them with what they needed. Obedience in only collecting the amount God prescribed was a step of faith each day—trusting that it would be enough, trusting that God knew what they needed more than they did, and trusting that He would supply their needs. Surely, they saw others carrying either more or less than they were back to their tents, so they were able to recognize the miracle of everyone ending up with the same amount. God was inviting the Israelites to lean on Him, and teaching them that He was worthy of their reliance.

God does the same for us in different ways every day. While it may not be revealed through obvious miracles, we bolster our faith and dependence on Him every time we walk in obedience. He honors those acts of obedience with blessings—either material or more often spiritual ones in the form of fruit in our lives (love, joy, peace, gentleness, etc.). Consider an example of obeying by extending kindness. Imagine you have had a stressful day, and to top it off, you forgot to buy a key dinner ingredient. You begrudgingly drag yourself to the car and drive to the store, and are almost hit by another driver who decided texting was more important than focusing on the road. You finally make it to the store, and the exact ingredient you needed is out of stock, so you are forced to think of an alternative. Compounding an already aggravating situation, the grocery store is crowded and you find yourself waiting in an express line behind people who clearly have more than the fifteen items permitted. It's just not your best day. After what seems like hours, it's your turn to check out, and the clerk looks like he's had an even rougher day than you have had. What do you do in this moment? Do you just keep quiet, pay for your groceries, and leave? Or do you say a kind and encouraging word to him, trusting God to use it to brighten his day?

Every time we choose to extend kindness in that situation, not only do we brighten someone else's day, *we* are blessed tremendously. Often after these acts of obedience, our entire perspective shifts and we walk away grateful and full of joy when we were annoyed and bitter before. Obeying God is not always easy, but it is always worth it, and we always reap some kind of blessing when we do. God uses even small and seemingly insignificant moments like this to strengthen our faith and accomplish His purposes. He is worthy of our utmost trust and reliance; recognizing and walking in obedience to that reaps countless benefits in our lives.

Unfortunately, the Israelites still have a way to go before realizing that truth:

> **Moses said to them, "Let no man leave any of it until morning." But they did not listen to Moses, and some left part of it until morning, and it bred worms and became foul; and Moses was angry with them. They gathered it morning by morning, every man as much as he should eat; but when the sun grew hot, it would melt. (16:19-21)**

No doubt inspired by God, Moses instructed the Israelites that they should not **leave any of it until morning**. God made it clear that an omer's worth of this bread would be sufficient to provide every individual with all the nutrition they would need for each day. Perhaps for some, such as children and people who were not feeling well, it was more than they needed. In this case, they would need to toss it out and destroy it at the day's end to ensure nothing was left by morning. But there was another, more likely possibility for this instruction: the Israelites were guilty of hoarding their supply. They likely did not eat as much as they should have because they intentionally wanted to save the bread and make it last as long as possible.

In one way, this is understandable. They had started out with a bunch of supplies from Egypt and needed to ration their food to make it last, especially in the past few days when they were running desperately low. So, it is understandable that they were still operating with a survival mentality, eating the bare minimum to ensure they had enough for the following day.

However, God did not call them to merely survive; His provision was enough to ensure they would thrive. He specifically told them how much to collect and then to eat all of His provision, not leaving any of it until the next day. Doing so would be yet another exercise of trust — consuming all the food even though they knew they had nothing to eat the following day. Except they did know, or at least should have known, that food would be provided the next day because God told them He would. All they needed to do was trust and obey, eat what God had provided, and trust Him to do so again. But... they didn't.

They did not listen to Moses, and some left part of it until morning. First, it needs to be clarified that only some of the Israelites did not listen or obey. This is actually progress because until this point, their grumbling and lack of faith has been expressed collectively — they all were guilty of it. Now, even that was a bit of a generalization because we know at least two people did not join in on their ungrateful whining sprees, Moses and Aaron. It is possible (and I would certainly like to believe) that there were at least a handful of others who remained faithful as well. But if a remnant did exist, it was too small to make special note of in previous passages. The Israelites were collectively grouped as guilty of grumbling and disbelief.

But here we are told that only **some** of the people disobeyed and **left part of it until morning**, which means that most did obey and ate God's provision. While that is an improvement, it is still not great. Disobedience is like a poison; it does not take much to negatively impact a whole community of people. Some kept bread overnight, and unsurprisingly, things did not go as expected. They were not able to eat the bread the next day because **it bred worms and became foul**. It takes a special kind of starvation to even think about consuming worm-ridden and malodorous food, and Israel was not there. The bread that had filled their bellies and met every nutritional need the day before had become foul to the point of repulsing their senses today. What was appealing was now repulsive.

Any hope of sneaking around God were dashed, and somehow Moses became aware of the transgression. We are not told how he found out, especially if only some of the people disobeyed by keeping it until the next morning. I can almost imagine one of the faithless approaching him, whining that their bread had turned foul: "Can you believe this?! Why did it go bad? I am hungry!" It is like when one of our daughters cannot find a particular outfit after not putting it back where it belongs, then acting appalled that it is not there (not like that has ever happened... in the past two hours anyway). The point here is that some of the Israelites were so immature and childish in their faith, they very likely went complaining to Moses about their worm-ridden bread. Even worse, they perhaps expected him to pity them.

He, however, did not. **Moses was angry with them**, first because they disobeyed and then because they seemed to be unashamed of their disobedience. God had just shown them overwhelming mercy and grace with the provision of quail and manna; how dare they proverbially slap Him in the face by blatant disobedience? Moses' anger is understandable and justified. Like a parent of a defiant child, he was losing his patience.

In this response, Moses shows us a couple of points worth considering. First, anger is morally neutral in itself. We typically associate anger with sin because of how we usually act in our anger. But there is such a thing as righteous anger, and we see examples of it throughout Scripture, particularly when Jesus overturned tables at the Temple. People had made the house of worship into a house of profit, and He was angry at their lack of reverence. His anger was justified and righteous, just as Moses' was over the Israelites' disobedience.

Moses did not lash out in his anger; he did not punish them or scold them (at least, there is no written record of it). He did what most of us should do in similar circumstances—he held his tongue and left it to God. While there are certainly times when we should speak up and discipline those under our charge, there are also times when we need to be silent and let God be the judge. Moses was following God's lead here. Even though he probably wanted to yell at the Israelites, he held his tongue because God did not tell him to do otherwise.

So the Israelites continued gathering the bread morning by morning, **every man gathering as much as he should eat**. As each day went by, they likely became better at gathering only what they needed. They would have gotten a feel for how much they needed; the omer as a measuring tool would become less and less necessary.

We learn another fact about this mystery bread in the following statement: **when the sun grows hot, it melts.** This could have been true from the start, or God could have caused it to be so after the greed of some Israelites became evident. Regardless, this bread was not an all-day buffet the Israelites could be lazy about. They needed to get up and collect it before **the sun grew hot**; otherwise, they would be out of luck because **it would melt.**

God's provision was sufficient, but not excessive. It was bountiful, but not boundless. God supplied Israel's needs within the parameters of instruction that He expected them to obey. This section began with a reminder that God heard Israel's grumblings and ended with them acting within the parameters He set forth for His response. Israel legitimately needed food, but they also legitimately needed to listen to and obey God. Some of them were starting to catch on, but others revealed their distrust in God by hoarding His provision. Yet God, the ever-patient and loving Father, withheld immediate punishment and allowed them to continue partaking in His blessing of food. The wilderness may have been barren to most, but it was a place of flourishing and abundance to God's people. Gathering food every morning according to God's instructions should have reminded them of the power, sufficiency, and love of God. Their faith should have grown with every morsel of bread they collected.

Exodus 16:22-36

> **Now on the sixth day they gathered twice as much bread, two omers for each one. When all the leaders of the congregation came and told Moses, then he said to them, "This is what the Lord meant: Tomorrow is a sabbath observance, a holy sabbath to the Lord. Bake what you will bake and boil what you will boil, and all that is left over put aside to be kept until morning." (16:22-23)**

Two main theories shape this text. First, some suggest that Israel unintentionally gathered twice as much as they needed every other day.[171] Israel did not know about the instruction to gather more because God had only revealed that to Moses, not to the entire Israelite community in 16:5. Thus, when Israel came back to measure their bread collection against the omer, the amount yielded two omers full and not just one. Under this theory, Israel was a somewhat complacent bystander in yet another miracle of God. Whereas He miraculously provided one omer previously, regardless of how much people were gathering from the ground, He now made it so that the amount gathered was exactly doubled. While this theory is possible, it is not likely. Just because Scripture does not specify that Moses told the Israelites about the double-portion gathering on the sixth day does not mean that he did not do so. That is an argument from silence, and while theoretically possible, it is not the most responsible interpretation of this text.

The second (and more likely) theory is that the Israelites had been instructed by Moses to gather **twice as much bread** on **the sixth day of the week** earlier, and doing so here was an act of obedience. They obeyed when the sixth day came and gathered double what they did on other days — two omers for each one. It is likely that God miraculously allowed the amounts to be equal as He did on previous days, but the Israelites were still acting compliantly and trying to gather two omers full of bread. Acting within the parameters God set forth for them reveals a growing trust in the Lord. Granted, it was not a challenging task. Gathering more than what was needed played to their concept of self-preservation and to some, their greed. Nonetheless, they obeyed, and when they did, **all the leaders of the congregation came and told Moses.**

Lest we forget, communication back then was limited to word of mouth, so it was slow. They did not have phones or the internet to spread word quickly; they had to tell someone, who told someone else, etc. Well, Israel had wisely established leadership within its community, a concept that we were introduced to much earlier in Exodus when Moses approached the Israelite leaders before going to Pharaoh (Exodus 4:29). The leaders of Israel acted as judges, counselors, and guides to the Israelite people. While Moses became the primary leader during the Exodus, Israel still had secondary leaders, and it was these men who **came and told Moses** that Israel had obeyed. They had gathered twice as much as on previous days, and now were curious about what they were supposed to do with it.

While Israel had likely been instructed to gather more bread, they had not been told why. The leaders came to Moses to find that out. Moses told them, **"This is what the Lord meant: Tomorrow is a sabbath observance, a holy sabbath to the Lord."** This is the first time the word **sabbath** is mentioned in Scripture, and the first time the Israelites were hearing about it. While God had foreshadowed the sabbath in the creation account (creating the universe in six days and then resting on the seventh), the concept had not trickled down into any kind of practice within the Israelite community. But that changed in this moment. Israel was now free from Egypt and at the beginning stages of being their own nation. God was establishing Himself as their King and revealing the sabbath as a way they could follow Him.

Obviously, the sabbath day would become a crucial observance to the Israelites and would soon be revealed as one of the Ten Commandments. But for now, the Israelites received a brief introduction to the concept. The seventh day would be **a sabbath observance, a holy sabbath to the Lord.** The word **sabbath** means "stoppage," which is an accurate portrayal of what the Israelites would be instructed to do on the sabbath day—intentionally discontinuing all voluntary work.[172] Observing the sabbath would mean rest from work, and "gathering food was the most basic sort of work anyone did in the ancient world," so gathering bread would hardly be appropriate.[173]

After gathering a double portion on the sixth day, Israel was to "**Bake what you will bake and boil what you will boil, and all that is left over put aside to be kept until morning.**" Numbers 11:8 provides a more detailed description of how the Israelites prepared the bread: "The people would go about and gather it and grind it between two millstones or beat it in the mortar, and boil it in the pot and make cakes with it, and its taste was as the taste of cakes baked with oil." Apparently, this bread was pretty easy to handle, and the Israelites had more than one option for how they prepared it. So, Moses told them to prepare and eat it like they normally would on the sixth day, and anything that was left should be **put aside to be kept until morning**.

> So, they put it aside until morning, as Moses had ordered, and it did not become foul nor was there any worm in it. Moses said, "Eat it today, for today is a sabbath to the Lord; today you will not find it in the field. Six days you shall gather it, but on the seventh day, the sabbath, there will be none." (16:24-26)

Continuing their fresh trend of obedience, Israel **put it aside until morning, as Moses had ordered**. This was, again, a rather easy request to follow because they had eaten their fill the day before and simply put away (instead of discarded) the rest. As a brief aside, we should be thankful for easy opportunities to obey! Walking in obedience to Christ can be challenging, but there are many occasions each day where compliance with His Word is sweet and enjoyable. Being present with your children as they play and giggle, working hard in a job you love, bringing cookies to the widow who lives next door to brighten her day—there are countless ways to bring Him honor that are pleasing and not difficult. All Israel had to do to obey here was put the bread **aside until morning**. It was not difficult, but it was pleasing to the Lord.

Unlike when they tried to hoard the bread a few days earlier and it became gross, this time **it did not become foul, nor was there any worm in it**. I am not the kind of person who looks for miracles in everything, but this absolutely was miraculous. On literally every other day except the eve of the Sabbath, any bread that had been kept over would rot and be infested with worms. It had quite a short shelf-life, which aided Israel's obedience (why keep something that you know would be rotten by morning?). But as the Sabbath dawned, they found their bread just as good as the day before. God had miraculously preserved it and confirmed once again His sovereignty and provision.

Moses continued God's instruction: **"Eat it today, for today is a sabbath to the Lord; today you will not find it in the field. Six days you shall gather it, but on the seventh day, the Sabbath, there will be none."** Not only would God miraculously preserve the leftovers from the day before, but He also would not provide the bread on the Sabbath. While this may seem obvious, it is yet another feature of His power. Every single other day, Israel would find bread in the field of the wilderness, just waiting to be collected. It is not as if the bread was available every day, and Israel was simply instructed not to collect it on the Sabbath. God removed the temptation entirely; there would be no bread at all available to them on the seventh day.

I am excited for heaven for countless reasons, and one of them is to hopefully be able to discover all the ways God worked in our lives while we remained completely oblivious to it. My husband and I often joke that our youngest daughter has a heftier allotment of angels protecting her because she comes close to serious injury far more often than any of our other girls did. Near-misses with head collisions against concrete, carelessness with flights of stairs (when she sneaks around our watchful eyes), adamantly walking forward while looking backward— all these and more lead to times that could have been her end. Despite constant supervision, she still manages to do dumb things, for which we are ever grateful for God's intervention and protection in her life.

Part of that protection, of course, is our supervision. When I see her about to walk into a wall, I either scoop her up or yell her name so she stops. When we observe her getting close to a flight of stairs, we stop everything and remove her from the situation. That is what God did for the Israelites by not providing them bread on the Sabbath morning. He removed the temptation entirely, so it was impossible for them to disobey Him and subsequently get hurt. And make no mistake, disobedience to God always results in our hurt. We may not realize it, but we are always worse off for disobeying God than we are for submitting to Him. Praise Him for sovereignly removing temptations so we do not even have to make that choice sometimes!

Israel now knew what and why they were to collect twice as much bread on the sixth day compared to any other day. They were fully informed, which, frankly, is another blessing in itself. There are many times in our lives when we are called to obey without being informed of why, but Israel had all the knowledge they needed to comply with God's command rather effortlessly. Unfortunately, their nice little streak of obedience did not last.

> **It came about on the seventh day that some of the people went out to gather, but they found none. Then the Lord said to Moses, "How long do you refuse to keep My commandments and My instructions? See, the Lord has given you the sabbath; therefore He gives you bread for two days on the sixth day. Remain every man in his place; let no man go out of his place on the seventh day." So the people rested on the seventh day. (16:27-30)**

Despite being told there would be no bread, **some of the people went out to gather** it on the Sabbath morning. I do wonder what was going through their heads. It cannot be that they forgot—gathering bread was still a new practice that had hardly had enough time to develop into a habit. No, it was a willing and intentional disobedience. They had both the command and the reason behind it, yet they still deliberately went out to collect something that God said would not be there.

The glimmer of good news is that once again, it was only **some of the people** who disobeyed; it was not the entirety of the congregation. But those who did transgress revealed the not-so-good news that their hearts were in a worse place than what we thought. Disobeying such a simple command reveals that "they cannot trust Yahweh to care for them; their disobedience is a rebellious rejection of the wisdom and goodness of his rulership over them."[174] They have never willingly followed a ruler before. Pharaoh's rulership over them was both forced and unwelcome. But despite God's countless ways of providing for them and showing them He could be trusted, some of them still refused to believe Him. They refused to trust and comply; they continued thinking only of themselves and prioritizing their self-perceived needs over His tried-and-true truth.

When those Israelites went out to gather bread, they obviously **found none**. I am not sure if this was a surprise (it certainly should not have been). We are not told how they responded, but that is not the point. The point is that they should not have even put themselves in a position to find out. They should have obeyed and remained where they were, content with the supplies they had been given the day before. Which brings up another point—why did they go out at all? They had everything they needed! They had plentiful bread leftover from the day before to feed themselves and their families; why would some of them go look for more? We can only speculate, but in the end, it is just flagrant disobedience. Despite having what they needed and being told not to, they disobeyed and went out for more.

Acting like children resulted in a scolding appropriate for children: **"How long do you refuse to keep My commandments and My instructions?"** God spoke this to Moses, but it was directed through Moses to the guilty Israelites. The necessity of this question is a sad commentary for people who were supposed to be God's people. But we also see a depressing irony within it. Only six chapters previously, God asked a similar question to Pharaoh through Moses: "How long will you refuse to humble yourself before Me?" (10:3). The Israelites are indirectly being compared with Pharaoh. The insolent authority they detested in Egypt is one they have now become. Both refused to submit themselves to God, both refused to obey His commands.

In the Bible study time of our homeschooling, the girls and I are currently talking about submission. It is an unpopular term and concept in our culture, but it is a beautiful aspect of Christianity that applies to everyone who bears the name of Christ. Submission is a willful yielding to another's authority, in our case, the Lord's as articulated through Scripture. Submission is a concept loaded with nuances and applications, from humility and acknowledgment of depravity to gratefulness in joining God's gospel work. As I often tell our daughters, it is not always (or even often) easy to submit to God's rule in our lives, but it is always worth it. Our lives are always full of peace, joy, patience, contentment, kindness, and more when we actively yield to His authority instead of trying to impose our misguided idea of authority upon Him.

The disobedient group of Israelites did not understand this. They kept bucking at the idea of a ruler being over them, despite God showing them over and over again what a gracious and loving Ruler He was. Did God actually expect them to answer His question of how long they refuse to keep His commandments? No. But He was reminding them to listen. They were not in control, nor did they have all the information.

They were responsible for what they did know—which was to observe a sabbath day of rest: **"See, the Lord has given you the sabbath; therefore, He gives you bread for two days on the sixth day. Remain every man in his place; let no man go out of his place on the seventh day."** God reiterated what He already told them, because, like children, they did not listen the first time. The deeper irony in all of this was that God was doing them a favor. Observing a sabbath day of rest is a gift! Countless studies have shown the importance of rest. It is not just something that is good to have every once in a long while; we need it regularly. Our bodies, minds, emotions, and souls need rest to function properly and thrive in accordance with how God created us. Therefore, by not listening to God, the Israelites were literally harming themselves.

Furthermore, the Israelites, of all people, needed extra rest. They had been slaves for four hundred years! They had been at the beck and call of their

227

Egyptian slave masters, doing whatever was asked of them, lest they be beaten into submission. We do not know how much, if any, regulated rest was observed in Egyptian culture of that day. But judging by how foreign the concept was to the Israelites (and using common sense), it is likely that rest was not a consistent part of the slavery they endured. Thus, God was quite literally giving them a much-needed gift with the observance of the S=sabbath. Yet, being distrusting, some of the Israelites were too dense to realize it.

The Israelites finally got the hint, some through obedience upfront, and others by not being able to collect bread because it was not there. Eventually, **the people finally rested on the seventh day**. This whole experience was akin to forcing someone to accept a gift that would benefit them tremendously. It reminds me of a conversation we occasionally have with one of our younger daughters. One of them will be acting up, not listening, and totally discontent with life at the moment. But one look at her red, swollen eyes reveals the culprit: she is exhausted. But has a child ever said that he/she *wanted* to go to bed? Of course not. So we have to (sternly at times) tell her it is time for bed and remove the choice. We obviously cannot force her to fall asleep, but we can instruct her to, explain why, and craft the environment to make it possible. It is very similar to what God did for the Israelites. He told them what to do, explained why to do it, and then took away the temptation of disobedience by not providing bread. Some, of course, still disobeyed, but God did everything He could to give them what they needed regardless of their receptivity to the gift.

> **The house of Israel named it manna, and it was like coriander seed, white, and its taste was like wafers with honey. (16:31)**

We are now finally told what the Israelites called the bread—**manna**. There is some disagreement among scholars about the origin of the term **manna**. Some believe the Israelites made up the name for it; others believe it was already a known term, and they simply adapted it to this miraculous bread. It hardly matters; **manna** is what they settled on, and it is what it would be referred to forever in Scripture.

The first description we received was that **it was like coriander seed, white**. Like much else in Scripture, there is quite a varying range of interpretations for this little note. One commentator believes that only the color is being addressed in this comparison. In other words, the only way that manna was like coriander seed was the fact that it was white.[175] However, coriander seeds are naturally brown, so others suggest that the comparison to coriander has nothing to do with color, but rather to its shape and size.[176] We were already told in Verse 14 that manna looked like frost, which is consistent with the color white. So its comparison to coriander most probably means "that the individual pieces of manna might have looked like small grains."[177]

Coriander seed is only mentioned twice in Scripture, and both instances directly reference and compare it to manna. The reference in Numbers 11:7 offers a small clarifying detail, namely, that "its appearance [was] like that of bdellium." Bdellium is "a transparent, yellow-ish gum-resin derived from a tree,"[178] so apparently, manna looked like that in some regard, only white. So we are left with a bit of a mystery. We know it was white, appeared like frost when the morning dew melted, and was flaky. Beyond that, we will just have to wait until we get to heaven to find out for sure.

While the color is helpful to know, the far more fascinating description of manna is how it tasted: **like wafers with honey**. **Wafers** were not nearly as common as bread and were basically thin cookies.[179] Similarly, **honey** was rare since it had to be found and collected in the wild (bee farms did not exist yet). Back in those days, processed sugar was not a thing. People sweeten their food in one of two ways: with fruit or honey.[180] It is unlikely, therefore, that the majority of the Israelites had ever tasted either **wafers** or **honey** during their slavery in Egypt, much less wafers made or garnished with honey. I love how one commentator describes how it tasted: **like wafers with honey** "was tantamount to saying that it was "the most delicious food imaginable."[181] In other words, God did not just provide food; He provided the best-tasting food that the Israelites had probably ever eaten. He gave them both what they needed and what they did not even know they wanted.

> **Then Moses said, "This is what the Lord has commanded, 'Let an omerful of it be kept throughout your generations, that they may see the bread that I fed you in the wilderness, when I brought you out of the land of Egypt.'" Moses said to Aaron, "Take a jar and put an omerful of manna in it, and place it before the Lord to be kept throughout your generations." (16:32-33)**

God wanted His provision of manna to be remembered and instructed that **an omerful of it be kept throughout your generations**. This memorial would serve to remind the Israelites that God was the one who **fed** them **in the wilderness** after He **brought** them **out of the land of Egypt.** The amount that was to be kept is no coincidence: **an omerful** was the amount each Israelite was given every day, personalizing this memorial. God took care of His people not just on a corporate and national level, but also individually. Not one Israelite was left behind either at the sea or as they gathered manna from the wilderness ground. Faith is both personal and corporate, and this memorial would exemplify both aspects for **generations** to come.

While Moses and Aaron would be the ones to set an omerful of manna aside, it must be remembered that God was the one miraculously preserving it. Again, manna lasted less than twenty-four hours five days a week, and only forty-eight on the sixth day of every week. It was a perishable item. But God would miraculously preserve this specific omerful for years so the Israelites could remember His provision. **Throughout** their **generations,** they would be able to **see the bread that** God fed them **in the wilderness** after He brought them **out of the land of Egypt.** It is therefore likely that at least occasionally, the manna would be taken out of the jar for the Israelites to see.[182] Children born in the Promised Land would be able to see the manna their parents and grandparents ate in the wilderness, and mediate upon God's provision for His people.

Through Moses, God instructed Aaron to **take a jar and put and put an omerful of manna in it.** We were not told what kind of jar it should be, but it does not matter. Not even the most air-tight jar could have preserved the manna. God would preserve it, and it was to be placed **before the Lord to be kept throughout** the **generations**. At this time, no official place of worship had been constructed. God's presence among His people was primarily through the pillar of cloud and fire as He led them. So perhaps the jar of manna stayed close to it and/or close to Moses and Aaron, since they were the ones closest to the Lord at this time.

> **As the Lord commanded Moses, so Aaron placed it before the Testimony, to be kept. The sons of Israel ate the manna for forty years, until they came to an inhabited land; they ate the manna until they came to the border of the land of Canaan. (Now an omer is a tenth of an ephah.) (16:34-36)**

Because Scripture was not written in real-time, occasionally, we see breaks in the narrative that were added to update the reader on what transpired. This is likely true of the verses above. Either Moses included it prophetically as directed by God, or Joshua (Israel's next leader) added it later per God's instruction. It is not relevant who penned it, we should just be grateful to have it.

In these verses, we first learn that God told Moses and Aaron to place the jar of manna **before the Testimony, to be kept**. The **Testimony** refers to the Ark of the Covenant, which would be built months after this moment in the wilderness. The Ark of the Covenant within the Tabernacle would eventually replace the pillar of cloud and fire as a representation of God's presence among His people. The manna would have a permanent place with the manifest presence of God, symbolizing its utmost importance as a memorial. Seeing the manna (which physically fed the Israelites) would remind them that their faith needed to be nourished as well. Manna could no more be separated from association with God than the plagues against Egypt could. It was a miraculous provision for His people, and they needed to meditate on it in order to nourish their souls for generations to come.

We next learn that **the sons of Israel ate the manna for forty years**. Those familiar with the narrative know the reason why the Israelites were in the wilderness **for forty years**. Familiarity tends to dull our minds, so I would like to pause to remind us that Israel was never supposed to be in the wilderness for that long. We have no idea how long the journey from Egypt to the Promised Land was supposed to take, but we know for a fact it was supposed to be much shorter than forty years. Israel's continued disobedience and persistent preoccupation with the chains of sin resulted in the consequence of an entire generation passing away in the wilderness. That generation would never see the Promised Land. Yet God did not abandon them in the wilderness in the meantime. He continued to provide manna for them and their children, supplying their every need day in and day out.

Eventually, **they came to an inhabited land; they ate the manna until they came to the border of the land of Canaan.** When they finally entered the Promised Land, God's provision of manna came to an end. God replaced manna with the land—a land they would be responsible for cultivating. Just as they had to make an effort to collect the manna from the wilderness, they would then need to work the land that God had given them. The overarching point here is that despite Israel's constant rebellion, God's care for them never ceased.[183] He remained faithful even in the face of their unfaithfulness, and He remained constant despite their fickleness.

Hebrews 13:8 says, "Jesus Christ is the same yesterday, today, and forever." He was faithful to the Israelites and remains faithful to us as His children, despite our many faults. Oh, how we should praise Him! Just as with Israel, He provides for our every need and goes far beyond what we could ever ask for or imagine. The question is not, "Is He faithful?" The question is, "Are we seeing His faithfulness and praising Him in response?" The people of Israel were still infants in their faith at this point. They did not fully trust God or humble themselves in obedience to His instructions.

If you are young in your faith, I encourage you to keep pressing on. For every Christian, young and old, we must strive to look for God's faithfulness in our lives. We must choose to focus on His provision more than what we lack. We must choose praise over grumbling, trust over doubt. We must fully embrace the freedom He gives us in Christ instead of continuing to wear the chains of sin that burdened us before accepting Him. He is faithful, my friends. May we always concentrate on that and allow our praise to shape our worldview.

The last verse in this section may seem a bit out of place, but it does provide us with an important detail: "**Now, an omer is a tenth of an ephah.**" We discussed this when we covered verses 16 and 18 earlier in this chapter. Just as a quick reminder, an omer was approximately two quarts, which was **a tenth of an ephah**. This sentence was probably included because, at the time of writing (or years later when a scribe added it), people were more familiar with an ephah than with an omer. Neither has any direct relevance to us in modern times, but I am always thankful when God includes extra details that make His Word easier to understand.

Thus concludes our current section from 16:22-36. The most prominent and important concept introduced in this text was the institution of the sabbath. The Israelites had legitimate needs during their time in the wilderness. The most obvious need was food, which God supplied with manna. They had no way to provide enough food for themselves, considering they numbered nearly two million people! But God provided and did so with flair, giving them bread that was as luxurious in taste as it was nutritionally satisfying.

The crux of this passage does not stem from what Israel knew they needed but from what they did not realize they needed: rest. They had been working hard at nearly a constant pace for the last 400 years as slaves in Egypt. Their schedules were dictated to them, and it is highly doubtful that they had any consistent periods of rest. Slaves are not typically allowed to take vacation days. Though it is impossible to know for sure, the only times they might have been able to rest were when they were sick, injured, or perhaps needed to care for someone who was. Regardless, they were clueless about their need for rest, but God knew. In His miraculous and sovereign provision, He instituted a life rhythm grounded in the creation account and later solidified in the letter of the law: the sabbath. For six days, Israel would work, but on the seventh, they would rest.

This life rhythm would continue for generations, as well as their reminder of God's provision of manna by keeping an omerful near God's manifest presence among them. God was making it clear that He alone knew what His people needed, He alone could provide for them abundantly, and He alone was worthy of all their praise for it. The Israelites still had a lot to learn, but He was doing everything possible to set them on a healthy and vibrant track of faith.

Summary

As the well-known hymn declares, God's grace is truly amazing. These passages both began and ended with grace. God **heard** Israel's grumblings, and instead of punishing them for it, He graciously appeared in the cloud and spoke to them through Moses. He told them they would **eat meat** that evening, **and they would be filled with bread in the morning**. They deserved to go hungry, yet God filled them with food and a reminder that they would **know** that He was God, and gracious at that.

As expected, that evening, **quails came up and covered the camp**. The Israelites ate to their full that night. We do not know the last time they were truly full. They likely had been rationing the food they brought with them from Egypt to make it last as long as possible. But on this night, they ate as much as they wanted. I bet they slept well, knowing their bellies were full and that God was providing for them.

When they woke up the next **morning, there was a layer of dew around the camp**. When it **evaporated, behold, on the surface of the wilderness, there was a fine, flake-like substance, as fine as the frost on the ground**. Israel had never seen anything like it before, and they had no idea what it was, as they asked each other, **"What is it?"** This must have been quite a sight among nearly two million people. But Moses knew exactly what it was, for he had been looking for the fulfillment of God's promise. His faith allowed him to recognize it for what it was, and he declared, **"It is the bread that the Lord has given you to eat."** God supplied yet another gracious provision to His people.

Moses further explained God's commands regarding the bread. The Israelites were to go out and gather it, taking **an omer apiece according to the number of persons in each of** their families. An omer was some sort of ancient measuring device, likely a specific-sized jar that could be consistently replicated. While we do not know the exact amount, scholars estimate that it was approximately equivalent to two quarts.

God's provisions continued. The Israelites obeyed and went out to gather this mystery bread—**some gathered much, and some little**. While this may have been due to greediness on the part of those who **gathered much**, I am inclined to give them the benefit of the doubt since they had never done it before and needed to go back to measure how much they had collected. Miraculously, **when they measured it with an omer, those who had gathered much had no excess, and those who had gathered little had no lack; every person gathered as much as they should eat**. God miraculously adjusted the amounts they brought in to equal exactly an omerful, regardless of how much they had collected. What a blessing!

Israel then received further instructions from Moses: they were not to **leave any of it until morning**. They were supposed to discard any that had not been used that day. Unfortunately, **they did not listen to Moses, and some left part of it until morning**. The somewhat good news is that we are told only **some** of them disobeyed, which is quite an improvement from the whole congregation whining as they did at Marah and in the wilderness of Sin. But it is still disappointing, and the result was that the bread **bred worms and became foul, and Moses was angry with them**. To Moses' credit, he kept his anger under control. We are not told how he responded (if he did at all), but from that day forward, **they gathered it morning by morning, every person as much as they should eat**. Then we learned that they had to collect it first thing in the morning because **it would melt when the sun grew hot**.

They had presumably gotten the hang of it, but needed one more word of instruction, particularly for the sixth day of the week. Israel was told to gather **twice as much bread, two omers for each one,** on the sixth day. Moses then told them why: **"Tomorrow is a sabbath observance, a holy sabbath to the Lord."** They should eat their portion for Friday, and **all that is left over put aside to be kept until morning**. Israel obeyed, and sure enough, the bread **did not become foul, nor was there any worm in it**. This was yet another miracle, another direct gift of God's grace.

Moses also warned Israel that there would be no bread on the seventh day, which further proved they needed to collect a double portion on the sixth. Unfortunately, **it came about on the seventh day that some of the people went out to gather, but they found none**. Again, it was only **some of the people**, but their lack of faith and frankly, outright disobedience was still grievously disappointing. God responded to Moses, asking, **"How long do you refuse to keep My commandments and My instructions?"** He was referring to those who had disobeyed, not Moses himself, but it still must have stung. Leaders want those under their charge to be the object of God's approval and praise, not discipline and disappointment.

After presumably another lecture, something clicked, **and the people rested on the seventh day**. Then the people named the bread **manna, and it was like coriander seed, white, and its taste was like wafers with honey**. We do not have much context to understand what that means, but to them, it was the most luxurious food they had ever tasted. They had been slaves their entire lives, and sweet foods were reserved for the wealthy. They likely had never tasted anything so good, which reveals yet another facet of God's grace. He did not just provide them with the basics of what they needed. He could have given them dry, crusty bread and told them to deal with it, especially after the attitude they had displayed earlier. But He did not. He provided them with lavish bread to confirm His lavish grace.

The last command that God gave Moses regarding the manna was to "**let an omerful of it be kept throughout your generations, that they may see the bread that I fed you in the wilderness, when I brought you out of the land of Egypt.**" God wanted them to remember His lavish grace and miracles displayed through the manna, and this was how He wanted it done. So Moses obediently complied. He told Aaron to **take a jar, put an omerful of manna in it, and place it before the Lord to be kept throughout your generations.** Aaron did so. God would miraculously preserve the manna in this jar, just like He miraculously preserved His people in the wilderness who could not even meet their most basic needs.

Concluding these passages is a note about the size of an omer, and, more importantly, another revelation of the breadth of God's provision: **the sons of Israel ate the manna for forty years, until they reached an inhabited land**. God provided manna for them six days a week, every week, for forty years. It always amounted to exactly what they needed—never too little, and never too much. Their wilderness experience was literal but also represented far more profound truths. One of them shone brightly in these passages: as they traveled through their wilderness of faith, they were never far from the oases of God's grace.

GROUP STUDY

Introduction

Grace pours living water on the barren earth of our souls.

As Christians, we've all been recipients of grace (receiving something we don't deserve) through the gospel. We deserve hell, but in Christ, we receive eternity with Him instead. He saves us, redeems us, sanctifies us, and unites our hearts with His. Realizing this truth makes our souls exhale deeply with relief and leap with elation. And if that isn't enough, He continues to bestow grace-filled blessings in our lives every day.

- In what ways have you been the recipient of grace lately?
- Have you been able to extend grace to someone else recently? Share about the experience if so.

The Word

Israel quickly revealed their immaturity in faith. Their immediate reaction to trials in their short time of freedom was to whine, grumble, and complain. Like a toddler throwing a tantrum, they deserved swift punishment. But God extended them grace upon grace. Instead of figuratively whooping their backsides, He literally filled their bellies. He provided them with quail to eat that evening and a whole new experience of bread the next morning:

> **In the morning, there was a layer of dew around the camp. When the layer of dew evaporated, behold, on the surface of the wilderness there was a fine flake-like thing, fine as the frost on the ground. When the sons of Israel saw it, they said to one another, "What is it?" For they did not know what it was. And Moses said to them, "It is the bread which the Lord has given you to eat." (Exodus 16:13-15)**

- What was on the ground in the morning?
  - What was Israel's reaction to it?

- What does Moses' response reveal about his faith that was lacking in the Israelites?

A new kind of bread came with new instructions. Israel didn't know what it was or what to do with it, so God gave them clear instructions to gather an omerful for each person every morning. Then, He miraculously made everyone's collection an omerful—**when they measured it with an omer, he who had gathered much had no excess, and he who had gathered little had no lack; every man gathered as much as he should eat** (Exodus 16:18). God was lavishing His grace upon them, providing miracles even within miracles. Yet Israel still struggled to trust and obey Him.

> **Moses said to them, "Let no man leave any of it until morning." But they did not listen to Moses, and some left part of it until morning, and it bred worms and became foul; and Moses was angry with them. (Exodus 16:19-20)**

> **Moses had told them to collect a double portion the day before the Sabbath. On the Sabbath, Moses said, "Eat it today, for today is a sabbath to the Lord; today you will not find it in the field…it came about on the seventh day that some of the people went out to gather, but they found none. Then the Lord said to Moses, "How long do you refuse to keep My commandments and instructions?" (Exodus 16:25, 27)**

- How did Israel disobey the first time?
  - What was Moses' reaction?
  - What do you think yours would have been?
- How did they disobey the second time?
  - What was God's reaction?

Fortunately for Israel, God's grace surpassed their childish distrust and disobedience. God not only wanted them to learn a lesson through this experience, He wanted them to remember it for generations to come:

Then Moses said, "This is what the Lord has commanded, 'Let an omerful of it be kept throughout your generations, that they may see the bread that I fed you in the wilderness, when I brought you out of the land of Egypt.'" (Exodus 16:32)

- How much manna was to be kept as a memorial?

- What would this remind the Israelites of, along with their future generations?

- Why is it important to remember God's gracious acts towards His people?

Apply

> For of His fullness we have all received,
> and grace upon grace.
> The Apostle John, John 1:16

> And He said to me, "My grace is sufficient for you,
> for power is perfective in weakness."
> Most gladly, therefore, I will rather boast
> about my weaknesses, so that the
> power of Christ may dwell in me.
> The Apostle Paul, Romans 6:1-2

God's grace is something we'll never fully understand, but that doesn't mean we should not try. Israel had a lot to learn, and one of the truths they missed was that His grace invites us to trust Him and live free from sin.

What shall we say then? Are we to continue in sin so that grace may increase? May it never be! How shall we do who died to sin still live in it?...Even so, consider yourselves to be dead to sin, but alive to God in Jesus Christ. Therefore do not let sin reign in your mortal body so that you obey its lusts, and do not go on presenting the members of your body to sin as instruments of unrighteousness; but present yourselves to God as those alive from the dead, and your members as instruments of righteousness to God. For sin shall not be master over you, for you are not under law but under grace. Romans 6:1-2, 11-14

- How should we, as Christians, consider ourselves?
  - Why is that challenging as we face struggles in this world?
- What masters us if we're continually falling into sin?
  - How does grace help us combat that?

The more we understand His grace, especially towards us in Christ, the more amazed we will be by Him, and the more we'll be transformed into His image. It takes effort, but it is absolutely worth it.

One practical habit that helps us focus on His goodness and grace is something I call "perceive and praise." The more we perceive His goodness and grace in our lives, the easier it is to trust, praise, and obey Him. When we start intentionally looking for His grace in our lives and then praise Him for it, we develop a habit of grace-filled worship and will grow leaps and bounds in our faith.

- What are five evidences of grace you can praise Him for right now—both in your life and in the lives of others around you?
- How can you practice "perceive and praise" daily in your life this coming week?

WEEK SIX

Learn From Your Mistakes...Or Not

Exodus 17:1-17:16

PERSONAL BIBLE STUDY QUESTIONS

1. Where did Israel camp next? (17:1)
2. What problem did they run into there? (17:1)
   a. How did the Israelites respond? (17:2-3)
   b. Was their response here better or worse than previously?
3. What was Moses' response? (17:4)
4. What did God tell Moses to do? (17:5-6)
   a. Did Moses obey? (17:6)
5. What did Moses name that place? (17:7)
6. Who came and fought against Israel at Rephidim? (17:8)
7. Who did Moses send out to lead the fight for Israel? (17:9)
   a. What did Moses tell him to do? (17:9)
   b. What did Moses plan to do? (17:9)
8. Who went with Moses up to the top of the hill? (17:10)
9. Israel made advances toward victory as long as Moses did what? (17:11)
10. How did Aaron and Hur assist Moses? (17:12)
    a. How long did they have to do this? (17:12)
11. Who won the battle? (17:13)
12. What did God tell Moses to do after the battle? (17:14)
13. What did Moses do in response to their victory? (17:15)
    a. What did he name it? (17:15)

COMMENTARY

Exodus 17:1-17:16

Knowledge is the accumulation of facts. Wisdom is knowing how to apply facts within proper contexts. Fools practice neither. They are unconcerned with expanding their knowledge and fail to exercise it wisely.

We have all known fools (and have been one at some point in our lives).

Some people lack intelligence. I am not trying to be cruel or unloving, but am merely pointing out an unfortunate reality. Some have not accumulated knowledge beyond the bare minimum of what they need to get by. Perhaps they dropped out of school at an early age, or maybe they just neglected education. Regardless, conversing with them about significant topics is challenging because they lack the ability to think critically. (We still love them and do everything we can to draw them to Christ, however. Our approach just may look different than with others).

Then there are fools who may be knowledgeable, but are just completely unwise. These people may be quite bright—they may have numerous degrees, a high IQ, or perhaps are simply proficient in several subjects. But, for some reason, their intellect never developed into perspective, and they never learned how to apply their knowledge wisely. I have known far more people in this category, people who are brilliant on paper but completely lack wisdom in their lives. For example, I knew a girl in college who was likely a certifiable genius. She excelled in her classes, and I believe she went on to become a doctor. But, mercy, she was unwise. She made terrible life decisions—dating unsuitable young men, having no concept of budgeting, etc. I was always intrigued by the dichotomy: how can someone so book-smart be so dumb in life?

We are not privy to the status of Israel's intellect, but they seem to fall into the second category of fools. They were so unwise, especially in their faith. God had conducted miracle after miracle, provision after provision on their behalf, yet they kept grumbling. They kept missing the point entirely, and it is frankly hard to read. How could people who had just witnessed what they did ever doubt God? How could they act that childish, knowing what they knew about Him?

Despite glimpses of obedience, as a whole, Israel still was not learning from their mistakes. But we can, and the next passages provide us with an excellent opportunity to do so.

Exodus 17:1-7

> **Then all the congregation of the sons of Israel journeyed by stages from the wilderness of Sin, according to the command of the Lord, and camped at Rephidim, and there was no water for the people to drink. Therefore the people quarreled with Moses and said, "Give us water that we may drink." And Moses said to them, "Why do you quarrel with me? Why do you test the Lord?" (17:1-2)**

Although God provided them with everything needed to progress on their journey of faith, the Israelites crumbled at the very next bump in the road. But before we delve into that, let's take a peek at the physical path God set them on.

- **All the congregation of the Sons of Israel journeyed in stages from the wilderness of Sin**, meaning they traveled as one large group, and their journey was divided into phases. A group of that size could not cover much ground for an extended period of time. They needed to stop and camp here and there, even if some stops were more temporary than others.

Numbers 33 provides a breakdown of the Israelites' journey, giving us a succinct, yet thorough recap of the places and the stages they traveled. According to verses 11-14 of that chapter, the Israelites camped at two smaller stops between the wilderness of Sin and Rephidim: Dophkah and Alush. These two stops are the **stages** mentioned in our passage as the Israelites continue their journey.

More importantly in this section is that the Israelites were not moving on their own volition but **according to the command of the Lord.** He was still present and guiding them via the pillar of cloud and fire. Again, the Israelites were quite helpless on their own in the wilderness. While they were likely strong from their years of manual labor as slaves, they had no clue where they were going or how to provide for themselves. They were wholly dependent on God for their survival and were following His lead.

God led them to camp **at Rephidim**. Now one knows where that was, despite numerous speculations. What we do know is that it was close to Horeb, which many believe to be synonymous with Mount Sinai.[184] It is also probable that **Rephidim**, along with many of the places Israel camped, was more of a general region than a precise location.[185] GPS did not exist back then; geographical markers in the wilderness consisted of mountains and oases, the latter of which were hardly permanent. Given the undeveloped wilderness, the descriptions of these locations were likely relatively vague, describing a general area more than a certified landmark. Being so far removed from them, we are left with educated guesses. As a side note, beware of anyone who claims to know with confidence where any of these locations were. It is a dangerous hermeneutical game to place certainty where none exists.

When they arrived at **Rephidim**, a familiar problem resurfaced: **there was no water for the people to drink.** Two primary interpretations exist regarding this water situation. First, there might have been a literal absence of water, at least not in the quantity necessary for the size of the population. Since the Israelites assumed there would be water, it is possible that drought conditions had dried up what was once there.[186] The second theory is that there was water, but the Israelites did not have access to it because "the hostile Amalekites were in control of this region and blocked the approaches to the sources of water."[187] Anytime we come to an interpretation that is called into question, we must remember that one of the main rules of hermeneutics is to interpret Scripture literally unless the context (narrow or broad) demands it be translated another way. Because there is no mention here or anywhere else in Scripture that the Amalekites blocked their access to the water, it is most reasonable to interpret this phrase literally—**there was no water for the people to drink.**

While this was an unwelcome surprise for the Israelites, remember, it was no surprise to God. He could have easily led them to a place with ample fresh water, but He chose not to. This was an intentional test for the Israelites, and it should have been an easy one for them to pass. They had just experienced two situations where they were without basic needs, handled them poorly, and yet the Lord graciously provided. When they realized the lack of water here, they should have immediately turned their attention to the Lord—praising Him for His continuous provision thus far, and asking Him to provide for them once again.

But they did not.

Instead, **the people quarreled with Moses and said, "Give us water that we may drink." Quarreled** (*rib*) is a different term than we have seen thus far. It is stronger than the previous word, "grumbling,"[188] and contains undertones of anger and fighting. The Israelites were not just whining, they were also mad that they were having to deal with another situation where they lacked water. Further, their tone was accusatory and can be translated as "argued a case with Moses:"[189]

> The verb is used two times in Exodus (17:2; 21:18). The verb...denotes a dimension of formal accusation even in this context. Elsewhere it denotes a formal legal charge (cf. Deut 25:1). This was a serious challenge to Moses' leadership.[190]

In their anger, they were, in a sense, formally accusing **Moses** of inept leadership and causing them harm. Going to Moses is somewhat understandable since he was obviously their human leader and had been the point of communication between them and God. However, they did not approach him humbly with the intent of making a contrite request to God through him. Rather, they angrily demand, **"Give us water that we may drink."**

I always try to give people the benefit of the doubt, reminding myself that I am not in their situation and am just as depraved as anyone. But the text removes any margin for sympathy for the Israelites. They are throwing a temper tantrum rivaling a toddler's, and a cowardly one at that. I believe one underlying reason they approached Moses is that they did not have the guts to approach God. Yes, Moses was God's representative, so he was the most obvious choice. However, we act much differently around a manager we work closely with every day than the owner of the company we rarely interact with. The pillar of cloud and fire was daunting; Moses was like them, and therefore, less intimidating. They wanted water, and they wanted it now. Moses was able to make the bitter water at Marah into sweet water, so he should provide water for them now.

But Moses was not one to back down, and he replied, **"Why do you quarrel with me? Why do you test the Lord?"** We have talked about it before, but it is worth mentioning again how far Moses has come since God approached him through the burning bush. It had likely been less than two years since that encounter, and God had transformed Moses into an entirely different person. The scared, pathetic weakling in faith who tried to weasel his way out of God's call numerous times is now an emboldened leader on God's behalf dealing with faith weaklings of his own. Why does this matter? Because God can and does radically transform lives. He did it in ancient times and continues to do so today. No one is beyond His ability to save; no one escapes His reach of love and transformation. Let this serve as a reminder to cling to Him and allow His Spirit room to work in your heart and life. Do not settle for mediocrity when He has an exceptional life waiting for you.

At this point, however, Moses is getting a taste of his own medicine. The immaturity and lack of faith he once possessed is now what he has to deal with in others. The Israelites **quarrel with** him and **test the Lord**. The term **test** (*nasa*) here is the same that was used in the last chapter, referring to how God tested them to see if they would obey gathering manna. But the and faithlessness of the Israelites prevent them from understanding one crucial point: God tests *us*; we are in no position to test the Lord. In fact, God would later inspire Moses to pen, "You shall not put the Lord your God to the test" (Deut. 8:2). Jesus would eventually quote this verse as well, shutting up Satan in one of his temptations. Pupils do not test their professors. By putting God to the test with their accusations, Israel was usurping God's authority and revealing a depressing lack of faith.

As one commentator writes, "Testing God always involves some degree of doubt about whether or not one's present circumstances are all that one deserves and whether or not God could or should have done a better job of providing one's needs."[191] The church today would be radically transformed if we all realized one simple truth: the only thing we deserve is hell. We literally deserve every accusation, judgment, condemnation, and punishment from God because of our sin. We do not stand a chance on our own, and as Scripture aptly points out, we are dead in our sins apart from Him (Colossians 2:13). How could walking corpses ever have the audacity to put the Living God to the test? Furthermore, how could we, as resuscitated people given life because of Jesus's sacrificial grace, even think of putting our resuscitator on trial? We can't. And it is laughable that we even try.

Unfortunately, spiritual realities do not always translate into temporal realm:

> **But the people thirsted there for water; and they grumbled against Moses and said, "Why, now, have you brought us up from Egypt, to kill us and our children and our livestock with thirst?" (17:3)**

Israel allowed their physical circumstances to dictate their reactions and beliefs. They unwisely chose to be led by their feelings instead of faith. "Forget the plagues! Who cares about being free from hundreds of years of slavery? The parting of the sea was not that big of a deal! Miracle bread every day is irrelevant.

We're thirsty!" This, in essence, is what the Israelites were saying as **they grumbled against Moses**. It was the pulse behind their question, **"Why, now, have you brought us up from Egypt to kill us and our children and our livestock with thirst?"** They seriously had the impulse control of a toddler, which is to say, nil.

Our youngest, a toddler right now, all but loses her mind when she gets hungry. We might be able to distract her here and there for a moment, but the inner beast inevitably comes back out until her physical needs are met. Has she ever actually gone hungry before? Have we ever neglected to feed or give her water? Absolutely not. She has never known real hunger and certainly has not come even remotely close to starvation. But her attitude would sometimes lead you to think otherwise. Why? Because she is a toddler and has to be taught to control her impulses.

As we have seen, Israel was a toddler in faith and, until this point, showed no interest in growing up. They were allowing themselves to be controlled by physical impulses rather than submitting to God's leadership in their lives. Everything God had done for them flew out the window the moment they encountered a hardship, and they got so worked up that Moses began to fear for his life.

> **So Moses cried out to the Lord, saying, "What shall I do to this people? A little more and they will stone me." (17:4)**

Unlike the Israelites, Moses turned directly to God when he encountered an issue. He had a legitimate concern. Quite frankly, he was at the mercy of the mob, at least from a physical standpoint. Some commentators believe that Moses was acting in error here, suggesting that his fear was based on a lack of faith and that he should have trusted God more. [192] I disagree. The people's anger grew with every passing minute, and Moses knew that the situation would not end well without God's intervention. He feared they would stone him. He had already asked the Israelites why they were testing the Lord, making it clear that his leadership was guided only by his submission to God. He knew he could do nothing on his own to resolve the situation; he certainly could not provide water for hundreds of thousands of people and animals. So, **he cried out to the Lord**, as God was his only salvation, and he asked Him what he should do.

Asking God what he should do further confirms that Moses was depending on Him in faith. Petitioning the Lord for guidance is never sinful, especially when He has not already revealed what He wants us to do. Moses may have been flustered, but he was trusting the Lord for direction. He did not lash out at the Israelites or take the situation into his own hands. Instead, he asked God what to do and patiently awaited His response, demonstrating trust, patience, and self-control.

Living a life of faith does not mean we are subject to a monk-life status where we are in a constant state of calm and humming meditation. Moses was upset with the Israelites and disassociated himself from them by saying **this people** instead of "my people" or "Your people," relating to God. "**This people**" hints at Moses' frustration in the same way an exacerbated parent might point to an ill-behaved child and tell a friend, "*That* child is driving me nuts!" No one boasts of association with someone who is acting poorly. We, of course, always love our children and never give up on them, but we all have moments when we are at our wit's end and cry out for help. Emotions are not inherently bad. However, like Moses, we must submit them to the Lord and seek His guidance over our impulses.

Both Israel and Moses had strong reactions to their current situation. The difference was that Moses directed his submission to the Lord while the Israelites used their circumstances as an accusatory weapon against Him. Moses recognized God's power and sovereignty over all trials and asked Him to intervene. Israel believed in the dominion of their circumstances more than the authority of God to overcome them. We will all face trials in this life; our faith will be tested. A genuine and thriving Christian is one who responds to those trials in faith, believing that Jesus has overcome the world and every trial within it (John 16:33). Moses turned to the Lord and waited for His guidance before proceeding. We must do the same.

> **Then the Lord said to Moses, "Pass before the people and take with you some of the elders of Israel; and take in your hand your staff with which you struck the Nile, and go. Behold, I will stand before you there on the rock at Horeb; and you shall strike the rock, and water will come out of it, that the people may drink." And Moses did so in the sight of the elders of Israel. (17:5-6)**

God responded to Moses and gave him clear instructions. Moses was to **pass before the people**, accompanied by **some of the elders of Israel** and carrying the **staff with which he had struck the Nile**. By having Moses pass **before the people**, God made His response public. While His typical method of communication with Moses involved private conversations and Moses relaying His messages to Israel, this time, it was more of a public spectacle. Moses was not just going to speak God's words; he was going to take action and make sure that everyone was watching.

Furthermore, God wanted him to take **some of the elders of Israel** with him. We are not told whether the elders were in agreement with the Israelites or if they had been standing up for Moses, but it was likely the former. The elders were the conduits of communication in Israel — how the masses of people communicated with leadership. It certainly was not possible for such a multitude of people to communicate effectively with Moses on an individual and regular basis. The people also had camaraderie with the elders, for they had been around during the years of slavery long before Moses entered the scene. If the elders had been trying to calm the people down, there would likely be some kind of record of that. Additionally, if the elders had been trying to steer the people toward faith and trust in God, the situation probably would not have escalated to the extent that it did. Thus, it stands to reason that the elders were just as guilty in their lack of faith as the rest of the people. Bringing **some of the elders of Israel** with Moses then was a strong statement by God. The elders were going to have a front-row view of what God would do; their lack of faith would be put to shame publicly.

Moses was also instructed to take **his staff with which** he had **struck the Nile**. God had been using Moses' staff as a conduit for miracles since the burning bush encounter in the desert. It had become a physical symbol of God's power, emphasizing the fact that the power was not coming from Moses directly. While God used Moses as an instrument, Moses could not make a stick perform miracles any more than we can. A stick is capable of nothing on its own. Therefore, using the staff was a powerful and repeated way for God to demonstrate His sovereignty.

Equipped with his staff and accompanied by the elders of Israel, Moses was instructed to **go.** This was not the first time God told Moses to go somewhere, and it would not be the last. God had previously directed him to leave the life of a shepherd and go to Egypt to free His people. As Moses walked in obedience (though reluctantly at first), God continued instructing him to go to Pharaoh and repeat the command to let Israel go. Obedience is a decision before it becomes an action. As God's appointed leader, Moses was required to physically move from one place to another (in this case, from Rephidim to Horeb) to signify obedience and submission to God. God was going to respond, but once again, it would be on His terms.

God told Moses that He would **stand before him** there **on the rock at Horeb**. I appreciate the progression of the people near Moses in this passage. He would pass before the (belligerent) people, escorted by (faithless) elders, and then come before the presence of God Himself. Symbolically, this is both powerful and sadly ironic. It is powerful because that is how our lives should look — we should actively be bringing others closer to God every day. Even if they do not follow, they should see us clearly moving toward Christ in our own lives. However, this is also sadly ironic because we, as the church, are supposed to be actively bringing each other closer to God. The elders and the congregation of Israel as a whole should have been supporting Moses as they all walked in obedience to the Lord. They should have encouraged, spoken truth, and exhorted each other with the promises and faithfulness of God. Instead, Moses was metaphorically dragging their sorry bums to take account before the Lord. In a moment of righteous vindication, they are the ones who were going "on trial" before God — to see His response to their horrendous behavior. This section begins with them hurling formal accusations against Moses; it turns around when God decides to **stand before Moses** and shut up their misplaced grievances.

The rock at Horeb ruffles all kinds of scholarly feathers, as most geographical points do. Yet again, no one knows with any kind of confidence where **the rock at Horeb** was. **Horeb** was often used in association or even synonymously with Mount Sinai, but it is not likely that they were one and the same. In fact, "Horeb most likely denotes a larger area, within which the Wilderness of Sinai and Mount Sinai were located."[193] While we do not know exactly where this was, it is quite certain that people back then did. **The rock at Horeb** was likely a known landmark, and early readers would be instantly familiar with this location.

A second point to note about **the rock at Horeb** is that the name Horeb "is derived from a Hebr. root that means to be dry or desolate."[194] In other words, this was not the place to go in search of water. Just as God brought them to Rephidim, knowing they would not find water there, He seemed to take them to an even more desolate place to respond to their childish outburst. Everyone was probably wondering what God was doing and why He was leading them toward a climate even more bereft of water than the one they were just in. Can you imagine how indignant they must have gotten on this walk? I do not know how far of a journey it was to this rock, but I can only imagine the tension was growing as tempers rose. They were already thirsty; exerting more energy and being led into a more desolate place might have fueled their outrage.

But alas, God knew what He was doing and told Moses about it beforehand. When they reached **the rock at Horeb**, Moses was to **strike the**

rock, and water would come out of it so that the people may drink. I often wonder what God thinks when He does something completely outside the box (which He does quite frequently). There are so many accounts throughout Scripture that made me scratch my head and go, "But why?" Why make a big fish swallow Jonah? Why have Jesus born in a stable, of all places? Why save Israel from Haman through the winner of a rather scandalous beauty pageant? So many head-scratching moments, and this is one of them. A rock? Hitting a rock so **water will come out of it?**

Good thing God does not have to make sense to us in order to accomplish His purposes and garner our faith. I believe that one reason He does the unexpected is to remind us once again that He cannot be put in a box. He is the Creator of the universe; He is not subject to the minds of His created beings. A God we could figure out would be a God we could control, which would not be God at all. By taking them to a place of increased desolation, God was trying to show Israel a need far deeper than their physical need for water. They were thirsty for Him and the satisfaction He alone could bring them. They desperately needed the living water of salvation. Since their stubborn immaturity was impeding their awareness of that need, it is likely having water come out of a rock might shock their senses enough to get their attention.

Moses asked for direction, and when God answered, he obeyed: **Moses did so in the sight of the elders of Israel.** We should once more give Moses credit. Even though God's instruction must have seemed strange to him, he was to the point in his walk with the Lord that he did not question it. He simply complied. He got up, took his staff and the elders with him, met God at the rock of Horeb, and struck it. No pause, no hesitation, no doubt. Oh, that we might be the same in our obedience to Christ! We have been given so much direction in God's Word. We have sixty-six books full of special revelation from God Himself, preserved by the Holy Spirit for thousands of years. Not that it is an excuse for their behavior, but the Israelites had nothing in writing. We have a ton. And we have the preserved witness of countless lives God has used throughout history to draw others to Himself as well. We are also indwelled with His Holy Spirit! We are without excuse, and we desperately need to do better—to believe better, to trust Him, and to act accordingly.

We are not told what the result of this narrative was. We can safely assume a couple of points, namely, that water came out of the rock like God said it would and that it was sufficient to meet the needs of hordes of people and animals. The rock of Horeb was probably no small pebble. Perhaps it was an enormous boulder fallen from a nearby mountain, which is why so many people knew where it was. Or maybe that is a completely erroneous conclusion, and the rock was rather small and insignificant, making God's provision that much more miraculous. (Jesus did, after all, feed thousands with only five small loaves of bread and two fish). Perhaps this event was the reason a smaller rock became famous, and its size served to embellish the narrative. No one knows for sure, but whatever size it was, God supplied more than enough water from it to satisfy a whole lot of people and animals. God's provision is always enough and far beyond just meeting physical needs:

> Thus says the Lord who made you and formed you from the womb, who will help you, "Do not fear, O Jacob My Servant; And you Jeshurun whom I have chosen. For I will pour out water on the thirsty land and streams on the dry ground; I will pour out My Spirit on your offspring and My blessing on your descendants; and they will spring up among the grass like poplars by streams of water." (Isaiah 44:2-4)

Israel, as a whole, did not realize their spiritual needs yet, but God was patiently revealing it to them one step at a time. He wanted them to crave Him, to love Him back, and to live fully in and through His blessings. His desire was for their attention to shift from their physical circumstances to their Heavenly Father, learning that He was sovereign and would always take care of them.

The Israelites' reaction to the miracle, first the elders and then the people, is also not recorded. Did their anger fizzle out like a hose extinguishing a small flame? Did their pompous hearts deflate like a popped balloon? Or did some of them tenaciously hold onto their skepticism and doubt, allowing God's provision to fuel their sense of entitlement? I imagine it was probably a bit of both. Undoubtedly, some repented of their behavior and sought God's forgiveness. Others likely complained that the water was too late in coming and whined about the method with which God provided it. Or maybe the water was too warm or too this or too that. There always seems to be both kinds of people in any given group. While we cannot control or be responsible for how others act, we can control our own responses, and prayerfully, we will recognize God's provision for what it is—a gift and blessing that should not be taken for granted.

> **He named the place Massah and Meribah because of the quarrel of the sons of Israel, and because they tested the Lord, saying "Is the Lord among us, or not?" (17:7)**

Massah literally means "trial," and **Meribah** literally means "quarrel." [195] Both names accurately depict the events that occurred in this location. By choosing them, Moses ensured that the Israelites would not remember these places wearing rose-colored glasses. Life is pockmarked with failures. We are sinful people, and even those of us saved by grace and indwelled with the Spirit continue to battle against the sinful nature that easily entangles us (Hebrews 12:1). However, some of our most significant failures can become powerful lessons that God uses to transform our lives. It is wise to reflect on past mistakes, glean lessons from them, and apply these lessons to future situations to avoid repeating the same errors.

By taking the time to name this place after Israel's sinful actions, Moses was inviting them to learn from their mistakes so they would not repeat them in the future. For those who felt convicted as they drank fully from the water flowing from the rock, the names **Massah** and **Meribah** were a punchy, humbling reminder that would serve them well in the future. Remembering past failures may not be enjoyable; it can evoke a sinking feeling in the pit of your stomach, and all the embarrassment comes flooding back. Yet, remembering the feelings along with the facts motivates you to never act that way again. This is what Moses hoped for by making this rock a memorial for the Israelites. He hoped they would remember their shame and what it felt like to be schooled by a rock so they would not doubt God again.

More than once, this passage mentioned how Israel had **tested the Lord**. They brought formal accusations against Moses, and God by extension. They put them "on trial," so to speak, so they could see if God was with them: **"Is the Lord among us, or not?"** Though explicit mention of God's manifest presence was never articulated in these verses, the underlying motif was certainly there. [196] (It is also possible that the Israelites did ask this question previously; it just was not recorded.) They wanted to know if God was really with them and, if so, why He had not provided them with water.

Psalm 95:8-10 reflects on this event. The Psalmist writes:

> Do not harden your hearts, as at Meribah, as in the day of Massah in the wilderness. "When your fathers tested Me, they tried Me, though they had seen My work. For forty years I loathed that generation, and said they are a people who err in their heart, and they do not know My ways."

I cannot think of a worse judgment pronounced against someone than to be someone who tries God despite ample proof of His presence, someone who errs in their heart and does not know God's ways. I often plead with God to let me know Him so well now in this life that when I meet Him face-to-face one day, I will be overcome with relief more than shock. I yearn for my first glimpse of Him to result in me falling on my face in tears, saying, "I knew it! I really, really knew You...thank You for letting me truly know You then." I want to run full-speed into heaven and immediately immerse myself in all the wonders we will behold there, Jesus first and foremost. To me, success in this life will mean a short transition period there. I long for my heart and mind to be so caught up with Him in the here and now that the transition to heaven will resemble an exhale of relief more than a gasp of shock.

For this generation of Israel, that was not the case. God provided them with countless miracles—irrefutable signs of His presence, love, and provision in their lives. They certainly "had seen [His] work," as the Psalmist declares. Yet they tested and tried Him, and in doing so, erred in their hearts and did not know His ways. They were trying to prove God's presence, but all they did was prove that they refused to enter His.

Exodus 17:8-16

Then Amalek came and fought against Israel at Rephidim. (17:8)

Amalek is synonymous with the Amalekites, an ancient nation about which we know little. The first mention of them as a people group in Scripture is in Genesis 14:7, where they are listed among the people groups conquered by Chedorlaomer during the war when Lot, Abraham's nephew, was taken captive. The first time **Amalek** is introduced in Scripture individually is in Genesis 36:12, where we learn that he was Esau's grandson, the son of Eliphaz by a concubine. Because his name is given later than the first reference to the Amalekite people, we have two options for interpretation. Either Esau's grandson Amalek had nothing to do with the Amalekite people, and their names just happened to be similar, or Amalek's descendants eventually joined with or took over the people mentioned in Genesis 14, and they were given the name Amalekites because that's what they ended up being known by. While the ultimate significance might be minimal, I am inclined to associate Esau's grandson with the Amalekite people. First, because the name **Amalek** is used here, not "the Amalekites," "people of Amalek," or another such moniker. Second, Esau was not known for fearing the Lord; his line of descendants was not the one God claimed as His own. Therefore, it would not be surprising that his offspring were in conflict with God's people, as is the case here.

Regardless of their origin, **Amalek came and fought against Israel at Rephidim**. This attack seems unprovoked; we are given no indication that the

Israelites caused any trouble or threatened them in any way. One possible explanation for the attack is that "the Amalekites interpreted the sudden appearance of the Israelites in this region as a menacing encroachment upon their territory and as a threat to their control of the oases and trading routes."[197] If true, this confirms yet again the size of the Israelite people. They were not merely a couple of thousand people roaming through the wilderness. Rather, they were a mass of people and animals that could have easily been perceived as a threat to other people groups trying to maintain control of their land. Furthermore, we must remember that political diplomacy was not a refined process back then. Nations ruled by brute force, and when they wanted something, they went to war to get it. Israel very well may have come off as a threat to the Amalekites, and while it would have been wise for them to seek peace, they opted to try to eliminate the threat through battle.

I believe this attack served a couple of purposes, the first of which was to punish Israel for their distrust and despicable behavior at Rephidim. It does not seem coincidental that Amalek came while **Israel** was still at **Rephidim**. Israel had miserably failed every test the Lord had given them so far, including Rephidim, yet God's faithfulness continued. He kept testing them, putting them in situations where they needed to trust Him so they could learn how to depend on Him. "Punishing" them by allowing the Amalekites to attack them was similar to sending the Egyptians back to them at the sea. God wanted them to realize they were utterly helpless without Him. They could not provide their own basic needs like food and water; they certainly had no hope of successfully defending themselves against a trained enemy army. This punishment, like every punishment of a loving parent, served to correct the Israelites' erroneous beliefs and behaviors, as well as reinforce truth in their hearts and minds.

Secondly, this attack served as a healthy dose of reality for the Israelites. Their situation in Egypt was far from an ordeal, but one major benefit was never having to deal with the threat of war. Egypt was like a cocoon, a place of great trial and struggle with the hope of great transformation when they emerged from it. They were a family of seventy when they came to dwell in Egypt; they left as a nation over a million strong. But this butterfly needed to continue its transformation. Their wings were still wet, so to speak, when they left Egypt—they were clueless about the outside world and how to be an autonomous nation. They could see the world outside Egypt, but they were ill-prepared to be on their own in it. These tests, therefore, served to show them that they literally could not survive without God. Food and water are the most basic needs in life, but being able to be victorious in battle was nearly as important in a world ridden with war. The Amalekites attacking them was their first introduction to what life outside their "cocoon" of Egypt would be like. War would be a near-constant threat, and they desperately needed to learn how to submit and depend on the Lord for deliverance.

This practical dose of reality also embodied a spiritual one: God was fulfilling His promise of bringing them to the Promised Land. But the Promised Land was not sitting there vacant. It was currently established and occupied by people groups who refused to bend the knee to the true God, so God would displace them via military exertion from His grossly unprepared people. Fighting Amalek would give Israel not only a general glimpse of what a war-filled world was like, but would also reveal what *their* world would be like when they got to the Promised Land. They did not just need to trust God for deliverance now; they would need to continue to trust and obey Him to receive the blessings He promised them. Israel's "wet wings" needed to dry with the wind of the Spirit of God, not only establishing and strengthening their military forces but also solidifying their faith and dependence on Him.

> **So Moses said to Joshua, "Choose men for us and go out, fight against Amalek. Tomorrow I will station myself on the top of the hill with the staff of God in my hand." Joshua did as Moses told him, and fought against Amalek; and Moses, Aaron, and Hur went up to the top of the hill. (17:9-10)**

Moses sees the situation and responds with haste. He tells **Joshua** to "**Choose men for us and go out, fight against Amalek.**" This is the first mention of Joshua in Scripture thus far, but it certainly will not be the last. Joshua was someone Moses had taken a special interest in. Neither he nor Moses may have realized it yet, but Joshua would become the next leader of Israel. Moses obviously already had a relationship with him and trusted him; he certainly would not have chosen someone at random to lead the **fight against Amalek.** We do not know when or how they met, but we do know that they had a special bond that would continue to strengthen for the rest of their lives together. We learn in Numbers 13:16 that at some point (presumably before this encounter with Amalek), Joshua's name used to be Hoshea, but Moses changed it to Joshua, which means "Jehovah is salvation." [198] Moses must have known that there was something special about Joshua (likely prompted by God), and made it a point to start mentoring and grooming him for leadership.

Joshua was given three instructions: **choose men for us, go out, and fight against Amalek.** Remember, Israel did not have a designated (or even trained) army. Joshua was not an elite military commander with years of experience supervising a fleet of meticulously skilled warriors. He was a novice leader stuck with a faithless band of former slaves, clueless in the art and form of warfare. The Israelite men may have been strong, but muscle alone does not make an elite soldier.

The need for men willing to fight is obvious, but it is also a good reminder that we do not fight battles alone. Moses did not tell Joshua to go and fight the Amalekites by himself; that would have been crazy. While there are records of extraordinary individuals accomplishing significant feats individually in battle. [199] But those are rare exceptions, and even then, they typically did not fight completely alone against an enemy. God empowers and protects those fighting in accordance with His will, and that usually begins by raising up men to join together in the fight. Joshua would not be alone in his fight; he had the Lord guiding him and the men who went with him.

We are not told how Joshua chose the men who would fight, nor how many he chose. But we do know that **Joshua did as Moses told him**, so he had no significant trouble choosing his men. I am inclined to believe that Joshua had already been tasked with forming (or at least thinking about) a militia of sorts before receiving this instruction because of how quickly he was able to do it. The more we learn about Joshua, the more we realize what a capable leader he was.

He and his chosen men were to **go out** and do so on behalf of the people: **for us**. As is commonly known, when there is a conflict that requires military action, a select group of soldiers goes out to fight on behalf of the people. Many women, children, the elderly, and the ill have physical limitations that prevent them from contributing to military efforts protecting their nation. Soldiers represent these people and take the place of society as a whole by fighting on their behalf. The beauty of this kind of selflessness and sacrifice is often forgotten. Soldiers and veterans have not received nearly enough support, encouragement, and thanks for their service, to our shame. Their sacrifice is weighty; our appreciation should be just as substantial.

As with many things in life, the concept of war reflects what God does for us in Christ. We are constantly in a battle with sin, yet Christ has made it possible for us to be victorious over it. He was the chosen man tasked **to go** out and fight against Satan, securing ultimate victory over sin through His death and resurrection. Jesus did what we could never do, dead as we were in our sins. He fought a battle that was not His, so we could gain a victory that could have never been ours without Him. As we read earlier in Exodus 15:3, "The Lord is a warrior;" He fights for His people because He loves us and knows we would not have a chance on our own.

It is no coincidence that the man tasked with militarily saving Israel shared the name "Jehovah is salvation" with Jesus, which is a later rendition of that same name.[200] Joshua was a foreshadow of the Ultimate Warrior who would conquer death and sin once and for all. While Joshua would gain earthly victories, making it possible for Israel to follow God's lead to the Promised Land, Jesus would gain the heavenly victory, making it possible for us to enter the Promised Land of Heaven one day. Joshua's calling was much more than just fighting a battle. It would symbolize hope for the Israelites and generations later, and provide us with confirmation of that hope as we read about it. Joshua was set apart, as Jesus would be too one day, and we should all fall on our faces in gratitude for their responses to their callings.

In addition to having a willing and capable military leader, another blessing they had was a bit of time. Moses told Joshua that they would fight **tomorrow**, which meant they had a day (or at least part of one) to gather up men to fight and prepare for battle. In all likelihood, Israel had this bit of time because the Amalekites were arriving in waves as opposed to one large army mass.[201] Deuteronomy 25:17-18 provides further clarity on how Amalek attacked Israel:

> Remember what Amalek did to you along the way when you came out from Egypt, how he met you along the way and attacked among you all the stragglers at your rear when you were faint and weary; and he did not fear God.

If the Amalekites had arrived all at once in mass, Israel very well may have conquered Israel due to Israel's ill-prepared state. (God obviously could have saved them by supernatural means, but the Israelites would have had no way of defending themselves without it). Instead, a wave of Amalekites arrived and attacked them from behind. We are not told if they attacked and then pulled back or if the Israelites were able to ward off this presumably smaller number of Amalekites on the spot. Regardless, this attack from behind was brief, and it gave the Israelites the gift of time. God provided Israel with time, enabling them to respond to this threat purposefully, not just act in a reactionary manner. He wanted them to think and consciously put their faith, hope, and trust in Him, so He gave them several hours to do so.

To their credit, Israel stepped up to the challenge under Moses' leadership. Moses put Joshua in charge of the military efforts; he would be the hands and feet of the battle. But Moses knew they needed a lot more than physical force to be victorious over the Amalekites, so he committed to fight via prayerful intercession throughout the battle. Moses said, **"I will station myself on the top of the hill with the staff of God in my hand."** He knew where he would be most effective and knew the true battle was not being fought with swords and shields. Moses would place himself as physically near the Lord as possible—**on the top of the hill**, and would once again bring **the staff of God in** his **hand.** God told him at the burning bush to keep that **staff** with him; he would not leave it behind when interceding on behalf of the people.

As we previously mentioned, **Joshua did as Moses told him and fought against Amalek.** He was faithful to the call and showed much courage, faith, and trust in the Lord in doing so. Joshua is the antithesis of the rest of the Israelites at this moment. Where they just failed a test of trust for water, Joshua was acing a test of much more intensity. **Moses, Aaron, and Hur** were stepping up as well, committed to fighting through prayer as they **went up to the top of the hill**.

The symbolism of their locations cannot be missed, for it portrays both the physical and spiritual realms of the battlefield. Joshua and his men went to fight the Amalekites; **Moses, Aaron, and Hur** went to fight on their behalf in prayer and supplication. Joshua went out for battle; Moses, Aaron, and Hur **went up.** They were enacting what each of us should be doing every day as we walk in faith. The physical world ("out") is important; we have to act in obedience as we go about our day—taking our thoughts captive, speaking truth in love, and working in ways that bring honor and glory to God. Most of us do not fight actual, physical battles like Joshua did, but we are engaged in a spiritual battle. And like Joshua, we need to equip ourselves with more than just physical armor:

For our struggle is not against flesh and blood, but against the rulers, against the powers, against the world forces of this darkness, against the spiritual forces of wickedness in the heavenly places. Therefore, take up the full armor of God, so that you will be able to resist in the evil day, and having done everything, to stand firm. (Ephesians 6:12-13)

Moses, Aaron, and Hur went to do battle ("up") in the heavenly realms on Joshua's (and Israel's) behalf. Joshua had done everything right to prepare both physically and spiritually by humbling himself under God's authority and obeying His instructions through Moses. **Moses, Aaron, and Hur** were going to bolster Joshua's faith by storming the throne of the Lord.

We know about Moses and Aaron, but **Hur** is another new introduction. With all likelihood, **Hur** was a man of leadership within Israel. He may have been an elder during Israel's years of slavery and continued in his role of leadership under Aaron and Moses. He would later be appointed as a magistrate with Aaron when Moses went to another mountain to be with the Lord (24:14), so he was certainly trusted.

Jewish tradition claims that Hur was also the grandfather of Bezalel, who was from the tribe of Judah and would become the chief workman in the tabernacle later in Exodus. [202] According to tradition, he was also thought to be "the husband of Miriam, Moses' sister," though Scripture does not verify that. [203] Regardless of the details, Hur was a man held in high regard, for he accompanied Moses and Aaron to **the top of the hill**.

The exact location of this **hill** is unknown, but we gather from the text that it afforded a good view of the battlefield below. **Moses, Aaron, and Hur** were able to watch the battle below while petitioning the Lord on Israel's behalf. Their efforts were not easy. In fact, in some ways, their form of battle was just as strenuous as the battle against the Amalekites.

> So it came about when Moses held his hand up, that Israel prevailed, and when he let his hand down, Amalek prevailed. But Moses' hands were heavy. Then they took a stone and put it under him, and he sat on it; and Aaron and Hur supported his hands, one on one side and one on the other. Thus his hands were steady until the sun set. (17:11-12)

Because of its brevity, this is one of the most curious parts of this narrative. The facts are simple: **when Moses held his hands up, Israel prevailed. But when he let his hands down, Amalek prevailed**. But why? What was special about holding up his hands? And what is meant by **"so it came about?"** Did Moses have to figure out this "trick" out on his own, as an observation made as the hours progressed? Or did God tell him about it beforehand? Unfortunately, we do not know, and the multitude of theories from commentators attempting to figure it out shows us we may never know with certainty. But we can explore it within its context and shed some light on it.

We do know that Moses, Aaron, and Hur ascending the hill was no accident. Moses knew that his part in this battle was spiritual, indicated by his resolve to take **the staff of God** in his **hand**. We have seen God use both the **staff** and the posture of raised hands before in our narrative. God told him at the burning bush that the staff would be an important tool and representation of God's power in and through His work through Moses. God used it numerous times through the plague and sea-parting narrative (7:10, 20; 8:16), combined with having Moses raise his hands (9:23, 10:13, 14:16). In the previous volume, we also discussed the significance of one's hand, especially how it symbolized power in the ancient world (3:20, 7:4, 9:3, 13:3). Thus, Moses either intentionally or under the compulsion of habit **held his hand up** with the staff of God to intercede and/or plead for God's intervention in the battle against Amalek.

God also could have prompted Moses with what to do to attain victory over Amalek. No conversation is recorded in this narrative, but a lot of details are left out. One primary piece of evidence for this theory is that Moses was acting swiftly and with confidence. Whereas the previous moments of testing Israel left Moses still and waiting for God's lead, this one rendered him jumping to action immediately. He was far from a warrior, so it is not like he was tapping into some former military experience. While he has been rash in reacting before (10:29), that was with words, not action, and certainly not leading a military campaign on the spiritual front. Thus, it is quite possible that God had told Moses what to do, and Moses was once again obeying His instruction.

While it is likely God told Moses what to do, it is unlikely that Moses took the time to spell it out for everyone else except by giving Joshua his basic commands. They were in a hurry, after all; they had been attacked and needed to step up to fight off Amalek in battle. The phrase **"so it came about"** cues the reader into the perspective of the general Israelite population at the time. They were figuring things out on the fly, so to speak. This battle lasted all day, and the link between Moses' raised hands and victory over the Amalekites probably became apparent quickly. Moses acted in accordance with what the Lord either prompted or instructed him to do, and as he did so, the **Israelites prevailed**.

The problem, however, was that **Moses' hands were heavy**. Often, during our morning homeschooling sessions, the girls and I transition between subjects with exercises to get our blood flowing and help them release some energy so they can focus better. Interestingly, they complain the most about arm-related exercises, like circling or keeping their arms raised during squats. Keeping your arms elevated is quite an exercise, and our girls cringe imagining what Moses had to endure all day during this battle.

Not much research can easily be found regarding how long people generally can hold their arms up. One blogger states that the record for keeping two arms up is about 9 minutes, while most people can only hold their arms up for two or three minutes.[204] I conducted a little test of my own with some willing participants (ahem, family members), and our seven-year-old was able to hold her arms up for seven minutes, so this blogger's information cannot be accurate unless adults are more restricted than children for some reason. However, it is still very difficult, and holding arms up longer than fifteen or twenty minutes is a significant challenge that most people would not be able to do. One reason why it is so difficult is that raising your arms causes the blood to rush out of them, and you start feeling that pretty quickly. Your hands start to hurt because the lack of blood is decreasing oxygen and causing muscle cramps, etc. In other words, it is more of a sprint exercise than a marathon one, which did not bode well for Moses.

Moses' adrenaline probably got him through the first minutes effortlessly, and it is even possible he thought it would be a quick victory over the Amalekites, so he was not thinking about it much. But when it started sinking in that the battle would be more challenging than anticipated, and gravity started weighing on his arms, he grew tired. We must also not forget that Moses was over eighty years old at this point. Granted, the life expectancy was much longer back then (Moses lived until he was 120), but still, eighty is no spring chicken. He was weary, and **his hands were heavy**.

The symbolism in this action is rich. God's hand of power had extended against Israel's enemies, specifically Pharaoh, numerous times in this narrative thus far. Moses raising his hands here, then, especially with his staff in them, also represented God's power. Once again, God worked through Moses' hands to save the Israelites.

Calvin suggests another aspect of symbolism, namely that God provides ministers with His power on earth:

> Moses speaks chiefly of himself to show that this charge was entrusted to him by God. For he did not only offer his prayers as a work of charity but because God had chosen him as intercessor, to conquer the enemies from afar by the stretching forth of the rod, and by his secret earnestness in prayer; and in this respect, he was a type of Christ; although the similitude does not hold in all its parts. [205]

For reasons we will never fully comprehend, God uses His chosen believers to be His hands, feet, mouthpiece, and heart in the world. He has made all of us ambassadors for Christ in one way or another and has set apart a smaller percentage of His people for full-time vocational ministry and leadership (2 Corinthians 5:20). Moses belonged to the latter category and was used by God in a distinct way as a conduit of His word and power among the people. Scripture provides us with numerous examples of God providing His chosen leaders with special abilities and tasks as they led His people—David, Elijah, Solomon, Samuel, and others. Each of these leaders acted in the power of God's Spirit as He led them, ultimately pointing to Christ as our true Intercessor and King.

Just as the Passover foreshadows the coming of Jesus, the ultimate sacrificial Lamb who would take away the sins of the world, so Moses represents (although certainly imperfectly) Christ coming as our Intercessor. God used Moses as a human intercessor and conduit of His power as a visible reminder that His strength is made perfect in our weaknesses, and that He uses His followers as ambassadors to this world. By raising his hands, Moses boldly declared that he was not acting on his own initiative but on God's. He relied on God's power to overcome Amalek. While Christ had all power and authority over heaven and earth, He still acted in accordance with God's will and humbled Himself to the point of death, even death on a cross (Philippians 2:8). Moses readily admitted he had no power of his own but, like Jesus, humbled himself and raised his arms to intercede to the One who did.

Jesus remained obedient to His calling, despite being under unfathomable pressure and strain to the point of shedding blood through His sweat (Luke 22:44). Moses, too, experienced pressure, especially physically. He could only hold his arms up for so long before lowering them, and when he did, **Amalek prevailed**. But he remained committed to his calling and was helped by Aaron and Hur. This is one glaring difference between Moses and Christ in this particular comparison—Moses' companions helped him; Jesus' disciples abandoned Him. Moses' friends supported and encouraged him in his time of trial; Jesus' disciples fell asleep (Luke 22:44-46). Christ was sustained solely by the Spirit and His Father. While there were times when Moses was alone in his faithfulness, during this battle, he was supported by two men who remained faithful throughout the entire day.

When it became apparent that Moses could not hold his arms up any longer, Aaron and Hur **took a stone and put it under him, and he sat on it; and Aaron and Hur supported his hands, one on one side and one on the other**. Aaron and Hur could not relieve Moses of his task, but they aided him and made it possible for him to continue. They first relieved the pressure of standing by taking **a stone and** putting **it under him** so he could sit. Holding your hands above your head is challenging enough, but having to do so while standing increases the difficulty. Aaron and Hur presumably found a nearby stone that was suitable for Moses to sit on and helped him to do so.

While not explicitly mentioned, it is likely that this stone was short enough for Aaron and Hur to support Moses' hands, one on each side, without needing to stand on stones of their own. If Moses was positioned lower, their arms would have been raised at a ninety-degree angle from the elbow, rather than raised above their heads, making it far more sustainable for longer periods of time.

Aaron and Hur willingly assisted Moses so that Israel could prevail in battle. This action reveals a couple of noteworthy points. First, it suggests that Moses was not merely holding his hands up but was actively interceding on Israel's behalf through prayer. There is no record of him asking for Aaron and Hur's help, so it stands to reason that he was so engrossed in prayer that he did not even think about it. He had one focus, and every ounce of his energy was directed toward the Lord and keeping his arms raised to Him. Aaron and Hur saw this and were that much more willing to help, enabling Moses to maintain his focus.

Second, Aaron and Hur's intervention reveals that God provides for His people through His people. Aaron and Hur originally went with Moses to help, and when they realized they could not take turns lifting the staff for him, they proactively changed the circumstances to make it possible for Moses to continue. Moses would soon realize that he could not lead the Israelites on his own, and Aaron and Hur were providing a glimpse of that fact at that moment. It is important for us to remember the same. Leaders can sometimes fall into the trap of pride or delusion, thinking they can do everything on their own and do not need anyone. This perspective often stems from an erroneously high view of oneself. While Moses was God's chosen instrument and was tasked with raising his staff alone, he could not do it on his own. If left only to Moses, Israel might have lost the battle. However, Aaron and Hur came alongside him, lifting him up to the Lord in more ways than one.

Though everyone has some kind of influence over others, not everyone is a leader. God created each of us to serve unique, complementary roles within the body of Christ, serving each other and glorifying His name on earth. Aaron and (likely) Hur were leaders, but they were not the primary human leaders of Israel. Their actions here reveal humility and obedience within the roles God called them to. They willingly went with Moses to help and actively looked for ways to do so. They did not need to be pushed, nor did they sulk because they were not in top leadership positions. They did not sit in the background with crossed arms and furrowed brows because they had secondary roles. Instead, they eagerly sought opportunities to be helpful, and when one presented itself, they took action. They did not just wait to be told what to do, nor did they present a list of options to Moses. They observed what he needed, took action, and significantly contributed to the battle efforts that day.

Their contribution highlights the beauty in God's design for kingdom work. Most successful kingdom efforts require at least three components: prayer, obedience, and unity within the body of Christ. Moses (and possibly Aaron and Hur) was dedicated to praying and obediently lifting up the staff to God. They also worked together, displaying great unity. Yet only part of the battle was being fought on that hill. Joshua and his willing army were engaged in the physical work below. Time did not permit them to pray continuously while wielding their swords (although many "help us!" prayers were likely uttered). Nevertheless, they remained faithful in their obedience and unity with each other in battling Amalek. They understood they were not the most skilled warriors, but their obedience to the Lord would lead them to victory.

Our battles must be fought in the same way.

If we are to have any hope of victory over sin in our lives, we must be diligent in prayer, obedient to the Word of God, and united with His people. People who embody these three components will not be perfect, but they will allow ample room for their faith to grow and will be formidable foes against the enemy. If you find yourself consistently falling prey to sin in your life, chances are you are weak in one (or more) of these areas. Strengthen your fight by praying to the Victorious One, walking in His way, and standing united with His people. You may not win every battle, but you will certainly experience more victories than defeats.

Another crucial component to pursue is dedication. It is one thing to pray, obey, and fellowship with other believers. However, none of these will accomplish much if you do them infrequently. Instead, they need to be practices and life rhythms you are dedicated to. Moses was committed to keeping his arms raised for the duration of that battle. He did not do it for five minutes and then give up, wishing Joshua luck. The same goes for Aaron and Hur. They assisted Moses and were prepared to do so for as long as it took. Thanks to them, **his hands remained steady until the sunset**. The same can be said for Joshua, who continued to fight even when it was challenging and exhausting. Each of them displayed dedication in their prayer, obedience, and commitment to each other, and the result was as expected: **Joshua overwhelmed Amalek and his people with the edge of the sword**.

It might have taken a while, but there was no ambiguity about who emerged victorious from that battle. Under the leadership of Moses and Joshua, the Israelites overcame **Amalek and his people**. Former slaves with no military training defeated a well-known army of the day because they followed God's instructions. Israel had not been particularly impressive in the narrative thus far, but even the weakest among us can be used by God in astonishing victories. Amalek was unwise to come against the King of Kings and Lord of Lords, and they paid dearly for it.

What happened next is of utmost importance to note:

> **Then the Lord said to Moses, "Write this in a book as a memorial and recite it to Joshua, that I will utterly blot out the memory of Amalek from under heaven." Moses built an altar and named it "The Lord is My Banner; and he said, "The Lord has sworn; the Lord will have war against Amalek from generation to generation." (17:14-16)**

Once victory was secure, God wanted to ensure that it would be remembered among His people. Entire books could be written on the importance of remembering, specifically how crucial it is for us to remember what God has done in both Scripture and our personal pasts. Remember the "Forgetting Curve" from Chapter One? It shows how much we forget if we do not make it a point to actively remember. Even details of major moments like our wedding day or children's births start fading with time. We are finite people, and one of the biggest hindrances to our finiteness is our sorely limited memory.

If we ever find ourselves growing distant from God (and let's be clear, we are the ones who move, not Him), it is almost guaranteed that we are filling our minds with something other than the truth. When we fail to remember His truths and promises, we open ourselves up to spiritual weariness and defeat. To help prevent this in Israel, God instructed Moses and the Israelites to be proactive in their memory. Before they even left Egypt, God established the observance of the Passover as a way to remember their salvation and point to their coming Savior. They needed annual celebrations to provide structured time and space to reflect on what God had done in order to renew their faith, praise Him for His faithfulness, and grow even closer to Him.

The defeat of Amalek, though not nearly as dramatic as the exodus, was still something worth remembering, and God declared it to be so. Instead of making it an annual observance, God told Moses, "**Write this in a book as a memorial and recite it to Joshua.**" The book was obviously not the kind of book we have today, but rather a scroll. In a highly oral culture, taking the time to write something down was significant and required intention. Ink pens did not exist, nor was there an abundant supply of paper. Every letter written needed to be intentional and carefully composed; otherwise, the integrity of the scroll would have been compromised. If the words he wrote were the ones we now have in Scripture, the task of writing and subsequently copying them would have been taken that much more seriously. In fact, scribes who would later copy Old Testament texts were so careful that if they made any error whatsoever, they would burn the entire scroll. Writing, especially with religious texts that God inspired, was a sobering task, and we should thank God every day for their diligence and His preservation of those scrolls so we can have the treasure that is Scripture today.

As mentioned, it is unclear exactly what Moses wrote. Some believe it was the exact preceding verses; others think it was a more detailed account that is no longer available to us. Regardless, the account of Amalek's defeat was preserved, and it was to serve **as a memorial**. The word for **memorial** (*zikaron*) was the same used to describe the Passover and accompanying Feast of Unleavened Bread in chapter 12. God does not just want a record of what happened; He wanted the Israelites (and the world) to actively remember what He did.

What they were supposed to remember was clear: God was the victor in that battle. There would be little point in remembering a battle that occurred merely in the physical realm. Countless battles have taken place within countless wars throughout history, many of which have been forgotten. This battle would not seem all that significant to the world, but it was of utmost significance to

Israel because it was their first as a freed nation, and because their God secured the victory for them. This **memorial**, then, was not so much about the battle as it was about reminding the Israelites that God is the Undefeated King, and He was *their* King. This is a lesson they would desperately need (and fail) to remember as time progressed, which is why God wanted to ensure memories like this were preserved.

In addition to writing about the battle **in a book**, Moses was commanded to **recite it to Joshua**. Here, we get confirmation that Joshua was already in a leadership role in Israel, but also a foreshadow of the role he would fulfill as Moses' successor someday. God's command here may have been one of the first official glimpses into the fact that Joshua was God's chosen leader for Israel after Moses. It could also be that by reciting **it to Joshua**, Joshua was charged with preserving the account and keeping it constantly before the people in future generations.

It was important for all Israelites to remember the battle with the Amalekites, but it was especially important for Joshua to do so. As Israel's future leader, Joshua needed to remember, meditate upon, and actively submit to God's kingship, authority, and sovereignty. Joshua, like any other person in history, was nothing and could accomplish nothing without God. It was crucial for him to relive that day of battle, but especially from Moses' perspective. That day would have been a bit of a blur to Joshua on the battlefield as adrenaline pumped through his veins, fighting hour after hour. He needed to know and be reminded of Moses' "bird's eye view" to understand that God was the one who secured victory on their behalf.

God not only wanted the battle and victory remembered but also a promise: that He would **utterly blot out the memory of Amalek from under heaven.** This statement at first seems contradictory because God wanted His victory over Amalek preserved forever, yet also says He will **blot out the memory of Amalek.** Verse 16 causes more of a furrowed brow when we read that **the Lord will have**

war against Amalek from generation to generation. However, the apparent tension is relieved when we probe a bit deeper.

Israel would continue to **face war against Amalek from generation to generation**. God used the Amalekites to punish Israel's obstinacy during their wilderness wanderings, as described in Numbers 14:25-45. The Amalekites also caused trouble for Israel during the period of the Judges, as mentioned in Judges 6:3, 33; 7:12. Saul, who was Israel's first human king, was instructed to completely destroy the Amalekites. But he disobeyed and failed to do so, as narrated in 1 Samuel 15. David also waged war against the Amalekites, ensuring their complete destruction in 1 Samuel 30.

Despite the ongoing conflict between Amalek and Israel, which began in the wilderness and persisted for several generations, God ultimately promised to **blot out the memory of Amalek from under heaven**. Victory over Amalek was assured, even if it would not be completely realized at once. As one commentator pointed out, "it seems that it is precisely because the Amalekites will cease to exist that a memorial of some kind is needed to keep the lesson alive for Israel."[206] Therefore, Israel would continue to have conflicts with Amalek for generations, but one day, Amalek would be wiped out and forgotten, except as an ancient foe God ultimately destroyed.

In addition to reciting it to Joshua, **Moses built an altar and named it "The Lord is My Banner."** This was not the typical type of altar we think of where an animal was sacrificed to the Lord. Rather, this altar served "as a memorial and witness to the battle and its portents."[207] Moses was not the first person to construct and name this type of altar, nor would he be the last. The patriarchs did this, especially Jacob (Genesis 33:20; 35:7), and Joshua would do so when he took over the leadership of Israel after Moses. These altars were for worship and expressing gratitude (usually for a specific event) and reminded people to worship God for what He did every time they would see one.[208]

Moses called this particular altar **"The Lord is My Banner."** In this sense, a banner could better be translated as "signal pole," for "in all earlier texts, it refers not to something made of fabric or cloth but of a decorated pole held high and used as a signal marker or a signal pole."[209] In the battle with the Amalekites, the pole was Moses' staff. It was held high to secure the Lord's victory on their behalf, but it was also a visible reminder to the troops fighting below to keep going. Whenever they may have been tempted to give up, the Israelites could look at the staff and be reminded of who they were fighting for and who was fighting on their behalf. By naming this altar, **"The Lord is My Banner,"** Moses was reminding the Israelites that the power of a sword did not win the battle. This battle, like all others, was won by the power of the Lord. God was the **Banner** around which Israel should always rally and draw their strength—yes, in military pursuits, but also every day in their walks of faith.

Summary

God provided Israel with so many opportunities to trust and obey Him, but they were having a very difficult time getting it. After failing at every stage of their journey, God led them to the next stop, **and Israel traveled in stages from the wilderness of Sin, eventually camping at Rephidim**. Once again, they found themselves in a place **without water for the people to drink**. This was not accidental. It was not as though God was surprised to discover the lack of water there; rather, God was testing them, and once again, they failed.

Instead of humbly asking the Lord to provide, **the people quarreled with Moses**. As we discussed, the Hebrew word for **quarreled** is much stronger than the previous ones used for "grumbling." The people were furious and were essentially putting him on trial. Moses' rebuttals did nothing to calm them down. It got so bad that **Moses cried out to the Lord, saying, "What shall I do with these people? A little more, and they will stone me."** Moses was not faithless in this statement; he genuinely believed the people were out of control and needed God to intervene.

Sure enough, God responded. He told Moses to **pass before the people and take… some of the elders of Israel and the staff.** God would **stand before** him **on the rock at Horeb.** Moses would then **strike the rock, and water would come out of it so that the people may drink.** Unlike Israel, Moses obeyed the Lord without question or hesitation, and God once again provided for the needs of His people despite their horrendous behavior toward Him.

While not explicitly stated, an argument can be made that the next part of the narrative was another test for Israel. Though only a handful of verses, the account of the Amalekite battle carries powerful symbolism and truths that God wanted Israel (and us) to remember forever. We, like Israel, cannot always control our circumstances. **Amalek came and fought against Israel,** completely unprovoked. Similarly, we are often "attacked" by unfortunate circumstances like illness, financial hardships, etc. We often do not see trials until they confront us, and how we respond determines whether or not we will succeed against them.

Despite their gross lack of military skill and prowess, Moses immediately took action and prepared their defense on two fronts—spiritually and physically. He empowered Joshua to handle the physical battle by telling him, "**Choose men for us and go out, fight against Amalek.**" It is possible Joshua had already been a recognized leader charged with thinking about the development of Israel's military because he **did as Moses told him.** Given the speed with which he responded to Moses' charge, he must have had some idea of the men he would take with him to battle. Joshua's commission also reveals the trust and confidence Moses had in him. Moses and Joshua were responding to the threat with composure and clear minds. It was a problem they did not want, but neither wasted time whining about it.

Yet Moses knew the real battle was not only to be fought with flesh and blood, so he, **Aaron, and Hur went up to the top of the hill** to intercede on Israel's behalf with the Lord. Moses knew this battle needed to be fought in heaven just as it was on earth, and his job was to petition God on behalf of Israel.

They quickly realized a correlation between Moses' actions and those on the battlefield: **it came about that when Moses held his hand up, Israel prevailed, and when he let his hand down, Amalek prevailed**. There was nothing magical about the staff Moses was holding. It was not a wand that supernaturally ushered victory from God to the battlefield. But it did reveal God's power and provision to the Israelites. It was the same staff that He had used in the plagues against Egypt and the same staff used to part and then close the sea. It was a tool being lifted up to the glory of God, and while it was raised, God responded with glorious favor towards His people.

But they encountered a serious problem when they realized the battle was going to be hours long, not minutes: **Moses' hands were heavy**. He was north of eighty years old, and even if he was particularly fit, he could not keep his hands up for hours on end. That is where Aaron and Hur came in. **They took a stone and placed it under him, and he sat on it, and Aaron and Hur supported his hands, one on one side and one on the other. Thus, his hands were steady until the sunset**. Aaron and Hur were observant, humble, and eager to help however they could. The moment they noticed the problem, they took action to solve it, and the victory that day was largely due to their dedication.

Not every battle will have physical components, but every battle demands a spiritual response, and if we are wise, we will invite others into the fight through prayer, as Moses did with Aaron and Hur. Yet we should also seek to be "Aarons and Hurs" to others going through challenging times, meeting both physical and spiritual needs. Perhaps a new mother is struggling with postpartum depression. We can pray for her, provide meals, or even assist with her laundry and tidy up her house. Maybe a friend is struggling in her marriage. We can offer a positive, encouraging, listening ear and pray with her often. Examples are endless, but the point is twofold: we need Aarons and Hurs in our lives, and we need to be Aarons and Hurs in the lives of others. In this way, the body of Christ glorifies our Head, and many battles will be won rather than lost for the kingdom.

And that is precisely what happened that day: **Joshua overwhelmed Amalek and his people with the edge of the sword.** Joshua fought tirelessly throughout the day. He knew Moses would be interceding with the Lord on the hill, but he obviously could not participate in prayer too actively with the battle raging around him. Yet he remained composed, fought valiantly, and relied on God to secure the victory for His people. Everyone came together and played their part that day, trusting God and acting obediently.

God wanted them to remember this battle. God told Moses, **"Write this in a book as a memorial and recite it to Joshua, that I will utterly blot out the memory of Amalek from under heaven."** While the complete destruction of Amalek would not occur until hundreds of years later, God made a promise to Israel with this victory that it would happen. Israel needed to know and remember this, which is partially why **Moses built an altar and named it "The Lord is My Banner."** God was the banner in that battle—the One they could look to with confidence, knowing that their victory and salvation rested in Him. But none of these truths held much value if they were forgotten. As we discussed in Chapter One, we are fallible, and our memories are too. Israel needed to set aside specific times to remember what God had done for them to remind them of His goodness and affection toward them. They needed to remember and dwell on the truth more than on any difficult circumstances that might arise.

Similarly, we need to actively remember and remind ourselves of God's truth and what He has accomplished in the past. His victories, such as this one with Amalek, nourish our souls and serve as weapons that keep us armed against the enemy. Meditating on His power, sovereignty, faithfulness, and provision can't help but strengthen our faith, and by extension, empower the faith of others when we come alongside them. Israel failed many tests of faith and refused to learn from their mistakes. However, Moses, Joshua, Aaron, and Hur stepped up and showed them how to trust and obey. It was challenging, but they remained determined in their faith and steadfast in their trust. They chose to learn from the mistakes of Israel and obey, regardless of the circumstances.

GROUP STUDY

Introduction

> The wise learn from other's mistakes as well as their own;
> fools learn from neither.

- Share a time in your life when you either learned from the mistakes of others (or your own) or failed to.
  - How did it impact your life?

The Word

God provided Israel with ample opportunities to live in obedience to Him. He gave them chance after chance to trust and obey Him, but they remained obstinate in their faithlessness.

> **Then all the congregation of the sons of Israel journeyed by stages from the wilderness of Sin, according to the command of the Lord, and camped at Rephidim, and there was no water for the people to drink. (Exodus 17:1)**

- Was Israel's arrival at Rephidim (or the problem they encountered there) an accident?
  - What does that reveal about God and His plan for them?

> **Therefore the people quarreled with Moses and said, "Give us water that we may drink." And Moses said to them, "Why do you quarrel with me? Why do you test the Lord?" But the people thirsted there for water; and they grumbled against Moses...So Moses cried out to the Lord, saying, "What shall I do to this people? A little more and they will stone me." (Exodus 17:2-3a)**

- What was Israel's reaction to their difficult circumstances?
  - How was it worse than previous times?
  - What does this reveal about their faith, especially at this point in their journey?

The Israelites were fools—refusing to learn from their mistakes despite so many opportunities to do so. Fortunately, God preserved a remnant within Israel who were strong in their faith and did learn from the mistakes of Israel. When Israel faced another difficult and unexpected trial with the attack of the Amalekites, leaders of faith in Israel stepped up.

> **Moses said to Joshua, "Choose men for us and go out, fight against Amalek. Tomorrow I will station myself on the top of the hill with the staff of God in my hand." Joshua did as Moses told him. (Exodus 17:9-10a)**

- Moses immediately recognized this battle would be fought on two fronts: physical and spiritual. Who did he put in charge of the physical battle?
  o Did he obey?
  o Why would that have been a difficult task?

Moses brought Aaron and Hur with him to the top of the hill to intercede with God on Israel's behalf. They quickly discovered that when Moses kept the staff/his hands raised to God, Israel would win, but when Moses lowered his hands, Israel would lose. They encountered a problem, though:

> **Moses' hands were heavy. Then they took a stone and put it under him, and he sat on it; and Aaron and Hur supported his hands, one on one side and one on the other. Thus his hands were steady until the sun set. So Joshua overwhelmed Amalek and his people with the edge of the sword. (Exodus 17:12-13)**

- How did Aaron and Hur step up and join the fight?
  o While it may seem like an insignificant action, how was it critical to Israel's victory that day?

Apply

> Give instruction to a wise man, and he will be still wiser,
> Teach a righteous man, and he will increase his learning.
> King Solomon, Proverbs 9:9

> All discipline for the moment seems
> not to be joyful, but sorrowful;
> yet to those who have been trained by it,
> afterwards it yields the peaceful
> fruit of righteousness.
> Hebrews 12:11

We can never evade challenging circumstances in life. In fact, much like He did with Israel at Rephidim, sometimes God purposely leads us into trials with the specific intention of nurturing our faith and advancing our sanctification. We have all made mistakes and will continue to do so, but the hallmark of a wise person is learning from our own mistakes and the mistakes of others as well.

- What's one area of your life you're struggling to overcome at the moment—something where you continually find yourself making the same mistakes over and over?
    - How is your life and faith impacted by those repeated failures?
- And not just your own life, but the lives of others around you?

We certainly don't want to replicate the behavior of Israel in these passages, but we absolutely want to emulate the faith and obedience demonstrated by Moses, Joshua, Aaron, and Hur.

- What's one thing that stuck out to you reading about their faith that you can begin implementing in your own life?

WEEK SEVEN

SPEAK UP AND STEP UP

Exodus 18:1-18:27

PERSONAL BIBLE STUDY QUESTIONS

1. Who came to see Moses? (18:1, 5)
2. What had he heard? (18:1)
3. Who did he bring with him? (18:2-3)
4. What were Moses' sons' names, and what did they mean? (18:3-4)
5. What was Moses' reaction to seeing Jethro? (18:7)
    a. What does this greeting reveal about their relationship?
6. Once they settled in, what did Moses tell Jethro? (18:8)
    a. How did Jethro respond? (18:9-12)
    b. Who joined them that evening? (18:12)
7. What aspect of Moses' leadership did Jethro point out as unwise? (18:14)
    a. Why was it problematic, according to Jethro? (18:18)
8. What was Jethro's suggested solution? (18:19-23)
    i. What kind of men did he suggest Moses choose? (18:21)
    ii. What did Jethro say would happen if Moses listened to him? (18:23)
9. How did Moses respond? (18:24)
    i. What character traits does Moses' response reveal about him?

COMMENTARY

Exodus 18:1-18:27

Imagine a river with the most scenic, pure water you have ever seen. It stretches for miles, lazily winding its way down a picturesque mountain. If you followed it from beginning to end, you would see numerous waterfalls, wildlife sipping its refreshing waters, and stones sparkling like gems underneath its surface. You would hear the roar of water rushing over boulders in some places, birds chirping gleefully as they bathed themselves in others, and the trickling of water in serene pools that would inspire masterpieces from any artist attempting to capture them. It is a dazzling river that makes visitors catch their breath in wonder.

Now, let's imagine the water is God's Spirit moving in and through the banks of the river, which represent our lives. He fills us with His Spirit the moment we accept Christ as our Savior and then moves in and through our lives to accomplish His purposes. But occasionally, we turn our attention away from the waters and to the landscape. Despite having beautiful boulders and trees planted in the calm pools of our lives, we long for what we do not have—the trees and rocks on the land. So, we weaken the banks of our lives to accommodate them. We open ourselves up so they fall into the river, which inevitably restricts its flow.

The occasional tree or boulder is annoying but not catastrophic—the river adapts by moving around the impediment and carries on its way. It disrupts the flow temporarily and will always be an eyesore, but it will eventually settle and become part of the riverscape. But sometimes, it is not just one tree or boulder. Sometimes, we get stuck in sin and act like beavers in our lives, damming up God's Spirit flowing through us.

It may or may not be intentional. Sometimes, it is a deliberate, blatant sin. We cut those trees down one toothy bite at a time, then smack it over with defiant tails right into the middle of the river. We brazenly disobey God with eyes wide open and have to suffer the consequences for it.

Yet other times, it is far more subtle and unintentional. Sometimes, it is not so much a sin as a series of unwise choices. Perhaps we get hit with difficult circumstances and default into survivor mode, where all we are trying to do is survive one moment to the next. But maybe that turns into weeks or months instead of only days, like it was originally intended to be. Priorities get shifted, our wisdom erodes, and those trees fall because our soil is too weak to keep them upright.

That is where Moses finds himself in this chapter. He had been strong and steadily allowing God to flow powerfully in and through his life. But leading an obstinate people was proving to be quite the stressor, and his decisions started to impede the flow. He was damming up the river and not even realizing it. Fortunately, God sent someone to help break up the dam and get the river flowing powerfully again.

Exodus 18:1-12

> **Now Jethro, the priest of Midian, Moses' father-in-law, heard of all that God had done for Moses and for Israel His people, how the Lord had brought Israel out of Egypt. Jethro, Moses' father-in-law, took Moses' wife Zipporah, after he had sent her away, and her two sons, of whom one was named Gershom, for Moses said, "I have been a sojourner in a foreign land." The other was named Eliezer, for he said, "The God of my father was my help, and delivered me from the sword of Pharaoh." (18:1-4)**

At this point in the narrative, we take a break from focusing on Israel and their wilderness excursions and turn our attention to Moses' personal life. **Jethro, the priest of Midian and Moses' father-in-law** is reintroduced and will play a central role in this entire chapter. We first met **Jethro** in Exodus 2 (discussed thoroughly in the first volume of this study), though he was presented as Reuel then. Jethro and Reuel were the same person; he just had two names—one was a literal name, and one was a title. Reuel meant "friend of God," which was fitting for his role as the priest of Midian, though it could have been his literal name as well. Jethro meant "his excellency," which could also have been a title he was referred to out of respect for those under his spiritual authority.

Not only was he a priest, but Jethro was also the father of seven daughters, who were the first people Moses encountered in the wilderness after fleeing Egypt. If you remember from Chapter 2, Moses fled Egypt after killing an Egyptian whom he had witnessed beating a Hebrew slave. He originally thought no one had seen him do it, but the next day, when attempting to break up a fight between two Hebrew men, Moses realized that the word was out—people knew he was a murderer. Pharaoh found out about it and tried to kill Moses, so Moses ran away and ended up in the land of Midian, where he sat down by a well. Jethro's seven daughters came to the well to water their father's flock, but ran into trouble when other shepherds attempted to drive them away. Moses interceded on the women's behalf, drove the shepherds away, and then helped the women water their flock. The women told their father, Jethro, what had happened, and Jethro invited Moses to stay with them. Eventually, Jethro gave one of his daughters, Zipporah, to Moses as a wife.

Moses ended up living in Midian for forty years until God appeared to him in the midst of a burning bush and called him to deliver Israel from Egypt. Despite throwing every excuse at Him to get out of the call, Moses eventually conceded to go. In one final attempt to get out of it, he deceitfully told Jethro that he wanted to return to Egypt to see if his brethren were still alive. Jethro did not take the bait, however, and with all confidence and blessing said, "Go in peace." Jethro seemed to have far more wisdom than Moses, and was sensitive to God's work in Moses' life.

That was the last we have heard about Jethro until now. Now we learn that **he heard of all that God had done for Moses and for Israel, His people, in bringing Israel out of Egypt.** As we have discussed previously, ancient people groups may not have had internet or phones, but communication still occurred at an impressive pace. Through means such as caravanners, "messengers, general gossip, and the like, Jethro had been learning of how Moses and the Israelites were faring during the plagues and the exodus itself."[210] Events as momentous as the exodus and the parting of the sea would have been quite the hot topic of conversation for several months, even years, among the ancient people groups. They still are today!

Further, it is almost certain that Jethro had also been eagerly asking for news about Moses and the Israelites. He was not just passively hearing the word as it came about. We know this first because Moses was his son-in-law, and Jethro obviously cared about him and how God's "river" was flowing in and through his life and that of the Israelites. But he had a practical interest as well: his daughter and grandsons. **Jethro, Moses' father-in-law,** had taken **Moses' wife Zipporah, after he had sent her away, and her two sons** to live with him. Zipporah and her two sons had been living with Jethro presumably for several months, which raises quite a few questions.

Back in chapter 4, we were told that Zipporah and their sons went with Moses to Egypt. But at some unmentioned point in Scripture, they returned to Jethro. Some scholars believe this happened before they even arrived in Egypt, concluding that Zipporah and their sons turned back after the strange circumcision event on the journey. Others believe that they made it to Egypt, but once Moses realized that Pharaoh was not going to let the Israelites go with any reasonable speed, he sent them back for safety reasons.

Another theory is that Moses divorced Zipporah while in Egypt. This idea is largely based on the phrase that Moses **had sent her away**. While there may be a tiny thread of textual evidence to support that theory, the majority of evidence is against it.[211] It is far more likely that Moses had **sent her away** to protect her, knowing she would be in excellent hands with Jethro.

Obviously, it was not just Zipporah who was sent away; Moses sent their two sons with her:

Of whom one was named Gershom, for Moses said, "I have been a sojourner in a foreign land." The other was named Eliezer, for he said, "The God of my father was my help, and delivered me from the sword of Pharaoh." **Gershom** was introduced by name back in chapter 2, and his name reflected Moses' situation at the time—he sojourned in Midian, which was a **foreign land** to him. **Eliezer** was only subtly referenced in the use of the plural form of "sons" in chapter 4 when they left for Egypt originally. We learn his name now, and it also reflects a significant moment in Moses' life. **Eliezer** means "God is help" and was a common biblical name in those days. [212] Moses clarified that the help for which **Eliezer** was named was when God spared Moses **from the sword of Pharaoh** when Pharaoh sought his life for killing an Egyptian.

Moses naming **Eliezer** after his escape from Pharaoh inspires two interesting possibilities. First, his escape might have been far more dramatic than the brevity of the Scriptural text indicates. Pharaoh sought his death, and it is possible that Moses barely escaped. Perhaps he had more than one close call on his way out of Egypt, which leads us to a second thought: he knew that God was the only reason he got away. Something happened during that escape that made a profound impression on Moses, and he understood that God deserved the credit for his deliverance. Just as the altar at Rephidim would remind Israel of how God is their Banner, **Eliezer** was a living memorial of God's faithfulness to Moses. God delivered Moses **from the sword long** before He would deliver Israel from it; His faithfulness knows no limit. He continued protecting and delivering His people from harm and would do so for generations.

> **Then Jethro, Moses' father-in-law, came with his sons and his wife to Moses in the wilderness where he was camped, at the mount of God. He sent word to Moses, "I, your father-in-law Jethro, am coming to you with your wife and her two sons with her." (18:5-6)**

After hearing about what God had done for Moses and Israel, Jethro presumably determined it was a good time to reunite Moses' immediate family. He **came with his sons and his wife to Moses in the wilderness, where he camped at the mount of God**. Jethro is referred to as Moses' father-in-law over a dozen times in this chapter, which is quite a noticeable repetition. This indicates that Jethro should be seen primarily in his familial context with Moses, not so much in his priestly role or any authority he had therein.[213] Jethro was not there in any official capacity. He was there as a father, returning his daughter and grandsons to their husband and father.

The mount of God is Sinai, as confirmed a bit later in chapter 19:2— "When they set out from Rephidim, they came to the wilderness of Sinai and camped in the wilderness; and there Israel camped in front of the mountain." Perhaps Jethro knew or speculated that Israel would settle there for a while, so he decided it was a good location for the reunification. Whether coincidental or intentional, it seems as though it was, in fact, good timing on Jethro's part.

Before they came, Jethro **sent word to Moses,** telling him that he was coming with his **wife** and their **two sons**. Sending messengers ahead was a common practice back then; messengers could move far more quickly than caravans or other traveling groups. We see this many generations before in Genesis 32:3 when Jacob "sent messengers before him to his brother Esau in the land of Seir." While it was a completely different situation (Jacob was terrified because he thought Esau may still want to kill him), it is still a similar circumstance in sending a messenger ahead to prepare for a family reunion. Jethro wanted Moses to be prepared for their arrival, not in an arrogant way – "Be sure you have everything ready and waiting for us!" but in a humble, courteous way, "Hey, we're coming and wanted to give you a heads up so you can do what you need to in order to get ready." Moses surely appreciated the notice and was able to make preparations for his family's arrival. He had been traveling solo since Israel left Egypt; his focus had been on leading Israel and following God closely. Now, he needed to shift gears and wrap his mind around settling down a bit, providing not just for Israel but for his family as well.

> **Then Moses went out to meet his father-in-law Jethro, and he bowed down and kissed him; and they asked each other of their welfare and went into the tent. Moses told his father-in-law all that the Lord had done to Pharaoh and to the Egyptians for Israel's sake, all the hardship that had befallen them on the journey, and how the Lord had delivered them. (18:7-8)**

Sending messengers ahead was typical, and so was Moses' response. He **went out to meet his father-in-law**, Jethro. Moses did not just go about his business and let them arrive whenever they did. He eagerly and actively awaited them and then **went out to meet** them, presumably before they even got to the camp. This indicates that Moses was excited to see them, and goes even further to rebuke the theory that Moses had divorced Zipporah. Extended family dynamics are difficult enough. It is doubtful Moses would have been enthusiastic about seeing the father of his ex-wife if they had divorced.

When Moses reached them, **he bowed down and kissed him**. Bowing and greeting with a kiss were customary actions in the East back then.[214] Going back to our Jacob and Esau example from above, we read that Jacob "bowed down to the ground seven times," and Esau "ran to meet him and embraced him, and…kissed him" (Genesis 33:3, 4). These were signs of respect and affection, which Moses held for his father-in-law.

Also customary was **asking each other about their welfare**, which Moses and Jethro did. Similar to today, they asked (and genuinely wanted to know) how each other was and **went into the tent** to discuss it further. Some things do not change over the years. When someone we hold in high esteem comes over, we do not go outside to greet them only to keep them outside. We invite them inside and settle in to hear the news of what has been going on in their lives. This is exactly what Moses did. Jethro, Zipporah, and the boys had just finished a journey, and this was a momentous reunion of a family. Moses eagerly asked how they were and invited them into his tent to get comfortable, perhaps enjoy some refreshments, and settle into a conversation centered around what God had been doing in their lives.

Their family was now reunited, and things had come full circle. Jethro had always extended hospitality and kindness to Moses, and now Moses has the chance to reciprocate the blessing to him. One commentator notes the following circle of blessings: Jethro sent Moses away in peace to go to Egypt (4:18); now Moses greeted him in peace. Jethro brought Moses into his home and family after learning what Moses did for his daughters; Moses now received Jethro into his home, thankful for Jethro bringing his family to him.[215] Unlike his former father figure in Egypt (Pharaoh), Jethro has extended only blessings to Moses and was excited to hear a firsthand account of all God's actions on behalf of His people.

Moses complied and **told his father-in-law all that the Lord had done to Pharaoh and to the Egyptians for Israel's sake, as well as all the hardship that had befallen them on the journey and how the Lord had delivered them.** I love this recap sandwich Moses gives Jethro. He starts and ends with the **Lord**, which is the best way to tell any story. I imagine Moses started at the beginning when he told **Jethro all that the Lord had done to Pharaoh and to the Egyptians for Israel's sake.** This probably took a while, considering all the details there were to share. He would have likely begun with the first meeting with Pharaoh, which did not go very well, then talked about the plagues and continued interactions with Pharaoh. Moses probably recounted his rising frustration with Pharaoh for his stubbornness and then with Pharaoh's backtracking—sometimes agreeing to let the Israelites go and then changing his mind. He must have recounted so many details not recorded in Scripture, and I can just imagine Jethro wide-eyed in amazement as he listened to the story unfold.

After telling Jethro all about the exodus, Moses moved on **to all the hardship that had befallen them on the journey** in the wilderness. Though not expressly stated, it is implied (and was well-known at the time) that the hardship was the fault of the Israelites. They were acting like angry beavers, damming up the flow of God's power and affection in their lives. The Israelites watched God deliver them from the Egyptians with plague after plague, and then the parting of the sea that destroyed the elite of the Egyptian army. But after all that, their faith failed, and failed hard. They barely made it to the wilderness before grumbling about a lack of water, then about the scarcity of food, then disobeyed when God provided them with food, and complained yet again when they arrived at another location with insufficient water. Of course, the Amalekites were a hardship not of their own doing, though I still believe that God orchestrated that battle to wake them up to their dependence on Him.

Egypt was a pagan nation that did not have a good track record with God. But Israel, God's own people, were not doing such a great job themselves. Moses' frustration with Pharaoh likely shifted to the Israelites as he recounted **all the hardship** they brought on themselves. Perhaps he was kind in his recounting of the facts to Jethro, especially since they had just experienced a powerful victory over the Amalekites. Or maybe he stuck to the straight facts and relayed the narrative exactly as it happened—warts and all.

Fortunately, God did not give Israel what they deserved—abandonment. Instead, Moses told Jethro **how the Lord had delivered them**. The Israelites were not capable of anything on their own. They were former slaves who had literally never known any other way of life. They were skilled in manual labor but had no idea how to function as their own nation. Without God, they literally had no hope of surviving in the wilderness, as Moses undoubtedly told Jethro. God remained faithful, and He **delivered them**. Despite not deserving it, and most of the time, not even asking for it with any kind of respect or politeness, God remained faithful and delivered them from every hardship they encountered. He provided above and beyond what they could have asked for and did so miraculously with each provision—water, food, and victory over Amalek.

Can you imagine listening to Moses telling Jethro all of this? If you are anything like me, you live for conversations like this—catching up with longtime friends or family, especially when weaving God's hand in and through everything. I recently had the blessing of spending a couple of hours with a longtime family friend whom I had not seen in thirteen years. We grew up together, and our families did almost everything together for the first twenty years of my life. Things happened; we moved states apart from each other and did not really keep in touch other than occasional social media interactions. Getting together with her again was so wonderful! She made the comment as she was about to leave that getting together felt like being home again. There is just something about catching up with someone you grew up with—especially in a theological/church context that refreshes your very soul.

I can imagine Jethro beaming as Moses told him all the things God had been doing in and through his life and for Israel. Moses had changed so much since he left Midian for Egypt. He was scared and immature when he left; now, he is a strong leader, dependent on God, and steadfast in following after Him. Jethro must have been proud not only because he was Moses' father-in-law but also from his position as someone with spiritual authority. Every indication we have of Jethro was that he was a man of faith (even if he was not fully aware of the true God yet). And there is no greater joy a parent can have than seeing their children (and children-in-law) growing in their faith and being used by God to accomplish His purposes.

> **Jethro rejoiced over all the goodness which the Lord had done to Israel, in delivering them from the hand of the Egyptians. So Jethro said, "Blessed be the Lord who delivered you from the hand of the Egyptians and from the hand of Pharaoh, and who delivered the people from under the hand of the Egyptians. Now I know that the Lord is greater than all the gods; indeed, it was proven when they dealt proudly against the people." Then Jethro, Moses' father-in-law, took a burnt offering and sacrifices for God, and Aaron came with all the elders of Israel to eat a meal with Moses' father-in-law before God. (18:9-12)**

As expected, Jethro received the news from Moses warmly. He **rejoiced over all the goodness that the Lord had done for Israel**, especially **in delivering them from the hand of the Egyptians**. Interestingly, the word **rejoiced** (*hada*) is only used three times in Scripture, but its meaning is clear: Jethro was glad and celebrated **all the goodness that the Lord had done for Israel**. Moses faithfully communicated God's sovereignty in and through all the Israelites' adventures, and Jethro eagerly picked up on it. He saw Israel's deliverance from Egypt for what it was—divine intervention by God Himself. Being delivered **from the hand of the Egyptians** brings us back to the "hand" motif that has been referenced several times in our narrative thus far. When God's hand went against Pharaoh's, He won, and it was not even a competition. God's power surpasses all others, and that was where Jethro directed the conversation next.

After celebrating God's deliverance of Israel, Jethro confessed that he now knows **that the Lord is greater than all the gods. Indeed, it was proven when they dealt proudly against the people**. While Jethro was a priest, that does not mean (nor should we assume) that he was a priest of Yahweh, or that he was intimately familiar with Him. Jethro was not an Israelite, so anything he knew about God would have had to be learned from outside sources, like Moses when they lived together in the wilderness for forty years. By all accounts, he was receptive to the truth. It stands to reason that when Moses told him about his encounter with the Lord at the burning bush, Jethro's interest was piqued, and he followed the hand of God closely from then on.

Jethro's confession here, **that the Lord is greater than all the gods**, could very well have been a conversion experience to the true God. Some scholars believe that this was a great awakening moment for Jethro, and that he fully and totally converted on the spot to become a worshipper of Yahweh. While that may be true, the text seems to indicate a confirmation of faith that was already there more than an introduction to faith in God. Again, Jethro was a spiritual man who had been wisely observing the movement of God for quite some time. He may have believed in the existence of other gods before, but he remained astute and hungry for the truth. Now, he believed in Yahweh, **that the Lord is greater than all the gods.** He stood amazed by what Moses had told him, and was excited to let God start flowing through his life as well.

The last part of his statement has confounded even the brightest of scholars: **Indeed, it was proven when they dealt proudly against the people.** Its confusion lies in the fact that the Hebrew words are unusual, and it seems to be an incomplete thought.[216] I will spare you all the technicalities, but most believe it means the Egyptians received what they had coming—that their pride became their downfall. God proved His sovereignty with ease, even over the vastly considered "powerful" gods of Egypt. So Jethro's overall point is that God **is greater than all the gods,** a fact that was confirmed in that even Egypt's gods did not stand a chance against Him or His people.

Jethro then did what anyone back then would have done to praise and thank God—he **took a burnt offering and sacrifices for God, and Aaron came with all the elders of Israel to eat a meal with Moses' father-in-law before God.** The official sacrificial system and its requirements had not yet been articulated by God at this point, but sacrifices had been practiced since nearly the beginning of time. The point of contention between Cain and Abel early in Genesis was that God accepted Abel's sacrifice, and not Cain's. Thus, sacrifices were an established form of worship, even if the exact specifications of sacrifices had yet to be officially announced within any kind of official law for the Israelites.

It seems as though this sacrifice was more for celebration and fellowship around God's sovereignty than one for repentance.[217] The communal aspect of the **burnt offering and sacrifices for God** affirms this, for it was partaken of with **Aaron** and **the elders of Israel.** The perception of Aaron and the elders seems to indicate that "Jethro's confession of YHWH was warmly welcomed by the Israelite leaders."[218] They embraced Moses' father-in-law and joined in his celebration of God on their behalf.

This celebratory meal was undoubtedly uplifting for Jethro, but it must have been quite an encouragement to the Israelite leaders as well. Until this point, Israel did not have any human allies outside their caravan. God was obviously on their side and claiming them as His own, but every other people group Israel had encountered so far viewed them as enemies, not friends. It must have been so refreshing to have an outsider come into their presence, eagerly hear about and rejoice over what God had done for them, and join them in celebrating it. Here, we see quite a contrast between Jethro and Israel.

Jethro, a bystander at best in this narrative, was hungry for the Lord, excitedly embraced all that He was doing, and worshipped Him immediately for it. In contrast, as the direct recipient of God's deliverance and blessing time and again, Israel had only taken dedicated time to praise God once (after the sea closed on the Egyptians). Jethro was responding the way Israel should have been responding every step of the way. Perhaps the Israelite leaders' faith was bolstered by Jethro's acts of worship, or at the very least, they felt the sting of conviction seeing him so naturally worshipping a God he had not even truly known until now. If a relative stranger could see the goodness of God and praise Him for it, surely the Israelites could step it up and do the same. The elders learned a lesson from Jethro that evening, and Moses would become a student of his father-in-law as well.

Exodus 18:13-27

> It came about the next day that Moses sat to judge the people, and the people stood about Moses from the morning until the evening. Now when Moses' father-in-law saw all that he was doing for the people, he said, "What is this thing that you are doing for the people? Why do you alone sit as judge and all the people stand about you from morning until evening?" Moses said to his father-in-law, "Because people come to me to inquire of God. When they have a dispute, it comes to me, and I judge between a man and his neighbor and make known the statutes of God and His laws." (18:13-16)

After an evening full of wonderful conversation and worship, they woke up, and Moses returned to his usual duties. One of Moses' responsibilities that we discovered **was to sit in judgment of the people**. People came to him **from morning until evening**, asking him to render judgments for them. This made sense, as he was the leader of the people and undoubtedly the one closest to the Lord.

Jethro, the observant patriarch that he was, **saw all that he was doing for the people**. Jethro did not just deliver his daughter and grandsons to Moses, listen to some gossip, and then go on his way. Nor did he simply sit in the tent, relax, and expect to be catered to or entertained. Instead, he went out and observed his son-in-law as he carried out his leadership duties. Notice that the text does not say that he inserted himself into the judgments, nor did he take over. Rather, he sat to the side and observed what Moses did.

After taking the time to gain insight into Moses' leadership, Jethro felt comfortable enough to gently confront him about something. He asked Moses, **"What is this thing that you are doing for the people? Why do you alone sit as judge and all the people stand about you from morning until evening?"** The purpose of this question was not to discover what kinds of judgments Moses was making or why he was making them. As he would soon elaborate on, Jethro wanted to know why Moses **alone** sat **as judge**.

Moses responds with an explanation of his duties: **"Because the people come to me to inquire of God. When they have a dispute, it comes to me, and I judge between a man and his neighbor and make known the statutes of God and His laws."** We do not know whether this was a role established by God for Moses among the people or if it was something that naturally evolved when Israel left Egypt and began to require a judge to handle internal domestic issues. It's essential to remember that this was not a small group of people traveling together on a vacation. It was an enormous population who had never functioned as an independent nation before. While there were undoubtedly some basic laws among them, they had no official legal system or designated judge. As a result, Moses assumed this position by default, and it appears that it consumed most of his time.

People would stand around him, presumably forming some kind of line, **from morning until evening**. I can only imagine the kinds of issues that were presented to him. Did these issues range from relatively insignificant matters like, "This man killed my goat and refused to pay for or replace it?" to more substantial problems such as extramarital affairs or troublesome prodigal children? The text will soon reveal that there were both types of issues—both weighty and minor. The exact nature of these disputes will remain a mystery, as the content of them is not provided. However, we do know four things. First, the Israelites did have legal disputes among themselves. Second, they required a third-party judge to settle these disputes. Third, they still recognized and accepted Moses' position as their leader, knowing he would act and render judgment, **making known the statutes of God and His laws**. And fourth, that Moses was fulfilling that role as an arbitrator of legal issues that arose among and between the people.[219]

But the job far exceeded his ability to do it on his own.

> **Moses' father-in-law said to him, "The thing that you are doing is not good. You will surely wear out, both yourself and these people who are with you, for the task is too heavy for you; you cannot do it alone." (18:17-18)**

With the utmost respect, concern, and care for Moses, Jethro confronted him, expressing that his one-man system of justice **was not good.** Before delving into his reasoning, we must commend Jethro for the manner in which he conveyed this message to Moses. He chose to confront Moses privately. He did not call Moses out in front of the elders of Israel or even during their family dinner that evening. Nor did he interrupt Moses' judgments that day to voice his opinion and criticize Moses in the presence of the people. Instead, he had a private and discreet conversation with Moses.

There is much to learn from Jethro's approach. Let's begin by considering what Jethro refrained from doing. First, he did not ignore Moses' shortcomings. He did not turn a blind eye to the issues he had identified, hoping they would miraculously disappear. Ignoring Moses' errors would have conveyed a lack of genuine concern for his son-in-law. As the proverb goes, "Iron sharpens iron, so one man sharpens another" (Proverbs 27:17). If we care for someone, we strive to support them in their best interests. Jethro's silence would also have had significant consequences for both Moses and the Israelites. One person cannot effectively lead nearly two million people on their own. Eventually, people would grow impatient waiting for Moses and might take justice into their own hands, leading to various other issues in Israel. Additionally, Moses would have experienced burnout. Just as he could only keep his arms raised for a short time on his own in the previous narrative, he could only lead Israel single-handedly for a limited time before burning out. Jethro's decision not to remain silent was significant, and we will soon see how everyone appreciated his intervention.

Jethro also did not gossip. When we notice a problem, we like to talk about it. But our first instinct typically is not to approach the accused party. We like to go around his/her back and chat about it with others first. Women are particularly prone to this kind of behavior (though I have known some men who err in that sin as well), and it is gossip. If Jethro had struck up a conversation with Aaron or other elders of Israel criticizing Moses, he would have caused a rift between Moses and the elders, cast doubt on Moses' leadership, and caused significant turmoil in Israel. He would have undermined Moses and caused people to question his abilities instead of following him as he followed the Lord. Gossiping is sinful, and it harms all parties involved. As Ephesians 4:29 states:

> Let no unwholesome word proceed from your mouth, but only
> such a word as is good for edification according to the need of
> the moment, so that it will give grace to those who hear.

Jethro did not ignore Moses' unwise leadership method, nor did he gossip about it. Lastly, he refused to criticize Moses in front of others. He could have been loud or made sure other people could overhear his conversation with Moses. This would have had similar results as the gossip scenario—undermining Moses' authority, inviting distrust into the ranks of Israel, etc. Thankfully, Jethro did not ignore it, gossip about it, or confront Moses loudly in front of others. Rather, he took Moses aside and spoke to him privately. This act in itself proves Jethro's maturity, wisdom, and care for his son-in-law.

While Jethro's approach was gentle, his message was strong. The way Moses was judging the people was **not good**. Further, if Moses continued on this path, Jethro told him that he would "**surely wear out, both yourself and these people who are with you.**" This would happen because **the task** was **too heavy** for Moses; he could not **do it alone**. Jethro was not demeaning Moses or implying that he was an inept or incapable leader. Rather, he was doing something that far more mentors should tell the younger generation—we are not invincible. We have limits, and we will burn out if we are not careful.

According to Barna, 38% of pastors have considered leaving ministry in the last year, and 46% if they are a pastor under the age of 45.[220] Here are some other disturbing statistics from WordPartners.Org:[221]

- 1,500 pastors leave the ministry each month due to moral failure, spiritual burnout, or contention in their churches
- 80% of pastors and 84% of their spouses feel unqualified and discouraged in their role as pastors
- 50% are so discouraged that they would leave the ministry if they could, but have no other way of making a living
- 80% of seminary and Bible school graduates who enter the ministry will leave the ministry within the first five years
- 90% of pastors said their seminary or Bible school training did only a fair to poor job in preparing them for ministry
- 80% of pastors believe their ministry negatively affects their families

- 45.5% of pastors have experienced burnout/depression and had to take a break from ministry

Ministry is not an easy career or calling, and it has never been. We do not answer that call because we aspire to be rich, famous, or to have a life of ease. Quite the opposite. We enter the ministry to serve the Lord and dedicate our lives to help His church grow and thrive. Our focus is on the kingdom of God, not the kingdom of this world, and maintaining that perspective is increasingly challenging.

Those serving in ministry enter a spiritual battlefield every day, and the risk of burnout is overwhelming. Regardless of their specific ministry roles, the tasks are always too demanding for us to handle on our own. Without the utmost dependence on the Lord through the Word and prayer, support from family and friends walking alongside us, and wisdom in time and priority management, those in ministry will experience burnout and/or fail quickly and intensely.

Moses was carrying out his duties to the best of his ability. He was depending on the Lord and had at least some people encouraging him. But unfortunately, he was not being wise in his time and priority management. To be clear, he did not seem to be sinning in his approach to ministry. It was not arrogance or pride that had him acting as the sole judge for the Israelites. It is not as if people had tried to help and he pushed them away, arrogantly thinking he could handle it on his own. Rather, he sincerely did not know better. He was in survival mode, and the banks of his river were eroding at an alarming rate without him even realizing it. He also was not aware that there was another option.

Until now.

Jethro had been in ministry for several years and had learned a thing or two that he was willing and ready to pass along to Moses. He began by serving a slice of humble pie—Moses could not (and should not) attempt to do everything by

306

himself. We are not God; we cannot handle everything on our own, especially the problems and disputes of nearly two million people.

> **Now listen to me: I will give you counsel, and God be with you. You be the people's representative before God, and you bring the disputes to God, then teach them the statutes and the laws, and make known to them the way in which they are to walk and the work they are to do. (18:19-20)**

After pointing out that Moses' current situation was not good, Jethro paused to make sure Moses was paying attention. He told Moses to **listen**, for he would give him **counsel.** Using language like this emphasizes the importance of what was about to be said. Moses was already probably attentive, but in case he was not, Jethro told him to **listen.**

The **counsel** began by reassuring Moses that his position was not in jeopardy. Moses was undeniably **the people's representative before God.** God had chosen him from birth to lead His people out of Egypt and into freedom. Moses was faithfully fulfilling his role as a leader to the Israelites and representing them before the Lord. Moreover, he was not in error by bringing **disputes to God.** The people needed counsel, and Moses was the most qualified person to provide it to them. No one was questioning Moses' position as the leader, and Jethro reaffirmed that. Moses should continue as the **people's representative** and judge.

However, Moses was not being wise in his approach to leadership by trying to do it all by himself. As a brief side note, it is intriguing how it took Jethro, a complete outsider, to make this observation. It is difficult to believe that no one among the two million people in Israel recognized the issue. Perhaps some people did notice it earlier but were too nervous to voice their concerns. It is also possible that they were intimidated by Moses and assumed he knew better than they did. Or perhaps some were jealous and secretly hoped for his failure, so they kept their concerns to themselves. Some may or may not have realized the problem, but regardless, it took an outsider less than a day to notice, care, and have the courage to speak up.

Jethro noticed and advised Moses to **teach them the statutes and the laws, and make known to them the way in which they are to walk and the work they are to do.** It is likely that the Israelites knew some of God's laws, but they were unfamiliar with the majority of them. Furthermore, although they were a people associated with God through their ancestors, many of them did not possess direct knowledge of Him. Up to this point, the majority of the Israelites had known and approached God through the elders of Israel, but now they turned their attention to Moses.

To be fair, Moses had been teaching the people "the statutes of God and His laws," as he mentioned to Jethro in verse 16. However, the problem was that he was doing it on an individual, case-by-case basis. He would reveal God's **statutes** about something as it directly related to the case at hand. Essentially, he was putting out fires rather than preventing them, and he could not keep up.

Another issue, of course, is that no mere mortal can be the sole mediator between God and humanity. Jesus, of course, ultimately fulfilled that role, and He is the only one who could have. Witnessing Moses falter in this capacity is actually reassuring to us, because it reminds us of our complete incapability to approach God on our own. But it also underscores the enormity of what Jesus did for us. Israel needed a mediator, and always would. However, neither Moses nor the priests to come would be sufficient on their own, just as no sacrifice would ever prove adequate to endure. Jesus, on the other hand, became both the Mediator and the ultimate Sacrifice—fulfilling roles that no human could fulfill—so that we can be reunited with God for all eternity.

Part of Jethro's counsel, then, was for Moses to directly teach **the statutes and laws** to the people. The Israelites, as a nation comprising individual people, needed to learn **the way in which they are to walk and the work they are to do.** It was not sufficient for Moses to issue individual, specific judgments for every issue that arose. The people needed to understand these **statutes and laws** for themselves, thus reducing the necessity to consult Moses for minor matters and disputes. As the old saying goes, "Give a man a fish, and you'll feed him for a day. Teach a man to fish, and you'll feed him for a lifetime." Jethro was trying to teach Moses this same principle. Teach the people **the way in which they are to walk,** and they will be able to handle many issues on their own.

One question that arises at this point among many scholars is about chronology. How was Moses to teach the people God's statutes and laws if He had not yet articulated them? The Ten Commandments and subsequent laws will not be given until the next chapter. While this raises concerns for many, it does not bother me at all. Once again, the Israelites had some laws prior to leaving Egypt. They maintained their own national identity within Egypt, which would have included their own customs and rules that they were expected to observe. It is possible that God had provided them with some along the way. It is also possible that many of them were created through common sense. Even today, most laws merely reflect common morality—do not kill, steal, destroy, etc.

Further, God had already begun establishing laws on their journey, like with observing the sabbath and rules around manna. God had provided them with what they needed so far; the problem seems to be that the leaders of Israel were holding the laws captive in a sense and were not communicating them well to the people as a whole. This would have been problematic for many reasons, not the least of which was leaving Moses a ragged mess at the end of every day. Thus, while God had yet to write down all His laws for the Israelites, Moses was absolutely capable of sharing the laws and rules he knew without special prophetic intervention from God.

> **Furthermore, you shall select out of all the people able men who fear God, men of truth, those who hate dishonest gain; and you shall place these over them as leaders of thousands, of hundreds, of fifties and of tens. (18:21)**

Many problems could be avoided and/or resolved by teaching people the statutes and laws of God. But not all of them. Like today, there are issues that arise that need the direct involvement of an authority figure and/or judge. Jethro knew this, which is why he continued his counsel by telling Moses to **select out of all the people able men who fear God, men of truth, those who hate dishonest gain; and you shall place these over them as leaders of thousands, of hundreds, of fifties, and of tens.** Moses needed to divide up the work to relieve the burden of ministry that rested on his shoulders.

I wonder if, while hearing this or shortly thereafter, Moses' mind flashed back to the battle with the Amalekites. Moses was the one appointed to lift up the staff before God to ensure the Israelites' victory, but like being a judge, he was not capable of doing it alone for any extended period of time. He needed Aaron and Hur with him, encouraging him but also physically keeping his arms raised before the Lord. Aaron and Hur were ready, willing, and able to serve, and their assistance led to victory over the Amalekites.

In the same way, Moses needed to find other men who could assist him as judges and leaders within Israel. First, Jethro told Moses to **select out of all the people able men who fear God.** This instruction also brings us back to the battle with Amalek when Moses told Joshua to "Choose men for us and go out, fight against Amalek" (17:9). Joshua needed to make quick decisions, presumably based on knowing and having a relationship with at least some of the men he chose. Now it was Moses' turn to **select** men **out of all the people**. This, by definition, means that not everyone was qualified to serve in such a role. Indeed, we have seen ample examples of the Israelites' lack of faith in grumbling and distrust of God so far in the wilderness. There were doubtless "leaders" of those movements—men who rallied others against the Lord and Moses, rather than for them. There were others, of course, who simply did not have the faith or maturity to carry out such a task. These kinds of men were to be avoided. Moses' helpers were to be purposefully chosen, not randomly selected.

The first qualification Jethro insists on is that these men are **able men**. Being **able** to do the work sounds rather obvious, but it is a good reminder that not everyone *willing* to serve is *able* to serve. Hindrances could be physical; these men needed to be in decent health with enough stamina to be available every day. Another hindrance could be vocational. Despite not being established in the promised land yet, the Israelites were working in various capacities. Flocks needed to be tended to, clothing and sandals needed to be repaired and/or made, tools needed to be sharpened and mended, etc. Some men who may have been willing and wise enough to volunteer were perhaps not able to because of their current circumstances that needed to take priority.

I will not spend too much time on it, but because of the drama in our current culture, it needs to be articulated that these roles were limited to **men**, not women. This is neither the time nor place to conduct a full study of the roles of men and women in ministry, but in this particular case (and I would argue, in most positions of ministry leadership), these roles were reserved for men. God designed men and women to have a beautiful, complementary relationship with each other. Each was created to fulfill unique roles in life and in the kingdom of God here on earth. Men were created to be leaders—to protect, provide for, and guide women in ways that honor the Lord. Strong, masculine men are being viciously attacked in our culture, and it leaves a sour taste to anyone genuinely pursuing Christ. Christian women need to step up and be loud in our support, encouragement, and respect for our men. Masculinity is not a threat. It is a crucial necessity for the healing and restoration of much brokenness in our culture and church. Men were designed to lead, and we, as women, need to do everything possible to support them in those roles. Moses was to choose **able men** for these judgeship roles, but the qualifications did not stop there.

Once their ability was established, these men needed to **fear God**. Physical and vocational limitations were obvious and visible reasons for disqualification. Fearing God was just as important (perhaps more so), but a bit tougher to pinpoint. To know if a man fears God requires having a relationship with him.

Little can be ascertained about someone's faith from a distance (assuming they are not overtly pagan in their behavior). Many can put on a show well enough to fool people into thinking their faith is stronger than it actually is. Only when we get to know someone and/or hear of them through multiple testimonies of other people who know them well, can we begin to determine if they truly fear God.

In the last volume of this study, we talked a bit about what it means to **fear God**. The first time we encountered this concept was with the midwives in Egypt. Pharaoh told them to kill any and all male babies born to the Israelites. But the midwives feared God more than they did Pharaoh. Thus, they chose to honor what they knew was right—to do right in God's sight rather than obey an earthly king. This fear is not one of terror or anxiety, but more of a strong, humble reverence for who God is and our unworthiness to be in His presence. The more we understand who God is, the more we will tremble in awe of Him, and the stronger our faith will become.

Fearing God also implies a deep respect for any calling or service rendered to Him. In this case, the men whom Moses chose to serve as judges needed to recognize that their role extended far beyond the physical and temporal realm. These judgments were important because they revealed and confirmed God's laws and expectations for His people. These men, like Moses, would be representatives of God to His people, a role that should be taken very seriously. Only men who feared God could accomplish this with humility and effectiveness. Only men who feared God could get out of the way and issue judgments that aligned with His word more than their personal biases and opinions. Only men who feared God could draw people closer to Him through their counsel, which is the goal of every person serving in ministry.

Choosing **able men who fear God**, then, was crucial to establishing an effective method of judicial organization. But also imperative was that they be **men of truth**. It is dangerous when someone without integrity gains power. They abuse their positions and use their status for personal gain. Their number one concern is not for the people they (supposedly) serve, but for themselves. They will stop at nothing to get what they want, and one of their most dangerous weapons is their tongues. They say whatever sounds good to manipulate people into conforming to their agendas. This is exactly what Satan does, and has done since the creation of the world.

Anyone who knows me knows that I detest lying. It is my biggest pet peeve, though it seems far too serious for such a trivial term. Dishonesty does not just leave a sour taste in my mouth; it causes me to distrust and discredit someone immediately. My husband and I made a commitment early on in our parenting journey to never lie to our daughters. This includes being honest about the non-existence of childhood fantasies like Santa Claus and the Easter Bunny. We are not Scrooges who do not want them to have fun. They actually still have tons of fun going to see Santa and the Easter Bunny as silly characters that make them laugh. But as their parents, it is our job to lead them into the truth, specifically, the truth of God's Word.

How can we do that if we are simultaneously lying about other things? How can we expect them to trust us if we are lying about something as ridiculous as fictional characters being real? Further, why would we want to invite even a smidgen of distrust into our relationship with them? Even if they cannot articulate it yet, our children look to us to lead them to the Lord. They may not always like our answers, but our girls know that we will always speak the truth to them.

Just as parents have the responsibility of leading their children to the Lord and teaching them His truth, so these judges would be leading the Israelites to the Lord and teaching them His truth. We cannot lead anyone to the truth if we are busy living a lie. These men needed to be **men of truth**, inside and out.

They also needed to be men **who hated dishonest gain**. These positions were ones of authority, yet required utmost integrity in those filling them. Acting as a judge, especially as an extension of God's law, not just man's, was a sobering task. These men needed to be above and beyond any reproach. No one serving in this role could even be slightly tempted by things such as monetary bribes or other inappropriate compensation for ruling for or against a particular judgment. Judgments need to be made on the basis of truth and justice first and foremost; those with a reputation or tendency toward **dishonest gain** were not even to be considered.

After articulating these character traits for the men Moses would choose as judges, Jethro turns his attention to the practical side of things. It is one thing to have a solid group of men helping you, but exactly how were they going to help? What "jurisdictions" would they cover? How would it work logistically? Fortunately, Jethro had a plan: Moses should **place these men over groups as leaders of thousands, of hundreds, of fifties, and of tens**. Instead of Moses having everyone and their mother coming to him from dawn until dusk, he should have established tiers of leaders and judges to filter out the easier cases. A leader would be assigned to every one thousand Israelites. But leaders would also be assigned to smaller groupings within the thousand because a thousand people is still a large and overwhelming number for just one man. Thus, a leader would also be placed over groups of one hundred, another over an even smaller group of fifty, and another still over each group of ten.

Such a concept is not new today, and was not in ancient times either. Interestingly, this breakdown of leadership over smaller groups of people was a military concept that continued long after this time period. Chiefs and/or commanders were given charge over small groups of soldiers, and as they matured in their service, they would move up to a larger command over a larger group of people. The same is true today in our military services and also within corporations. Frankly, it is just common sense. Establishing specific points of contact and authority to smaller groups of people makes life far smoother and more enjoyable for everyone. The people know who to turn to when they find themselves in a pickle—the chain of command is clear, present, and established. Further, people understand that if an issue is outside the realm of the first authority figure, they can easily approach the next higher-up in command and continue that process until judgment can be rendered by someone with adequate authority.

That was exactly how Jethro suggested Moses should operate. The men Moses chose were to be assigned to specific positions, likely based on their life experience and spiritual maturity. Those who were less experienced were probably given positions over groups of ten, while those with more experience and solid reputations earned over time were likely granted positions over the groups of thousands. Jethro's point was that Moses needed to establish a system of judicial hierarchy. It was evident he could not do it by himself, nor would it have been wise to just pick a few men and distribute cases to them randomly as they arose. The Israelites needed a judicial system that was clear and easily understood.

> **Let them judge the people at all times; and let it be that every major dispute they will bring to you, but every minor dispute they themselves will judge. So it will be easier for you, and they will bear the burden with you. If you do this thing and God so commands you, then you will be able to endure, and all these people also will go to their place in peace." (18:22-23)**

Establishing this judicial hierarchy would significantly alleviate the pressure on Moses. Instead of Moses having to sit as a judge all day every day, the other leaders **would judge the people at all times**. Now, this does not mean that these men would have to be literally available 24/7 to the people within their jurisdiction. With the establishment of these positions likely came the establishment of certain times of day when these men were available to hear cases and/or be presented with issues. Again, these were not full-time ministerial positions. Some of them, perhaps those who were older and past their days of manual labor, could probably be available for large portions of the day. Others, however, were younger and still very much had daily responsibilities—work that required their attention. They could (and wanted to) give some of their time to this, but could not be available constantly for issues that were not urgent.

As we hinted before and as the hierarchy suggests, there would be issues too large and/or important for some of the lower-tier judges to handle. In those cases, Jethro told Moses **to let it be that every major dispute they will bring to him, but every minor dispute they themselves will judge**. Moses was still God's appointed leader to the Israelites and was expected to serve as a judge in some capacity. He needed to be available for disputes too complicated or heavy for other leaders to render judgment.

Sending cases to Moses would have, by the way, been another testament to the character of the lower-tier judges. Only those humble in their positions recognize their limitations and are responsible enough to send people "over their heads" to a higher authority figure. Insecure, selfish, and arrogant people hoard power; they do not relinquish it.

Doing this would make life **easier** for everyone, especially for Moses, because the judges would **bear the burden with** him. Again, just like Aaron and Hur bore the physical burden of holding Moses' arms up during Israel's battle with Amalek, so these men would bear the spiritual, emotional, and time burden that judging the Israelites had weighed on Moses thus far.

But it was not just good for Moses. It was good for the people. If Moses did this, not only would he **be able to endure**, but **all these people also will go to their place in peace**. Let's first chat about this concept of endurance. Life is hard, and sin makes it infinitely more difficult. Even with the Holy Spirit indwelling us, we fall, fail, and flail as we go about our lives trying to become more like Jesus and embrace His kingdom on earth as it is in heaven. Endurance is not an accessory for a Christian's life, it is a necessity. It is like oxygen. Without it, our faith cannot survive.

One of my favorite passages on endurance is Hebrews 12:1-3:

Therefore, since we have so great a cloud of witnesses surrounding us, let us also lay aside every encumbrance and the sin which so easily entangles us, and let us run with endurance the race that is set before us, fixing our eyes on Jesus, the author and perfecter of faith, who for the joy set before Him endured the cross, despising the shame, and has sat down at the right hand of the throne of God. For consider Him who has endured such hostility by sinners against Himself, so that you will not grow weary.

Endurance consists of discipline intently focused on something (or, in our case as Christians, Someone) greater than ourselves. When an athlete trains for a competition, his daily practice, exercises, and diet regimen can be grueling. Such discipline is not possible without him constantly dwelling on the competition before him—a specific goal that bolsters his determination and fuels his endurance to get there.

As the Hebrew passage states, Jesus is both the reason and motivation for our endurance as Christians. We fix our eyes on Him, desperately wanting to know Him, become like Him, and ultimately be with Him one day in heaven. Yet we also recognize that without Him, faith is not possible. We cannot manifest our own faith, nor can we cause it to grow by sheer will. Our faith and endurance thereof are a partnership predestined and worked out by the Holy Spirit in our lives in cooperation with Jesus and God the Father. While an athlete can discipline himself into excellence, we cannot discipline ourselves into faith. But we can create the right environment for our faith to flourish, which begins with laying "aside every encumbrance and the sin which so easily entangles us."

Earlier, we talked about how Moses' lack of wisdom in his approach to ministry was not a sin, and I believe that is true. But like every impediment to our growing faith and success in ministry (every tree that falls into our "river"), it was an encumbrance that directly resulted from a fallen world. Our struggles are not be limited to direct, personal sin. The earth and everything in it was cursed after the fall, and even honest mistakes can deter our endurance in pursuit of Christ.

Fortunately, Jethro was a blessing sent from God to inform Moses of a significant encumbrance that was causing great angst for both Moses and the Israelites in general. He told him about the trees damming up his river. Destroying the dam of sole responsibility as a judge would alleviate much stress and enable Moses to endure the race set before him. Further, it would remove encumbrances on the people's faith by allowing them to **go to their place in peace.**

Imagine for a moment how many people must have been waiting in line to speak with Moses every day. There could have been dozens, perhaps hundreds, of people needing advice and resolutions to a particular conflict they were experiencing. Only those with the ability and time to wait would have had the opportunity to get resolutions for their issues. It is quite possible that many of them gave up hours into their wait—their families and responsibilities calling them back to their tents. It is also probable that many were turned away each day after waiting for hours. At some point every evening, Moses needed to rest. Can you imagine waiting for hours in line—giving up an entire day's work and/or neglecting the responsibilities you had with your family and profession— only to be turned away at the last minute? These people were unable to **go to their place in peace**. In fact, they likely went to their tents angry, frustrated, hungry, and utterly disappointed. They came for a resolution and justice, they left unseen, unheard, and with their issues unresolved.

Establishing an organizational hierarchy of judges would have vastly improved, or to be more accurate, made possible a process for people to get answers to their questions and judgments to their issues in a timely fashion. They could be heard within a matter of minutes, not hours or days, and many of them would be able to receive a verdict with the same expediency. But even for those with more complicated cases, they would have been "passed along" to higher authorities and eventually to Moses in a far more accelerated fashion.

Both Moses and the Israelites would have experienced **peace** in this new judicial process. It would have fueled everyone's endurance and allowed them to get the resolutions they were so desperately seeking.

Jethro's advice was incalculably wise. It began with a quiet observation made out of concern for his son-in-law and was communicated to Moses privately and respectfully. Jethro presented Moses with a way to alleviate a significant encumbrance to his calling in ministry, and consequently eased countless burdens of the Israelites who needed counsel and verdicts in their daily struggles.

> **So Moses listened to his father-in-law and did all that he had said. Moses chose able men out of all Israel and made them heads over the people, leaders of thousands, of hundreds, of fifties and of tens. They judged the people at all times; the difficult dispute they would bring to Moses, but every minor dispute they themselves would judge. Then Moses bade his father-in-law farewell, and he went his way into his own land. (18:24-27)**

Great leaders embody humility. They must not be content with being "good enough," nor should they grow complacent in their abilities. Rather, they seek to grow and strive to make the most of what they have been given. Moses reveals the marks of a great leader in how he responds to Jethro here. Whereas a lesser man may have taken offense to Jethro's correction, Moses was hungry for it and receptive to it—he **listened to his father-in-law and did all that he had said.**

Every now and then, God brings someone into your life who truly amazes you. I have had the privilege of knowing some great people over the years, and all I want to do is sit with them and absorb every morsel of wisdom they are willing to give. Moses wisely took this approach with Jethro. His respect for his father-in-law opened the door for him to not only listen to his counsel, but take immediate and thorough action in carrying it out. It is one thing to hear wisdom; it is quite another to act on it. Moses does both, and with haste.

Just as Jethro advised, Moses **chose able men out of all Israel and made them heads over the people, leaders of thousands, of hundreds, of fifties, and of tens**. An official judicial hierarchy was established among the people, and relief must have been felt immediately by everyone. The leaders were able to judge the people at all times. They were available to the people when Moses could not be, and the people now had a specific person to go to with their concerns and disputes. As directed, **the difficult** cases would be brought to **Moses, but every minor dispute they themselves would judge.**

With one correction, Moses was able to raise up, establish, and empower leaders in Israel. Notice how additional leaders did not threaten or diminish his position. Quite the opposite. Raising up leaders to partner with him in ministry actually elevated his own ministry and allowed him to thrive in it. He could accomplish more and fulfill his calling with far more effectiveness by having a team than he ever could have on his own. Let this be a word of encouragement and a challenge to all the micromanagers out there. Let it go. Allow your team to help and take care of the smaller issues so you can direct your attention to the larger ones, and—gasp, be able to vision-cast and work on accomplishing even bigger goals. Get out of your own way and stop being an encumbrance to others' growth and flourishing. It is one thing to throw logs in your own river; it is quite another to throw them into others'. Remove obstacles, do not add to them. Lead as Moses did. Listen to wise counsel, take action, and allow your ministry, faith, and/or business to thrive.

Jethro accomplished his primary goal of returning his daughter and grandsons to Moses, and then was able to benefit Moses astronomically in his ministry pursuits. When that was finished, it was time for him to go home: **Moses bade his father-in-law farewell, and he went his way to his own land.** Jethro had responsibilities back home. It would not surprise me if he had followed his own advice years ago and established his own hierarchy system of leadership among his people. If so, this trip would have been taken with peace and surety that things would go well in his absence. Contrarily, could you imagine Moses ever being able to leave his position as leader over Israel at this time in their history? They would have been directionless and miserable; chaos would have ensued. But now he was actively taking steps to establish a pyramid of leadership and subsequently, peace among the Israelites.

The last time Moses and Jethro parted, Moses left to begin the journey of a lifetime—being God's appointed man to lead the Israelites out of Egypt and into freedom. Moses left to attain freedom for the Israelites. This time, Jethro left after helping Moses attain freedom in his leadership and service to the Lord. Both the Midianites and Israel were better for these men knowing, encouraging, and worshiping with each other.

Summary

Jethro's visit provides us with several valuable lessons worth learning and subsequently applying to our lives. First, God, His truth, and actions should never be kept quiet and to ourselves. Jethro had been ardently following the news of Moses and the Israelites after his son-in-law departed from Midian. He had **heard of all that God had done for Moses and for Israel, His people, and how the Lord had brought Israel out of Egypt**. He saw an opportunity to return **Moses' wife Zipporah… and her two sons** to Moses and seized it. Moses had likely sent his wife and sons back to Midian when things got rocky in Egypt—when it became clear that Pharaoh had no intention of letting Israel go anytime soon. Jethro gladly took them in and protected them, with every intention of bringing them to Moses when it was safe. He seized the opportunity when he heard the Israelites were near Sinai. He ended up accomplishing his goal and then some. He was able to reunite Moses' family and got the opportunity to hear all the amazing things God had done.

Moses was as eager to share as Jethro was to listen. After they settled in their tent, Moses told his father-in-law all that the Lord had done to Pharaoh and **the Egyptians for Israel's sake, all the hardship that had befallen them on the journey, and how the Lord delivered them.** I also imagine that Moses was eager for Jethro to see how much of a transformation he had undergone since leaving Midian. He was a different man than the one Jethro had known in Midian. Back then, he was a bit of a faithless wimp. Now Moses welcomed the opportunity to brag about God and all He had done for His people. We, too, should eagerly share what God has been doing in and through our lives. God should never be silenced in or by His people. Rather, our lives should be megaphones proclaiming His goodness, truth, and faithfulness to everyone around us.

The second lesson we can learn from Jethro's visit is that God gives us relationships that we should cherish and nurture. Unfortunately, not everyone has the best relationship with their in-laws, or even their parents for that matter. Not all authority figures are deserving of their role and influence in our lives. But make no mistake—we have people from our circles whom we can encourage, worship with, and learn from. Jethro entered into Moses' world and, after hearing his story, **rejoiced over all the goodness which the Lord had done to Israel, in delivering them from the hand of the Egyptians.** Then he **blessed** the Lord and **took a burnt offering and sacrifices to God.** Jethro may have had a conversion experience or at least a deeper realization of who God was through his conversation with Moses. He was thrilled for his son-in-law, mostly because God had shown Himself so powerfully through him.

When was the last time you entered someone else's life solely to listen to how God is working in and through him or her? When was the last time you prayed with someone as an expression of worship, or even held a time of worship through fellowship and/or singing outside of a church service? The point here is that we all need to be more intentional about nurturing the relationships God has given us, especially with those who can sharpen and encourage us in our walks with the Lord.

The third lesson is that there is a right way and a wrong way to offer advice to others. Jethro was superb in how he offered wisdom and counsel to Moses. He was patient, taking the time to observe Moses in his element and handle his duties. He observed Moses all day; he did not just watch/listen for 5 minutes and then spit out all the things he thought Moses was doing wrong. Once he identified the problem, he did not confront Moses in front of others, embarrassing or undermining him. Rather, he discussed the matter privately with him. There was no embarrassment or chastisement. While Jethro was firm in his opinions, he was not condescending or judgmental. He told Moses, **"The thing that you are doing is not good. You will surely wear out, both yourself and these people who are with you, for the task is too heavy for you."** His care for Moses was evident, and he genuinely wanted Moses to thrive in his leadership role in Israel.

Fourthly, Jethro did not offer criticism without a solution. He pointed out where Moses was not being wise, but then told him how to correct it. Per our river analogy, Jethro saw a dam and offered the dynamite necessary to demolish it. First, he told Moses to teach the people **the statutes and laws, and make known to them the way in which they are to walk and the work they are to do.** Knowing what was expected of them would ease many of the problems they faced. Next, Jethro told him to **select out of all the people able men who fear God, men of truth, those who hate dishonest gain; and you shall place these over them as leaders of thousands, of hundreds, of fifties and of tens.** These men would **judge the people at all times** regarding smaller disputes. Moses would still be the lead judge, handling **every major dispute.** But, allowing others **to bear the burden with** Moses would work out better for everyone. With this kind of judicial hierarchy, Moses would **be able to endure, and all these people** would be able to **go to their place in peace.** Jethro did not just tell Moses about the dam restricting his life, he told Moses exactly what to do to destroy it and get the river flowing powerfully again.

The fifth lesson we can glean from this narrative is that there is always room for improvement in the way we approach our lives. Moses was conducting ministry inefficiently and desperately needed Jethro's wise intervention. We may not be crumbling the banks of our rivers like Moses was, but there are always things we can do to make it flow more smoothly. A small, practical thing my husband and I did in our marriage a while ago was sharing a synchronized calendar on our phones. It took us way too long to figure out that little tip, but man, it has been a life changer! Now, when one of us puts something on the calendar, the other can see it, and usually, it is color-coded so we know what type of event it is. Let me tell you, with four young daughters, careers, and extracurricular activities, that little hack has resolved and prevented many a marriage woe. That is a small example, but it proves the point: we can always do something to improve the situations in our lives—our relationships, careers, ministries, volunteering, the organization of our home, etc. We should never be content with merely surviving; God created us to thrive.

The sixth lesson we can learn from Jethro's visit is that of intentionally raising up leaders to serve with us and lead after us. It will not look exactly like Moses' situation. Not many, if any, of us have the need to establish a judicial hierarchy for nearly two million people. But we are each called and expected to mentor someone and bring others along in our service to the Lord. I am currently mentoring three young women, and it is such a delight. To pour into these sweet teenagers and be there with them through life's trials and triumphs brings joy that can hardly be put into words. We, like Moses, need to teach others—especially those younger than us—the truth of God's Word and what He expects of us. In other words, we need to disciple others so they can grow and then one day, continue the process and begin making disciples of Christ themselves. We are not the end of the line, and we cannot do it all on our own. God wants us to choose, raise up, train, and empower leaders so they can thrive and His kingdom can expand on earth far more than if we were doing it alone.

Many more lessons can be gleaned from this passage, but the last one I would like to note is the importance of being a humble leader. Moses could have gotten a bit prickly when Jethro told him that his current approach to ministry was "not good." He had poured countless hours into his calling and was giving everything he had to fulfill it. But he was humble enough to realize that there were people out there much wiser than him, and that he still had a lot to learn.

He was humble enough to want the best for Israel more than the best for himself and was willing to set aside his ego in order to see it through. **He listened to his father-in-law and did all that he said**. He put Jethro's advice into action immediately and was rewarded for it with a more effective ministry and a more peaceful life. Only good things happen when we are humble enough to get out of our own way and allow God to work in and through those around us, even if it means being corrected from time to time.

GROUP STUDY

Introduction

Rivers flow powerfully when unobstructed.
Our lives will too if we remove the obstacles
that threaten to dam us up.

Each of us encounters obstacles in our lives every day. Some may be small, like getting a flat tire on our way to work. Others may be significant, like dealing with a chronic disease or illness that we have to struggle with on a daily basis.

- What are some obstacles you've experienced this week?

  o How did they make your life challenging?

  o How did you handle them?

The Word

Like logs protruding from a river, most obstacles in our lives are obvious. But some impediments are submerged, hidden from view and require assistance to uncover. Moses, dedicated to following God to the best of his ability, remained unaware that his ministry approach was creating a dam, hindering the flow of his leadership.

> **It came about the next day that Moses sat to judge the people, and the people stood about Moses from the morning until the evening.**
>
> **Now when Moses' father-in-law saw all that he was doing for the people, he said, "What is this thing that you are doing for the people? Why do you alone sit as judge and all the people stand about you from morning until evening?" Moses said to his father-in-law, "Because the people come to me to inquire of God. When they have a dispute, it comes to me, and I judge between a man and his neighbor and make known the statutes of God and His laws." (Exodus 18:13-16)**

- What was Moses' primary job during the day?
  - How much of his time did it take?

Fortunately, Moses' father-in-law, Jethro, cared enough about Moses and God's people to point out the obstacle and then offer counsel on how to remove it.

> **Moses' father-in-law said to him, "The thing that you are doing is not good. You will surely wear out, both yourself and these people who are with you, for the task is too heavy for you; you cannot do it alone." (Exodus 18:17-18)**

- What was Moses doing wrong/unwisely?

- What did Jethro say would happen if Moses continued on that path?

- What role do you think Moses and Jethro's relationship played in the process of this confrontation?

Jethro first instructed Moses to teach the people God's laws and statutes and how they should live and work. Subsequently, he provided insightful counsel, proposing the establishment of a judicial hierarchy. This involved elevating capable leaders to supervise groups of tens, fifties, hundreds, and thousands, allowing them to handle smaller disputes. Moses would retain the responsibility of judging major disputes, but by sharing the burden with others, the overall process would be more efficient and beneficial for everyone.

> **"If you do this thing and God so commands you, then you will be able to endure, and all these people also will go to their place in peace." So Moses listened to his father-in-law and did all that he had said. (Exodus 18:23-24)**

- What did Jethro say would happen if Moses followed his advice?

- How did Moses respond to Jethro's counsel?
  - What does this reveal about Moses' character?

Apply

> You younger men, likewise, be subject to your elders;
> and all of you, clothe yourself with
> humility toward one another,
> for God is opposed to the proud,
> but gives grace to the humble.
> The Apostle Peter, 1 Peter 5:5

> When pride comes, then comes dishonor,
> But with the humble is wisdom.
> King Solomon, Proverbs 11:2

So many lessons can be gleaned from Jethro's visit with Moses. But three clear points of application are summed up in the following prayer:

Lord, help us see the truth, speak up in love, and step up in humility.

- Why is seeing truth a crucial first step?
  - In what ways can we practice seeing truth more clearly in our lives?

Confrontation is never fun, but sometimes it's necessary. Jethro confronted Moses well—privately and with obvious concern for him. He cared for him enough to speak up and to do so in a loving manner.

- Why is it important to speak up and do so in love?
  - What happens when we do one without the other?

Once confronted, we're given a choice. Will we respond in humility and eagerly get the logs out of the water so the river can flow freely once again? Or will we get offended, shut down, and let the dam keep blocking the flow of God's Spirit in our lives?

- Why is it difficult to respond with humility to criticism?

- What can you do to make humility a rhythmic part of your life and faith?

BIBLIOGRAPHY

Alexander, T. Desmond. *Exodus*. Downer's Grove, Illinois: InterVarsity Press, 2017.

Brown, Francis; Samuel Rolles Driver, and Charles Augustus Briggs, *Enhanced Brown-Driver-Briggs Hebrew and English Lexicon*. Oxford: Clarendon Press, 1977.

Bruckner, James K. *Exodus*. Grand Rapids, Michigan: Baker Books, 2008.

Calvin, John and Charles William Bingham, *Commentaries on the Four Last Books of Moses Arranged in the Form of a Harmony*, vol. 1 (Bellingham, WA: Logos Bible Software, 2010), 471.

Calvin, John. *The Ten Commandments: An Exposition of the Moral Law*. Ichthus Publications, 2015.

Carpenter, Eugene. *Evangelical Exegetical Commentary: Exodus 1–18*. Bellingham, Washington: Lexham Press, 2016.

Cassuto, Umberto. *A Commentary on the Book of Exodus*. Jerusalem, Israel: Magnes Press, 1967.

DeYoung, Kevin. *The 10 Commandments*. Crossway: Wheaton, Illinois. 2018.

Douglas, J.D. and Merrill C. Tenney. *Bible Dictionary*. Grand Rapids, Michigan: Zondervan, 1987.

Enns, Peter. *The NIV Application Commentary: Exodus*. Grand Rapids, Michigan: Zondervan Publishing House, 2000.

Fanning, B. M. "Exaltation," in *New Dictionary of Biblical Theology*, ed. T. Desmond Alexander and Brian S. Rosner, electronic ed. Downers Grove, IL: InterVarsity Press, 2000.

Finley, Harvey E. "Watch," ed. Charles F. Pfeiffer, Howard F. Vos, and John Rea, *The Wycliffe Bible Encyclopedia*. Moody Press, 1975.

Garrett, Duane A. *A Commentary on Exodus*. Grand Rapids, Michigan: Kregel Publications, 2014.

Gowen, D.E. *Theology in Exodus: Biblical Theology in the Form of a Commentary*. Louisville, Kentucky: Westminster John Knox. 1994. 27.

Hamilton, Victor P. *Exodus: An Exegetical Commentary.* Grand Rapids, Michigan: Baker Academic, 2011.

Kaiser, W.C. *Exodus*: Grand Rapids, MI: Zondervan. 1990.

Kim, H.C. P. "Gender Complementarity in the Hebrew Bible." In *Reading the Hebrew Bible for a New Millennium: Form, Concept, and Theological Perspective,* edited by W. Kim et al. Harrisburg, PA: Trinity, 2000.

Ketcham, Henry. *The Life of Abraham Lincoln – 1901.* Cornell University Library (scanned the original 1901 edition cover to cover), 2009.

Kwok, Hon-Lee. "Warfare," ed. Douglas Mangum et al., *Lexham Theological Wordbook,* Lexham Bible Reference Series. Bellingham, WA: Lexham Press, 2014.

Mackay, John L. *Exodus*, Mentor Commentaries (Fearn, Ross-shire, Great Britain: Mentor, 2001), 236.

Merida, Tony. *Christ-Centered Exposition: Exalting Jesus in Exodus.* Nashville, Tennessee: B&H Publishing Group, 2014.

Motyer, J.A. *The Message of Exodus.* Downers Grove, Illinois: InterVarsity Press, 2005.

Myers, Allen C. *The Eerdmans Bible Dictionary.* Grand Rapids, MI: Eerdmans, 1987.

NET Bible® http://netbible.com copyright ©1996, 2019 used with permission from Biblical Studies Press, L.L.C. All rights reserved".

Oswalt, John N. "943 כָּבֵד," ed. R. Laird Harris, Gleason L. Archer Jr., and Bruce K. Waltke, *Theological Wordbook of the Old Testament.* Chicago: Moody Press, 1999.

Pink, Arthur W. *Gleanings in Exodus.* Chicago, Illinois: Moody Press, 1981.

Pfeiffer, Charles F. *Baker's Bible Atlas Revised Edition.* Grand Rapids, Michigan: Baker Books, 2003.

Powell, Mark Allan ed., "East Wind," *The HarperCollins Bible Dictionary (Revised and Updated)* (New York: HarperCollins, 2011), 211.

Sarna, Nahum M. *Exploring Exodus: The Origins of Biblical Israel.* New York, New York. Schocken, 1996.

Sarna, Nahum M. *The JPS Torah Commentary: Exodus.* Philadelphia, PA: The Jewish Publication Society, 2003.

Strong, James. *A Concise Dictionary of the Words in the Greek Testament and The Hebrew Bible.* Bellingham, WA: Logos Bible Software, 2009.

Stuart, Douglas K. *The New American Commentary: Exodus Vol 2*. Nashville, Tennessee: B&H Publishing Group, 2006.

Weber, Carl Philip. "507 הָמָם," ed. R. Laird Harris, Gleason L. Archer Jr., and Bruce K. Waltke, *Theological Wordbook of the Old Testament*. Chicago: Moody Press, 1999. 220.

Williams, William A. "Pride," ed. Douglas Mangum et al., *Lexham Theological Wordbook*,

Lexham Bible Reference Series. Bellingham, WA: Lexham Press, 2014.

Wittman, Dr. John. "The Forgetting Curve." *Stanislaus State University*, Stanislaus State University, https://www.csustan.edu/sites/default/files/groups/Writing%20Program/forgetting_curve.pdf.

END NOTES

WEEK ONE

[1] Francis Brown, Samuel Rolles Driver, and Charles Augustus Briggs, *Enhanced Brown-Driver-Briggs Hebrew and English Lexicon* (Oxford: Clarendon Press, 1977), 304.

[2] Stuart, Douglas K. *The New American Commentary: Exodus Vol 2*. Nashville, Tennessee: B&H Publishing Group, 2006. 295.

[3] NET Bible® http://netbible.com copyright ©1996, 2019 used with permission from Biblical Studies Press, L.L.C. All rights reserved".

[4] Sarna, Nahum M. *The JPS Torah Commentary: Exodus*. Philadelphia, PA: The Jewish Publication Society, 2003. 62.

[5] Alexander, T. Desmond. *Exodus*. Downer's Grove, Illinois: InterVarsity Press, 2017. 240

[6] Hamilton, Victor P. *Exodus: An Exegetical Commentary*. Grand Rapids, Michigan: Baker Academic, 2011. 194.

[7] Sarna, Nahum M. *The JPS Torah Commentary: Exodus*. 2003. 62.

[8] https://www.census.gov/quickfacts/houstoncitytexas

[9] Stuart, Douglas K. *The New American Commentary: Exodus Vol 2*. 2006. 301.

[10] Stuart, Douglas K. *The New American Commentary: Exodus Vol 2*. 2006. 302.

[11] Good News Translation and New Living Translation read just "men," the Holman Christian Standard Bible reads "soldiers on foot."

[12] Alexander, T. Desmond. *Exodus*. 2017. 241.

[13] Stuart, Douglas K. *The New American Commentary: Exodus Vol 2*. 2006. 299-300.

[14] Garrett, Duane A. *A Commentary on Exodus*. 2014. 93.

[15] Sarna, Nahum M. *The JPS Torah Commentary: Exodus*. 2003. 62.

[16] Stuart, Douglas K. *The New American Commentary: Exodus Vol 2*. 2006. 298.

[17] Sarna, Nahum M. *The JPS Torah Commentary: Exodus*. 2003. 62.

[18] Stuart, Douglas K. *The New American Commentary: Exodus Vol 2*. 2006. 303.

[19] This view represented as "wanderlust" expressed by Hamilton, Victor P. *Exodus: An Exegetical Commentary*. 2011. 195.

[20] Sarna, Nahum M. *The JPS Torah Commentary: Exodus*. 2003. 63.

[21] Stuart, Douglas K. *The New American Commentary: Exodus Vol 2*. 2006. 309

[22] Written by John H. Sammis (1887) and composed by Professor Daniel Towner

[23] Stuart, Douglas K. *The New American Commentary: Exodus Vol 2*. 2006. 303.

[24] Merida, Tony. *Christ-Centered Exposition: Exalting Jesus in Exodus*. Nashville, Tennessee: B&H Publishing Group, 2014. 74.

[25] Merida, Tony. *Christ-Centered Exposition: Exalting Jesus in Exodus*. 2014. 74.

[26] Wittman, Dr. John. "The Forgetting Curve." *Stanislaus State University*, Stanislaus State University, https://www.csustan.edu/sites/default/files/groups/Writing%20Program/forgetting_curve.pdf.

[27] Graphic derived from: Guide. "How Much Information Can We Really Retain? (and How to Increase Your Memory)." *Brain Based Solutions*, Brain Based Solutions, 26 Jan. 2022, https://brainbasedsolutions.org/how-much-information-can-we-really-retain-and-how-to-increase-your-memory/.

[28] Alexander, T. Desmond. *Exodus*. 2017. 250.

[29] Mackay, John L. *Exodus*, Mentor Commentaries (Fearn, Ross-shire, Great Britain: Mentor, 2001), 236.

[30] Calvin, John and Charles William Bingham, *Commentaries on the Four Last Books of Moses Arranged in the Form of a Harmony*, vol. 1 (Bellingham, WA: Logos Bible Software, 2010), 471.

[31] Sarna, Nahum M. *The JPS Torah Commentary: Exodus*. 2003. 67.

WEEK TWO

[32] Mackay, John L. *Exodus*, Mentor Commentaries (Fearn, Ross-shire, Great Britain: Mentor, 2001), 237.

[33] Garrett, Duane A. *A Commentary on Exodus*. 2014. 382.

[34] NET Bible® http://netbible.com copyright ©1996, 2019 used with permission from Biblical Studies Press, L.L.C. All rights reserved".

[35] Sarna, Nahum M. *Exploring Exodus: The Origins of Biblical Israel*. New York, New York. Schocken, 1996. 105.

[36] Alexander, T. Desmond. *Exodus*. 2017. 263.

[37] Alexander, T. Desmond. *Exodus*. 2017. 263.

[38] Stuart, Douglas K. *The New American Commentary: Exodus Vol 2*. 2006. 323.

[39] Sarna, Nahum M. *The JPS Torah Commentary: Exodus*. 2003. 69.

[40] Carpenter, Eugene. *Evangelical Exegetical Commentary: Exodus 1–18*. Bellingham, Washington: Lexham Press, 2016. 497.

[41] Stuart, Douglas K. *The New American Commentary: Exodus Vol 2*. 2006. 324.

[42] Exodus 17:8-16; Joshua 6:1-27, several accounts in Judges, etc.

[43] Enns, Peter. *The NIV Application Commentary: Exodus*. Grand Rapids, Michigan: Zondervan Publishing House, 2000. 270.

[44] Hamilton, Victor P. *Exodus: An Exegetical Commentary*. Grand Rapids, Michigan: Baker Academic, 2011. 207.

[45] Sarna, Nahum M. *Exploring Exodus: The Origins of Biblical Israel*. 1996. 108.

[46] Stuart, Douglas K. *The New American Commentary: Exodus Vol 2*. 2006. 326.

[47] Merida, Tony. *Christ-Centered Exposition: Exalting Jesus in Exodus*. 2014. 81.

[48] Douglas, J.D. and Merrill C. Tenney. *Bible Dictionary*. Grand Rapids, Michigan: Zondervan, 1987. 791-792.

[49] Alexander, T. Desmond. *Exodus*. 2017. 265.

[50] Garrett, Duane A. *A Commentary on Exodus*. 2014. 384.

[51] Enns, Peter. *The NIV Application Commentary: Exodus*. 2000. 270.

[52] Sarna, Nahum M. *Exploring Exodus: The Origins of Biblical Israel*. 1996. 111.

[53] Sarna, Nahum M. *Exploring Exodus: The Origins of Biblical Israel*. 1996. 112.

[54] Merida, Tony. *Christ-Centered Exposition: Exalting Jesus in Exodus*. 2014. 81.

[55] Ketcham, Henry. *The Life of Abraham Lincoln – 1901*. Cornell University Library (scanned the original 1901 edition cover to cover), 2009.

[56] Enns, Peter. *The NIV Application Commentary: Exodus*. 2000. 271.

[57] Carpenter, Eugene. *Evangelical Exegetical Commentary: Exodus 1–18*. 2016. 512.

[58] Alexander, T. Desmond. *Exodus*. 2017. 274.

[59] NIV, NET, RSV, HNV

[60] Stuart, Douglas K. *The New American Commentary: Exodus Vol 2*. 2006. 332.

[61] Sarna, Nahum M. *The JPS Torah Commentary: Exodus*. 2003. 72.

[62] Alexander, T. Desmond. *Exodus*. 2017. 276.

[63] Stuart, Douglas K. *The New American Commentary: Exodus Vol 2*. 2006. 336.

[64] Alexander, T. Desmond. *Exodus*. 2017. 277.

[65] Bruckner, James K. *Exodus*. Grand Rapids, Michigan: Baker Books, 2008. 132.

[66] Stuart, Douglas K. *The New American Commentary: Exodus Vol 2*. 2006. 338.

[67] Hamilton, Victor P. *Exodus: An Exegetical Commentary*. 207. 217.

[68] Stuart, Douglas K. *The New American Commentary: Exodus Vol 2*. 2006. 341.

[69] Pink, Arthur W. *Gleanings in Exodus*. Chicago, Illinois: Moody Press, 1981. 111.

[70] Cassuto, Umberto. *A Commentary on the Book of Exodus*. Jerusalem, Israel: Magnes Press, 1967. 166.

[71] Oswalt, John N. "943 כָּבֵד," ed. R. Laird Harris, Gleason L. Archer Jr., and Bruce K. Waltke, *Theological Wordbook of the Old Testament* (Chicago: Moody Press, 1999), 426.

[72] Myers, Allen C. *The Eerdmans Bible Dictionary* (Grand Rapids, MI: Eerdmans, 1987), 299–300.

[73] Powell, Mark Allan ed., "East Wind," *The HarperCollins Bible Dictionary (Revised and Updated)* (New York: HarperCollins, 2011), 211.

[74] Robards, Kate. "The Mind after Midnight: People More Likely to Make Bad Decisions Late at Night." *Sleep Education*, 17 Jan. 2023, https://sleepeducation.org/mind-after-midnight/.

[75] Stuart, Douglas K. *The New American Commentary: Exodus Vol 2*. 2006. 342.

[76] Douglas, J.D. and Merrill C. Tenney. *Bible Dictionary*. 1055.

[77] Finley, Harvey E. "Watch," ed. Charles F. Pfeiffer, Howard F. Vos, and John Rea, *The Wycliffe Bible Encyclopedia*. Moody Press, 1975.

[78] Weber, Carl Philip. "507 הָמַם," ed. R. Laird Harris, Gleason L. Archer Jr., and Bruce K. Waltke, *Theological Wordbook of the Old Testament*. Chicago: Moody Press, 1999. 220.

[79] Weber, Carl Philip. "507 הָמַם," ed. R. Laird Harris, Gleason L. Archer Jr., and Bruce K. Waltke, *Theological Wordbook of the Old Testament*. 220.

[80] Kwok, Hon-Lee. "Warfare," ed. Douglas Mangum et al., *Lexham Theological Wordbook*, Lexham Bible Reference Series. Bellingham, WA: Lexham Press, 2014.

[81] Stuart, Douglas K. *The New American Commentary: Exodus Vol 2*. 2006. 342.

[82] NIV, NET

[83] Judah. "Remember What It Cost." *7*, 2021.

[84] Stuart, Douglas K. *The New American Commentary: Exodus Vol 2*. 2006. 346.

WEEK THREE

[85] Sarna, Nahum M. *The JPS Torah Commentary: Exodus*. 2003. 75.

[86] Stuart, Douglas K. *The New American Commentary: Exodus Vol 2*. 2006. 347.

[87] Stuart, Douglas K. *The New American Commentary: Exodus Vol 2*. 2006. 347.

[88] Alexander, T. Desmond. *Exodus*. 2017. 297.

[89] Sarna, Nahum M. *The JPS Torah Commentary: Exodus*. 2003. 77.

[90] Fanning, B. M. "Exaltation," in *New Dictionary of Biblical Theology*, ed. T. Desmond Alexander and Brian S. Rosner, electronic ed. Downers Grove, IL: InterVarsity Press, 2000. 467.

[91] Carpenter, Eugene. *Evangelical Exegetical Commentary: Exodus 1–18*. 2016. 542.

[92] Sarna, Nahum M. *The JPS Torah Commentary: Exodus*. 2003. 77.

[93] Brown, Francis, Samuel Rolles Driver, and Charles Augustus Briggs, *Enhanced Brown-Driver-Briggs Hebrew and English Lexicon*. 627.

[94] Sarna, Nahum M. *The JPS Torah Commentary: Exodus*. 2003. 77.

[95] Williams, William A. "Pride," ed. Douglas Mangum et al., *Lexham Theological Wordbook*, Lexham Bible Reference Series. Bellingham, WA: Lexham Press, 2014.

[96] Strong, James. *A Concise Dictionary of the Words in the Greek Testament and The Hebrew Bible*. Bellingham, WA: Logos Bible Software, 2009. 47.

[97] Enns, Peter. *The NIV Application Commentary: Exodus*. 2000. 298.

[98] Carpenter, Eugene. *Evangelical Exegetical Commentary: Exodus 1–18*. 2016. 544.

[99] Carpenter, Eugene. *Evangelical Exegetical Commentary: Exodus 1–18*. 2016. 544.

[100] *The Lexham Analytical Lexicon of the Hebrew Bible*. Bellingham, WA: Lexham Press, 2017.

[101] *The Lexham Analytical Lexicon of the Hebrew Bible*. Bellingham, WA: Lexham Press, 2017.

[102] Carpenter, Eugene. *Evangelical Exegetical Commentary: Exodus 1–18*. 2016. 544.

[103] Enns, Peter. *The NIV Application Commentary: Exodus*. 2000. 299.

[104] Stuart, Douglas K. *The New American Commentary: Exodus Vol 2*. 2006. 355.

[105] Douglas, J.D. and Merrill C. Tenney. *Bible Dictionary*. 1987. 850.

[106] Sarna, Nahum M. *The JPS Torah Commentary: Exodus*. 2003. 80.

[107] Sarna, Nahum M. *The JPS Torah Commentary: Exodus*. 2003. 80.

[100] Sarna, Nahum M. *The JPS Torah Commentary: Exodus*. 2003. 81.

[109] Psalm 48:6, Jeremiah 6:24, 22:23, 50:43; Micah 4:9

[110] Elmer A. Martens, "207 בָּהַל," ed. R. Laird Harris, Gleason L. Archer Jr., and Bruce K. Waltke, *Theological Wordbook of the Old Testament* (Chicago: Moody Press, 1999), 92.

[111] Stuart, Douglas K. *The New American Commentary: Exodus Vol 2*. 2006. 359.

[112] Stuart, Douglas K. *The New American Commentary: Exodus Vol 2*. 2006. 359.

[113] Stuart, Douglas K. *The New American Commentary: Exodus Vol 2*. 2006. 358.

[114] Stuart, Douglas K. *The New American Commentary: Exodus Vol 2*. 2006. 358.

[115] Douglas, J.D. and Merrill C. Tenney. *Bible Dictionary*. 1987. 188.

[116] Garrett, Duane A. *A Commentary on Exodus*. 2014. 405.

[117] Carpenter, Eugene. *Evangelical Exegetical Commentary: Exodus 1–18*. 2016. 547.

[118] Stuart, Douglas K. *The New American Commentary: Exodus Vol 2*. 2006. 360.

[119] Carpenter, Eugene. *Evangelical Exegetical Commentary: Exodus 1–18*. 2016. 548.

[120] Carpenter, Eugene. *Evangelical Exegetical Commentary: Exodus 1–18*. 2016. 548.

[121] Garrett, Duane A. *A Commentary on Exodus*. 2014. 405.

[122] Sarna, Nahum M. *The JPS Torah Commentary: Exodus*. 2003. 82.

[123] Stuart, Douglas K. *The New American Commentary: Exodus Vol 2*. 2006. 362.

[124] Hamilton, Victor P. *Exodus: An Exegetical Commentary*. 207. 235.

[125] Sarna, Nahum M. *The JPS Torah Commentary: Exodus*. 2003. 83.

[126] Sarna, Nahum M. *The JPS Torah Commentary: Exodus*. 2003. 83.

[127] Hamilton, Victor P. *Exodus: An Exegetical Commentary*. 207. 235.

[128] Kim, H.C. P. "Gender Complementarity in the Hebrew Bible." In *Reading the Hebrew Bible for a New Millennium: Form, Concept, and Theological Perspective,* edited by W. Kim et al. Harrisburg, PA: Trinity, 2000. 274-276.

WEEK FOUR

[129] Alexander, T. Desmond. *Exodus*. 2017. 311.

[130] Sarna, Nahum M. *The JPS Torah Commentary: Exodus*. 2003. 84.

[131] Stuart, Douglas K. *The New American Commentary: Exodus Vol 2*. 2006. 362.

[132] Alexander, T. Desmond. *Exodus*. 2017. 312.

[133] Stuart, Douglas K. *The New American Commentary: Exodus Vol 2*. 2006. 366.

[134] Sarna, Nahum M. *The JPS Torah Commentary: Exodus*. 2003. 84.

[135] Exodus 5:8, 15; 8:12; 14:10, 15

[136] Garrett, Duane A. *A Commentary on Exodus*. 2014. 413-14.

[137] Carpenter, Eugene. *Evangelical Exegetical Commentary: Exodus 1–18*. 2016. 561.

[138] Carpenter, Eugene. *Evangelical Exegetical Commentary: Exodus 1–18*. 2016. 561.

[139] Sarna, Nahum M. *The JPS Torah Commentary: Exodus*. 2003. 84.

[140] Garrett, Duane A. *A Commentary on Exodus*. 2014. 413-14.

[141] Garrett, Duane A. *A Commentary on Exodus*. 2014. 413-14.

[142] Stuart, Douglas K. *The New American Commentary: Exodus Vol 2*. 2006. 367.

[143] Carpenter, Eugene. *Evangelical Exegetical Commentary: Exodus 1–18*. 2016. 558.

[144] Sarna, Nahum M. *The JPS Torah Commentary: Exodus*. 2003. 84.

[145] Alexander, T. Desmond. *Exodus*. 2017. 314.

[146] Alexander, T. Desmond. *Exodus*. 2017. 314.

[147] Enns, Peter. *The NIV Application Commentary: Exodus*. 2000. 323.

[148] Carpenter, Eugene. *Evangelical Exegetical Commentary: Exodus 1–18*. 2016. 561.

[149] Sarna, Nahum M. *The JPS Torah Commentary: Exodus*. 2003. 85.

[150] Pink, Arthur W. *Gleanings in Exodus*. Chicago, Illinois: Moody Press, 1981. 122.

[151] Alexander, T. Desmond. *Exodus*. 2017. 321.

[152] Stuart, Douglas K. *The New American Commentary: Exodus Vol 2*. 2006. 370.

[153] Stuart, Douglas K. *The New American Commentary: Exodus Vol 2*. 2006. 370.

[154] Stuart, Douglas K. *The New American Commentary: Exodus Vol 2*. 2006. 371.

[155] Sarna, Nahum M. *The JPS Torah Commentary: Exodus*. 2003. 86.

[156] Alexander, T. Desmond. *Exodus*. 2017. 321.

[157] Stuart, Douglas K. *The New American Commentary: Exodus Vol 2*. 2006. 371.

[158] Pink, Arthur W. *Gleanings in Exodus*. Chicago, Illinois: Moody Press, 1981. 124.

[159] Howe, Frederick. *"Glory,"* ed. Charles F. Pfeiffer, Howard F. Vos, and John Rea, *The Wycliffe Bible Encyclopedia* (Moody Press, 1975).

WEEK FIVE

[160] Carpenter, Eugene. *Evangelical Exegetical Commentary: Exodus 1–18*. 2016. 571.

[161] Sarna, Nahum M. *The JPS Torah Commentary: Exodus*. 2003. 88.

[162] Alexander, T. Desmond. *Exodus*. 2017. 324.

[163] Carpenter, Eugene. *Evangelical Exegetical Commentary: Exodus 1–18*. 2016. 571.

[164] Sarna, Nahum M. *The JPS Torah Commentary: Exodus*. 2003. 88.

[165] Stuart, Douglas K. *The New American Commentary: Exodus Vol 2*. 2006. 378.

[166] Hamilton, Victor P. *Exodus: An Exegetical Commentary*. 207. 255.

[167] Stuart, Douglas K. *The New American Commentary: Exodus Vol 2*. 2006. 378.

[168] Sarna, Nahum M. *The JPS Torah Commentary: Exodus*. 2003. 92-93.

[169] Alexander, T. Desmond. *Exodus*. 2017. 328. (NLT, HCSB, TEV)

[170] Alexander, T. Desmond. *Exodus*. 2017. 325.

[171] Alexander, T. Desmond. *Exodus*. 2017. 326.

[172] Stuart, Douglas K. *The New American Commentary: Exodus Vol 2*. 2006. 381.

[173] Stuart, Douglas K. *The New American Commentary: Exodus Vol 2*. 2006. 381.

[174] Carpenter, Eugene. *Evangelical Exegetical Commentary: Exodus 1–18*. 2016. 580.

[175] Stuart, Douglas K. *The New American Commentary: Exodus Vol 2*. 2006. 384.

[176] Sarna, Nahum M. *The JPS Torah Commentary: Exodus*. 2003. 91.

[177] Alexander, T. Desmond. *Exodus*. 2017. 327.

[178] Alexander, T. Desmond. *Exodus*. 2017. 327.

[179] Stuart, Douglas K. *The New American Commentary: Exodus Vol 2*. 2006. 384.

[180] Stuart, Douglas K. *The New American Commentary: Exodus Vol 2*. 2006. 384.

[181] Stuart, Douglas K. *The New American Commentary: Exodus Vol 2*. 2006. 384.

[182] Alexander, T. Desmond. *Exodus*. 2017. 328.

[183] Carpenter, Eugene. *Evangelical Exegetical Commentary: Exodus 1–18*. 2016. 583

WEEK SIX

[184] Sarna, Nahum M. *The JPS Torah Commentary: Exodus*. 2003. 93.

[185] Alexander, T. Desmond. *Exodus*. 2017. 333.

[186] Sarna, Nahum M. *The JPS Torah Commentary: Exodus*. 2003. 93.

[187] Sarna, Nahum M. *The JPS Torah Commentary: Exodus*. 2003. 93.

[188] Enns, Peter. *The NIV Application Commentary: Exodus*. 2000. 328.

[189] Carpenter, Eugene. *Evangelical Exegetical Commentary: Exodus 1–18*. 2016. 585.

[190] Carpenter, Eugene. *Evangelical Exegetical Commentary: Exodus 1–18*. 2016. 585.

[191] Stuart, Douglas K. *The New American Commentary: Exodus Vol 2*. 2006. 389.

[192] Stuart, Douglas K. *The New American Commentary: Exodus Vol 2*. 2006. 390

[193] Alexander, T. Desmond. *Exodus*. 2017. 335.

[194] Alexander, T. Desmond. *Exodus*. 2017. 335.

[195] Sarna, Nahum M. *The JPS Torah Commentary: Exodus*. 2003. 94.

[196] Alexander, T. Desmond. *Exodus*. 2017. 336.

[197] Sarna, Nahum M. *The JPS Torah Commentary: Exodus*. 2003. 95.

[198] Douglas, J.D. and Merrill C. Tenney. *Bible Dictionary: "Joshua."* 1987. 547.

[199] 2 Samuel 23:8-39

[200] Douglas, J.D. and Merrill C. Tenney. *Bible Dictionary: "Joshua."* 1987. 547.

[201] Stuart, Douglas K. *The New American Commentary: Exodus Vol 2*. 2006. 394.

[202] Douglas, J.D. and Merrill C. Tenney. *Bible Dictionary: "Hur."* 1987. 456.

[203] Douglas, J.D. and Merrill C. Tenney. *Bible Dictionary: "Hur."* 1987. 456.

[204] Bhandari, Sandeep, "How Long Can a Person Hold Their Arms up (and Why)? -." *Exactly How Long*, 2 Dec. 2022, exactlyhowlong.com/how-long-can-a-person-hold-their-arms-up-and-why/.

[205] Calvin, John and Charles William Bingham. <u>*Commentaries on the Four Last Books of Moses Arranged in the Form of a Harmony*</u>, vol. 1. Bellingham, WA: Logos Bible Software, 2010. 293.

[206] Enns, Peter. *The NIV Application Commentary: Exodus*. 2000. 350.

[207] Sarna, Nahum M. *The JPS Torah Commentary: Exodus*. 2003. 96.

[208] Stuart, Douglas K. *The New American Commentary: Exodus Vol 2*. 2006. 400.

[209] Stuart, Douglas K. *The New American Commentary: Exodus Vol 2*. 2006. 400.

WEEK SEVEN

[210] Stuart, Douglas K. *The New American Commentary: Exodus Vol 2*. 2006. 403.

[211] Stuart, Douglas K. *The New American Commentary: Exodus Vol 2*. 2006. 404-408.

[212] Sarna, Nahum M. *The JPS Torah Commentary: Exodus*. 2003. 98.

[213] Alexander, T. Desmond. *Exodus*. 2017. 348.

[214] Sarna, Nahum M. *The JPS Torah Commentary: Exodus*. 2003. 99.

[215] Alexander, T. Desmond. *Exodus*. 2017. 349.

[216] Sarna, Nahum M. *The JPS Torah Commentary: Exodus*. 2003. 99.

[217] Alexander, T. Desmond. *Exodus*. 2017. 350.

[218] Alexander, T. Desmond. *Exodus*. 2017. 350.

[219] Enns, Peter. *The NIV Application Commentary: Exodus*. 2000. 371.

[220] "38% of U.S. Pastors Have Thought about Quitting Full-Time Ministry in the Past Year." *Barna Group*, 2021, www.barna.com/research/pastors-well-being/.

[221] Halloran, Kevin. "Christian Ministry Burnout: Prevention, Signs, Statistics, and Recovery." *WordPartners*, 3 Jan. 2020, wordpartners.org/resources/christian-ministry-burnout-prevention-signs-statistics-and-recovery/.

www.ingramcontent.com/pod-product-compliance
Lightning Source LLC
Chambersburg PA
CBHW050747100426
42744CB00012BA/1922